AF522026

DORA ROMANO

RICE AND BEANS AND TASTY THINGS

A Puerto Rican Cookbook

Edition and translation by JAIME ROMANO.
Illustrations and design by Jaime Romano.
Cover photograph by Jochi Melero
Photographic portrait by Tec Color Laboratories

First printing: July 1986
Second printing: July 1989
Third printing: July 1992
Fourth printing: September 1993

Printed in Puerto Rico by RAMALLO BROS. PRINTING, INC.
227 Duarte St., Floral Park, Hato Rey, P.R. 00917

To Jimmy. For the first fifty years.

TABLE OF CONTENTS:

INTRODUCTION

Since its original 1970 and through two subsequent augmented and revised editions, *Cocine conmigo* has been a success, appearing several times in Puerto Rico's best-seller list. The colloquial use of language and extremely detailed step-by-step recipes has endeared it to the inexperienced who like to eat well but who view cooking with some apprehension. Even for those experienced cooks who do not follow recipes slavishly, Doña Dora's book has become a reference source for points of departure and for hints.

The core of *Cocine conmigo* is a compilation of traditional Puerto Rican recipes learned from the author's mother, to which a good amount of other Caribbean and international recipes adapted to the Puerto Rican taste has been added. The recipes attest to the influences which have acted upon the tastes and ways of cooking in the Island: the Indian, the Spanish, the African, the North American, and to a lesser extent, the Italo-French presences show strongly. Traditional recipes from other Caribbean islands that arose from similar regional transformations have been taken in happily. Imported products have been Puerto Ricanized. Traditional dishes from other centuries have been made more accessible through modern marketing and kitchen tools such as freezing and the food processor.

A brief perusal of *Cocine conmigo* will make a reader aware of the vitality of this ethnic cooking which is still undergoing an exhuberant growth. It is not depurated and refined like the classical French and Chinese cuisines, but its aggressive vitality makes Puerto Rican cookery exciting. As it refines its traditional recipes, it constantly brings in new ones.

During the past decade or so, there has been an increased interest in ethnic foods. The proof is in the proliferation of specialized restaurants and markets in North American cities.

They cater not only to immigrants, but to Americans who have discovered the delights of foods once thought of as exotic and unapproachable. There is also a third generation of Puerto Ricans in North America who hold firmly to their ways of eating, though not necessarily to their native Spanish. An English book of the Island's recipes ought to fill that gap. At the same time, it would make Puerto Rican food more accessible to other English-speaking persons who have become acquainted and fallen in love with it.

In translating *Cocine conmigo* we decided to go for more than merely that. We turned it into a total revision. Out of the 588 recipes which appear in the second augmented edition, some 350 were selected and some 35 more were added to fill gaps. The decisions on which recipes to include were based firstly on their traditional and regional values —for example, *pasteles, asopaos*, green papaya compote, and so on. Recipes that come from sources other than the traditional Spanish-African-Indian, were also included because they have entrenched themselves more recently in the Island's cooking through the local availability of foreign products or through new ethnic influences: the sauteed canned corned beef, the Cuban *congrí*, the Dominican *malarabia*, stand as examples. Some of these newcomers were integrated without major changes, others have been transformed to conform to local taste. The third group of recipes taken from *Cocine conmigo* were, of course, those highly successful original or personally-transformed recipes of Doña Dora: the rice with chicken with saffron and vermouth, the award-winning rice with seafood and so forth. The recipes from the Spanish book that were not used were essentially those that can be found elsewhere in general cookbooks —roast beef, hamburgers, mashed potatoes. Nevertheless, if any of those turned out with a distinct local character, through the use of regionally available products such as *culantro* or sweet chili peppers, they were included. Lastly, the new recipes added were mainly basic-process recipes that appeared as part of individual ones in *Cocine conmigo*, and some that, although obvious to the Islander, might be mistifying to the uninitiated. "How on earth do you peel a green plantain?"

Once the recipes were selected, the revising process began. Every recipe was rethought —some were left as they were, many took minor changes, some were drastically changed. All those with minor or major alterations were tested once and again. We wanted to make sure that the original fool-proof character of *Cocine conmigo* would remain. Some changes were made in the ingredients themselves —there is more emphasis on fresh products—; others, in the quantities. Some are in the processes or the tools involved. There is a wide use of the food processor.

The major revision was dietary. The unhealthy effects of the overuse of saturated fats and salt has been amply proven. The attitude has changed favoring healthier and less fattening foods; thus, most recipes had their fat and salt contents reduced. Puerto Rican food, though not hot, is spicy, so it adjusts very easily to these changes without altering the nature of the dishes or their flavor. As you reduce salt, you add more spices: one more garlic clove —which is good for you— or a pinch more of oregano. The reader is urged to try the recipes with the amount of salt indicated. Getting rid of the salt habit is not a one-day thing. Persons who have broken it attest to a better taste in foods and to an intensified awareness of the national flavors of products. What was before considered tastiness is eventually understood as saltiness. Give yourself time and eventually you will find that the amounts of salt indicated in the recipes can be lowered even further. As for fats, use vegetable oils —apparently olive oil is the healthiest— and in the vastly reduced quantities suggested in this book. Only a few recipes retain the original amounts of oil, and that is because it is intrinsic to the dish's character. Eat those sparingly and only once in a while. That should also apply to desserts, which following latin taste, are very sweet. One other reduction was made, and that was in the amount of food per servings. Considering that rice and beans, the universal side dish of the Island's kitchen, is almost a complete protein source, there is no need for large amounts of meat proteins.

The second major revision of *Cocine conmigo* was in the way the actual recipes were written. In the Spanish book they are self-contained, highly detailed and usually chatty. In the translation we have simplified them. They are shorter, yet clear and complete. They simply assume that you are familiar with the very basic processes of cooking, such as simmering, beating egg-whites and so forth. We have not attempted a how-to-cookbook, but rather a collection of dishes enjoyed by Puerto Ricans. Nevertheless, all basic recipes or processes needed were included. These are presented as separate recipes which are the starting point for many others, witness the *picadillo*, or ground meat stuffing, that appears in nineteen other dishes. Another example is the reconstitution and de-salting of salt-codfish that preceedes those recipes where it is used. All are clearly cross-listed in the indexes and recipes, and thus are easily found.

A glossary was definitely needed. For those familiar with the ingredients used in Puerto Rican food, it will still be useful, since some products in markets outside the Island are sold under unfamiliar names. For the reader not acquainted with the products, its usefulness is obvious. We have tried to be as complete as possible, yet sometimes we ran into a wall. For example, after many consultations in books and with botanists we could not come up with a common English name for the *ají dulce*, or be sure of its scientific one (possibly *C. chinense* var. *rocotillo*). This pepper which is present in almost every savory dish, has either not been classified or its nomenclature has eluded our research. Thus, we decided to translate it literally as sweet-chili-pepper. It sounds like a contradiction in terms, but so does its Spanish name. This brings us to the question of nomenclature and recipe titles. As to these last, we went for the literal translation when it was not awkward, such as roast chicken. With others we used a non-literal, descriptive one such as braised chicken for *pollo al caldero*, literally chicken in a pot. With other recipes we simply threw up our arms in the air and used the Spanish name —*pasteles, ajilimójili, surullitos*. A descriptive title could have been used, but since they are so typical, you will probably encounter these dishes more readily in your eating and cooking experience under their Spanish name. We have also tried to reflect this in the indexes and glossary, where not only the recipes' titles, but other terms appear in Spanish as well as English. It was surprising to find so many of the terms already accepted in the English language, the difference sometimes being merely one of an accent: pimenton against *pimentón*. We have kept to this usage as you will gather from the glossary, the recipes and the indexes, where Spanish terms appear in italics.

What started out in 1980 as the translation of a highly successful book, ended up as a complete revision and rethinking of the concepts and actual recipes, of the ideas and structure of the original *Cocine conmigo*. It has been a long process of researching, retesting, translating —we thank Glenna Haynie of Washington, D.C. for revising the translation—, redacting, editing, and so forth. We are satisfied and proud. Enjoy!

J.R.

GLOSSARY

English common terminology is followed by its Spanish equivalent. This is followed by the scientific name and by any other common names. Spanish terms refer the reader to the appropriate English entry. Where no English equivalent exists, the description is given under the Spanish nomenclature. An asterisk means a recipe appears elswhere in the book.

A

Acid lime - *limón agrio (Citrus aurantifolia), lima.*
The fruit of a tropical citrus that takes its English common names from the point of origin, thus West Indian Lime, Key Lime. Known in Spanish as *limón* (lemon), this is a different fruit from the true lemon *(Citrus limon)*. It is properly a lime with thin skin, of 1½" diameter, and very acid juice. In this book when true lemon is called for it is thus specified, although it can be substituted for the ripe acid lime if it is not too acid. This is common usage in Puerto Rico. The grated rind of the green acid lime is used frequently as a flavoring agent of desserts. If unavailable, substitute the rind of any available green lime.

Achiote - v. annatto

Adobo - Either a dry or wet marinade for meats. It refers mainly to one which includes salt, pepper, garlic, oregano, olive oil and vinegar.*

Aguacate - v. avocado

Agua de azahar - v. orange blossom water

Ají bravo - v. peppers

Ají de Cayena - idem.

Ají de Tabasco - idem.

Ají dulce - idem.

Ají picante - idem.

Alcaparrado - A combination of capers, green olives and pimientos, or pimiento-stuffed olives, packed in salted water and sold commercially in jars. It is sometimes used in the *Sofrito*, v.

Amarillo - v. plantain

Ananas - v. pineapple

Annatto - achiote *(Bixa orellana), bija, bijol.* The sienna-red seed of an American tree cultivated in the tropics. It is used to color cooking lard or oil, and to give a light, delicate flavor.*

Anon, *anón* - v. soursop

Anona - idem.

Apio - *(Arracacia xanthorrhiza), apio tuberoso*, arracacha. The tuberous root of a perennial herb native in Mexico to Peru. The branching roots of this plant have starchy yellow flesh and are eaten as a vegetable.* Apio is also the common Spanish name for the celery (*Apium graveolens*). Although both are from the *Umbilliferae* family, they are not interchangeable vegetables.

Apio tuberoso - v. apio

Apple Bananas - v. bananas

Araceae - A family of plants with more than 100 genera of which the *Xanthosoma* and *Colocasia* have tuberous rhizomes that are cultivated in the tropics as vegetables. From the *Xanthosoma saggitifolium* species comes the white yautia and tanier. From *Xanthosoma atrovirens* comes the yellow yautia. The *Colocasia esculenta* produces the taro, malanga and dasheen. The skin of these roots are usually dark brown, bark-like, and are sometimes covered with short bristles. Their flesh can be white, yellow, gray or purple. When buying they should feel firm to the pressure of the fingers. They can be kept at room temperature or refrigerated for up to a week. They are peeled, cut and boiled in salted water until tender, and eaten very much like potatoes. Mashed yautias are particularly delicious. Sometimes they are peeled and grated to use in the mash of *alcapurrias, pasteles** and other tropical dishes of which you will find recipes in this book. Although they are interchangeable as an accompanying vegetable, they are not so for these dishes. The malanga, for example, is too smooth and sweet to substitute for the yautia in dishes where this is called for.

Aroids - plants of the *Araceae* family, v.

Aroides - v. aroids

Arracacha - v. apio

Arroz - v. rice

Arroz con habichuelas - v. rice and beans

Arroz guisado - v. rice

Avocado - aguacate *(Persea americana)*, palta. The fruit of an American tree of the tropical and sub-tropical regions. Pear shaped, it can weight as much as 2 pounds. Its smooth or rough skin can be either light or dark green, or even purple. It is easily peeled by quartering the fruit and pulling the skin off. The pulp of a perfectly ripe fruit is yellow and smooth, but firm. You can tell by pressing the fruit with your fingers. It yields without feeling mushy. If bought when green and hard, it will ripen at room temperature or in a paper bag in one or two days. If not used immediately after that, it can be kept in the refrigerator for up to two days. The varieties grown in the West Indies are particularly noted for their tenderness.

B

Bacalao - v. salt codfish

Bacalao salado - idem.

Bacalao seco - idem.

Banana - *guineo (Musa sapientium), plátano*. The fruit of a tropical herb with a tree-like shape native probably in India. This is the common banana which is edible without cooking in its ripe stage —*guineo maduro*. It has a yellow skin, mottled with black when fully ripe, and sweet pulp. In Puerto Rican cookery bananas are also used in their immature, green stage, cooked as a vegetable.* At that stage they are called *guineos verdes*. They can be found in Latin American markets. The *plátano* is the Castillian Spanish term for the banana and does not mean plantain *(Musa paradisiaca)*, v.

Ladyfinger bananas - *guineítos niños*, are another variety

(Musa sapientum Champa) much grown in the West Indies. They are about 5" long, with pale, thin skin. They are very sweet and although they can be eaten raw when ripe, they are usually fried.* Other varieties include the red bananas *(Musa sapientum rubra)*, the *manzanos* or apple bananas —extremely sweet with an acid tinge—, the *mafafo*, which are used green for lighter and crispier *tostones** than those made with plantains, and the *Monte Cristo* bananas.

Banana leaves - *hojas de plátano*. The leaves of the banana *(Musa sapientum)*, v., or the plantain *(Musa paradisiaca*, v. About 9 feet long by 2 feet wide. Their central rib is cut off, their edges trimmed and then they are cut into square or rectangular pieces in the desired dimensions. They are wilted over the range or in the oven to make them flexible and then used to wrap foodstuffs that will be boiled or steamed, such as *pasteles*.* Sometimes they can be found in Latin American markets in packets. The leaves can be frozen successfully if well wrapped. As a substitute you may use parchment paper, although this will not impart neither the flavor of the aroma that banana leaves do.*

Batata - v. sweet potato

Beans and Peas - *habichuelas y guisantes* (Order: *Leguminosae)*. The seeds of plants which comprise a number of genera among which are the *Phaseolus, Vigna, Cicer* and *Cajanus*. These seeds grow in pods. In Puerto Rico the common nomenclature does not necessarily reflect the correct botanical classification, or varies from the usage of other West Indian isles or countries. To prevent confusion we will limit ourselves to Puerto Rican usage. In the Island's cookery, the beans and peas used are mostly in dried form with the exception of pigeon peas, v., mostly used in their immature, but shelled stage; some green beans used in *sopones**; and of course, the string or snap beans called *habichuelas tiernas*.

These are the ones most commonly used:

Black beans - *frijoles negros*. Turtle beans. Small, flat, black with a white dot.

Black-eyed peas - frijoles. Cowpeas. Small to medium, flat, with a black spot.

Chick peas - garbanzaos, v.

Lima beans - habas. Medium, flat, white.

Navy beans - *habichuelitas blancas*. Small, round, white.

Pigeon peas - gandules, v.

Pink beans - *habichuelas rosadas*. Medium, oval, dirty pink.

Pinto beans - *habichuelas pintas*. Medium, oval, light mottled pink.

Red Kidney Beans - *habichuelas marca diablo, habichuelas rojas*. Large, kidney shaped, reddish-sienna.

Bell peppers - v. peppers

Bija - v. annatto

Bijol - idem.

Bitter oranges - v. sour oranges

Black beans - v. beans and peas

Black-eyed peas - idem.

Blood sausage - v. sausages

Boniato - v. sweet potato

Breadfruit - *panapén (Artocarpus altilis), pana*. The fruit of a tropical tree widely cultivated in the tropics to use as a vegetable. It is round or semi-oblong with a diameter as wide as 8 inches. Its yellowish-green skin is sort of bumpy. Its flesh, cream colored, is eaten boiled, baked or fried.* It should be eaten at a stage where it is neither too green or too ripe. Some breadfruits are seedless; nevertheless, other varieties produce seeds which are boiled for eating.*, v.

Breadfruit seeds - *panas de pepita (Artocarpus altilis)*. The seeds of a seed-producing breadfruit, v., which are eaten boiled, with a texture and flavor not unlike chesnuts.*

Bullock's heart - v. soursop

Butifarras - v. sausages

C

Cabrito - v. kid

Caimito - v. star apple

Calabaza - v. West-Indian pumpkin

Caldero - This is a basic cooking pot ubiquitous in the Puerto Rican kitchen. It is used almost exclusively as an universal cooking utensil: for frying, braising, stewing, cooking rice, and even for desserts. Essentially it is a semi-spherical kettle or small cauldron with straight low sides tapering from a flat bottom. It has two small handles and a cover. *Calderos* are made either of heavy iron or thick aluminum and come in all sizes, from the very small to the gargantuan. Two of the more useful sizes are the two-quart (8½" x 3") and the four-quart (11" x 4"). The Puerto Rican cook will use nothing else for the rice, as it is essential for that prized side dish, the *pegao*, v. It is also perfect for fritters, as it is taller than a frying pan —thus having a large oil capacity— and low enough to let the vapor escape. It can be bought at Latin American markets, but a substitute can be a heavy iron, deep (3" high), chicken fryer.

California peppers - v. peppers

Caribbean land crab - v. great land crab

Carne cecina - v. jerked beef

Carrucho - v. conch

Casabe - v. yuca

Cashew apple - *pajuil (Anacardium occidentale), marañón.* The fruit of an evergreen native in all tropical countries. It has a kidney shaped, bright yellow or red receptable about 3" long and a nut that contains a poisonous kernel edible after roasting —the cashew nut. The flesh of the receptacle is tart and is used in compotes* and confections.*

Cassava - v. yuca

Cayenne peppers - v. peppers

Chayote - *(Sechium edule)*, christophine, *chuchu*, mirliton. A cucurbit native to the tropical Americas. Pear shaped, about 4 to 8" long, it can be either white or green, with smooth or striated skin. It is sometimes covered with soft spines. The flesh is firm and white and surrounds a single seed. It should be bought when firm. Refrigerate for up to a week if not using immediately. They are boiled to be used in salads, and their skin can be stuffed with their pulp and other ingredients.*

Cherimoya - v. soursop

Chicharrón - v. crackling

Chick peas - garbanzos *(Cicer arietinum).* The seeds of an herb native in West Asia which grow one or two per pod. They are usually found dried and must be soaked overnight before boiling and stewing.* They can be bought already boiled, canned in salted water.

Chili peppers - v. peppers

China - v. sour orange

Chorizos - v. sausages

Christophine - v. chayote

Chuchu - idem.

Cilantro - *(Coriandrum sativum),* coriander, Chinese parsley, *cilantrillo, culantro, culantrillo, coriandro.* An annual herb indigenous to southern Europe which is cultivated for its seeds and leaves, both of which are used as seasonings. The leaves are much used in Latin American cookery. It resembles the flat-leaf parsley, v., but the leaves are lighter in color and more pungent in smell and flavor. It is usually sold with the roots attached. Unless used immediately, keep roots and leaves attached. Do not wash until ready to use and keep wrapped in plastic in the refrigerator. The term *culantro* creates confusion, for in Puerto Rico this term is reserved for another plant, the leaves of which are widely used in cooking *(Eryngium foetidum),* v. Both form part of the *recao,* v., and the *sofrito,* v.* Since *E. foetidum* is seldom available outside of the Island, you may substitute cilantro for it, even though this is less pungent. Substitute in equal amounts of freshly finely chopped leaves. It can be found in Latin American and Oriental markets.

Cilantrillo - v. cilantro

Ciruela - v. golden apple

Cocolía - v. great land crab

Coco - v. coconut

Coconut - coco *(Cocos nucifera).* The fruit of a widespread palm which thrives in the tropics. It can be found either green *(coco verde)* or mature *(coco seco).* The green, or immature coconut is usually found unhusked at roadside stands where it is sold either at room temperature or refrigerated. The stem part is loped off with a machete until the nut is exposed. This is pierced and the sweet and refreshing water is drunk directly or with a straw. Once empty, the whole coconut is split to eat the immature, gelatinous, translucent flesh —also sweet— with a piece of the husk cut off in the shape of a small spatula. Both water and flesh are used in a sherbet* Ripe coconut is the familiar brown, hairy nut found in markets. This has been husked. From these nuts one gets the coconut water *(agua de coco)*, which is the transparent liquid drained out after piercing the eyes of the nut; the grated coconut *(coco rayado)*,* which is the grated sweet, firm, white flesh; and the coconut milk *(leche de coco)*,* which is the milky liquid extracted by squeezing the grated flesh. All are used extensively in recipes.*

Coconut milk - v. coconut

Coconut water - idem.

Coco rayado - idem.

Coco seco - idem.

Coco verde - idem.

Conch - carrucho *(Strombus gigas)*. The pink conch of the Caribbean. It is a large edible sea mollusk with a spiral shell. Its flesh is tough and must be tenderized by either pounding or boiling before using in salads or other recipes.*

Condimento crudo - v. uncooked condiment

Congo peas - v. pigeon peas

Cooked condiment - v. *sofrito*

Cooking banana - v. banana, plantain

Cooking ham - *jamón de cocinar*. A cured ham, sometimes sold as smoked picnic, sold in thick slices. It is basic to the *sofrito*, v.,* and not eaten by itself. It is one of the staples of the Puerto Rican larder. You may substitute any lightly smoked, cured ham as it is used diced and in small quantities.

Cooking pepper - v. peppers

Cooking tomato - v. tomatoes

Corazón - v. soursop

Coriander - v. cilantro

Coriandro - idem.

Corossol - v. soursop

Cowpeas - v. beans and peas

Crackling - *chicharrón*. An hors d'oeuvre prepared by deep frying pieces of pork skin to which some of the fat, and sometimes meat, is still attached.* Also used in *mofongos*.* They can be bought commercially in plastic bags, but they are usually tasteless compared to fresh. A Puerto Rican town, Bayamón, is known for its pork cracklings sold at roadside carts along with anisse-flavored lard bread.

Cuchifrito - Deep-fried morsels of pork sold at roadside stands. They can consist of ears, tail, stomach, intestines, and so forth. They are usually sold along *alcapurrias**, blood sausage, v., and fried sweet potatoes, v.

Culantro - *(Eryngium foetidum)*, Portorican coriander, *culantro de monte*, spiny coriander. A perennial herb of the *Umbilliferae* family, it is a thistle-like plant with deep green, spiny-toothed leaves, as long as 10 inches. It has a strong and pungent aroma and flavor similar to cilantro, v., but definitely much stronger. It is sometimes confused for cilantro *(Coriandrum sativum)* for this is also called *culantro*. Both form part of the *recao*, v., basic to the *sofrito*, v.* *Recao* is also used as a term for *E. foetidum* by itself. This herb is so much used in Puerto Rican cookery, that even though it is seldom found outside the Island, it is the one that is asked for in this book's recipes, just in case the reader happens to come upon it. If not available, substitute with an equal amount of chopped fresh cilantro leaves. 1½ teaspoon of *culantro* chopped into ¼" pieces equals one 8 inches long leaf. Fresh *culantro* leaves can be dried successfully in a 250°F oven. Rinse the leaves, shake well, and lay flat on a cookie sheet. Dry in the oven for 15-20 minutes. Once cool, crumble and keep in a tightly closed spice jar. Use one teaspoon dried *culantro* per tablespoon of fresh chopped leaves.

Culantro de monte - v. *culantro*

Culantrillo - v. cilantro

Custard apple - v. soursop

D

Dasheen - v. *Araceae*

F

Fatback - *tocino*. Strip of fat from the back of the pork which is cured by dry-salting. Usually found as a small slab about ¾" thick composed of the pork skin with the attached white fat. It is used in Puerto Rican cooking in the *sofrito*, v.*, in rice*, and other recipes. It is usually diced and rendered after removing the skin. The rendered fat is used for cooking, but the crispy pieces can be taken out or left in as part of the dish. It can be blanched for 10 minutes to reduce the saltiness. Sometimes it is called salt-pork, although technically this can come from other parts of the pork and be cured in a brine rather than with dry-salting.

Filete de bacalao - v. salt codfish

Flan - Properly speaking, a flan is an open tart with a sweet or savory filling. But in some parts of France it means a set-cream preparation. In Puerto Rico, as well as in other Latin countries, it means essentially a caramel custard baked in the oven and its variations. For the purposes of this book we will follow the Island's common usage and call flan any baked custard, and custards any stirred preparations done on the range top, such as ironed cream.*

Flat-leaf parsley - v. parsley

Frijoles - v. beans and peas

Frijoles negros - idem.

Frituras - Fritters of many kinds. They can be either savory or sweet. They can be made with batters flavored with shredded codfish —*bacalaítos**—, vegetables mashes enclosing a stuffing —*alcapurrias**—, fried vegetables such as *tostones,** and so forth. *Frituras* can be used either as side dishes or hors d'oeuvres.

Fruta bomba - v. papaya

Frying pepper - v. peppers

G

Galletas de soda - v. soda crackers

Gandules - v. pigeon peas

Garbanzos - v. chick peas

Golden apple - jobo *(Spondias dulcis)*. The fruit of a tree found in the tropics. It is ovoid, about 3 to 4 inches long and orange yellow. The acid-sweet pulp is also of a deep yellow color and surrounds a large spiny seed. It is eaten raw or made into conserves when ripe. There is a variety called *jobillo* or *ciruela (Spondias purpurea)* which is about 1" long and ovoidal. Its yellow variety is also found in Puerto Rico.

Great land crab - juey *(Cardisoma guanhumi)*, Caribbean land crab, white land crab, *guanhumi, tourlourou*. A crustacean highly prized for its meat in the Caribbean, much preferred over the blue sea crab, or *cocolía*, which is mainly used as bait. The carapace of the grayish-blue great land crab can measure up to 6 inches. It has large defensive pincers, one of which is very developed in the male. It lives far from the sea in sugar cane fields and coconut groves in holes that it digs down to six feet. This crab is nocturnal, and it is at night when it is caught. Not without giving a good fight, though, for they can feel ground vibrations and have good vision. The crabs, once caught, are kept in pens for a few days —males apart from females— and fed vegetables, fruits, grains and water to rid their flesh of any muddy flavor. Coconut meat and corn make them especialy tasty. They are boiled and used in many dishes.*
The mangrove crab —*juey de mangle (Aritus pisoni)* is another land crab that climbs mangroves above water level to feed on the leaves. Its taste is not as desirable as that of *Cardisoma guanhumi*.

Green banana - v. banana

Green pumpkin - v. West-Indian pumpkin

Grosella - v. star-gooseberry

Guanábana - v. soursop

Guanhumi - v. great land crab

Guava - Guayaba *(Psidium guajava)*. The fruit of a tropical-American tree or shrub. It is eaten raw when ripe, or cooked in conserves*, jellies, pastes or ice cream.* It can be round, oval, or pear shaped. Guavas range in size, but the common one is usually about 2 to 4" long, it is yellow skinned and has a white, yellow, or deep-pink flesh full of small seeds. They can be either acid or sweet. A ripe guava should yield to the pressure of the fingers without feeling mushy. They will keep in the refrigerator for several days.

Gueros - v. peppers

Guingambós - v. okra

Guinea - v. Guinea fowl

Guinea fowl - *Guinea.* The domestic Guinea fowl is a bird related to the pheasant that descends from a West African subspecies *(Numida meleagris galeata)* brought to Europe and the Americas by the Portuguese. It has a beautiful bright gray, spotted plumage. Its flesh, though delicious, has a tendency to dryness, so it is best when braised.*

Guineo - v. banana

Guineo maduro - idem.

Guineo mafafo - idem.

Guineo manzano - idem.

Guineo Monte Cristo - idem.

Guineo, guineíto niño - idem.

Guineo verde - idem.

Guisantes - v. beans and peas

Gumbo - v. okra

H

Habas - v. beans and peas

Habichuelas marca diablo - idem.

Habichuelas pintas - idem.

Habichuelas rosadas - idem.

Habichuelas tiernas - idem.

Habichuelas y guisantes - idem.

Habichuelitas blancas - idem.

Hojas de plátano - v. banana leaves

Hot chili pepper - v. peppers

I

Italian pepper - v. peppers

J

Jamón de cocinar - v. cooking ham

Jerked beef - tasajo, *carne cecina.* A sun-dried and salted beef usually sold in small slabs about 1" thick, covered with a layer of orange-colored lard. It has to be reconstituted and de-salted before cooking.* Even then, it keeps an agreeable chewey texture and salty flavor.

Jimbling - v. star-gooseberry

Jobo - v. golden apple

Jobillo - idem.

Juey - v. great land crab

Juey de mangle - v. great land crab

K

Key lime - v. acid lime

Kid - *cabrito.* The meat of the young goat, usually under a year old. *Capra egagrus hircus*, or the domestic goat, contrary to the popular view, is a very clean animal that prefers for food tasty leaves. Its meat is tender and flavorful when young.

L

Ladyfinger bananas - v. banana

Langosta - v. spiny lobster

Leche de coco - v. coconut

Lechón a la varita - v. roast pig

Lechón asado - idem.

Lechonera - idem.

Lechosa - v. papaya

Lerenes - v. sweet-corn root

Lima - v. acid lime

Lima beans - v. beans and peas

Limón - v. acid lime

Limón agrio - idem.

Limón maduro - idem.

Limón verde - idem.

Lobster - v. spiny lobster

Longaniza - v. sausages

M

Mabi - *mabí (Colubrina elliptica)*, naked wood. Small tree of Florida and the West Indies with a thin, scaly bark which is used to prepare a fermented beverage in the Caribbean islands.*

Mafafo banana - v. banana

Malanga - v. *Araceae*

Mamey - *(Mammea americana)*, mammee apple. The fruit of a tropical tree. It measures up to 6" in diameter and has a russet colored, rough skin. The juicy flesh is bright yellow or orangey and is eaten raw when ripe and also used in compotes and other recipes.*

Mammee apple - v. mamey

Mamón - v. soursop

Mandioca - v. yuca

Manioc - idem.

Mango - *(Mangifera indica), mangó.* The fruit of a tropical tree of Asian origin. There are many species which vary in size, shape, color and flavor. Most are oval or heart-shaped, about 3 to 5" long, although some varieties can be a lot larger. The skin is smooth, and when ripe, mostly yellow and reddish. The flesh of the ripe fruit adheres to a single large, flat stone, and is very sweet. They are easily peeled by piercing the skin and then pulling it off. Then they can be sliced to eat raw or used in recipes.* A ripe fruit should yield to the light pressure of the fingers and its skin should not be unduly mottled with black spots. Once ripe it will keep for several days in the refrigerator.

Mangrove crab - v. great land crab

Manzano - banana - v. banana

Marañón - v. cashew apple

Mirliton - v. chayote

Monte Cristo banana - v. banana

Morcillas - v. sausages

N

Nakedwood - v. mabi

Ñame - v. yam

Naranja agria - v. sour orange

Naranja amarga - idem.

Naranja de Sevilla - idem.

Navy beans - v. beans and peas

Níspero - v. sapodilla

O

Octopus - *pulpo* (Genus: *Octopus*): A mollusk with eight arms with suckers, a saclike body and a large head. As with the conch, v., its meat is tough and has to be either pounded or boiled for a long time, in order to tenderize it for serving in salad, or cooking in other forms.*

Okra - *guingambós (Abelmoschus esculentus)*, gumbo. The pods of a plant native in Africa and cultivated in southern climates. The pods can be as long as one foot, but they are eaten as a vegetable only when immature, for later they become woody. The most tender are less than 3" long. They should be bought when fresh and bright green. They are fried, used in gumbo soup or in the Puerto Rican manner, stewed with pork,* or in rice with okra.* They have a mucilaginous interior that is not to everybody's taste, thus dividing people into lovers or haters. This liquid is used as a thickener. If the okra are very small they can be cooked whole —just trim off the stems being careful not to pierce the pod and release the liquid. If they are to be cut, once they are sliced, dip them for 15 minutes in water and vinegar and then rinse. This eliminates most of the gummy liquid.

Orange - v. sour orange

Orange flower water - *agua de azahar*, orange blossom water. A distillation made of orange blossoms for flavoring desserts.

Otaheite gooseberry - v. star-gooseberry

P

Pajuil - v. cashew apple

Palta - v. avocado

Pana - v. breadfruit

Pana de pepita - v. breadfruit seeds

Panapén - v. breadfruit

Papaya - *(Carica papaya)*, pawpaw, lechosa, *fruta bomba*. The fruit of a tropical American tree. Its thin smooth skin, when mature, ranges from yellow to orange. The flesh is thick and yellow with black seeds. It can grow as large as 20" long and weight as much as 10 pounds. It is eaten raw when mature for its sweet, melonlike flavor. The immature or green papaya is prepared as a compote in Puerto Rico.*

Parchment paper - *pergamino de cocina*. A grease and water resistant paper for wrapping foodstuffs to be cooked. A substitute for banana leaves, v.

Parsley - *perejil (Petroselinum crispum)*. The commonly used curly leaf parsley. The species *Petroselinum latifolium*, or flat leaf parsley can be used as a substitute for either the cilantro, v., or the *culantro*, v., although it is far from being as pungent in aroma or flavor as these.

Patitas de cerdo - v. pig's feet

Pawpaw - v. papaya

Peas - v. beans and peas

Pegao - From *pegado*, literally, stuck. Cooking rice in a *caldero*, v., in the Puerto Rican manner will produce a crust of toasted and crunchy rice that sticks to the bottom of the pot. Once the rice is served on a platter, this *pegao* is scrapped off the bottom of the *caldero* and served as another side dish. Everybody gets some to mix with the rice, or to eat by itself, as it is highly prized. The sound of scraping off the *pegao (raspar el pegao)* is one of the most typical sounds coming from the Puerto Rican kitchen.

Peppers - *pimientos y ajíes*. The fruits of *Capsicum frutescens* and its derivatives, all of New World origin. They are pod-like, seeded and fleshy. They vary widely in size, shape, color and pungency. So much so, that many are still not botanically classified. Some of those used in the Puerto Rican kitchen are:

Frying peppers - *pimientos de cocinar,* Italian peppers, California peppers. Thin skinned, from 3 to 5" long, 2" wide, crooked and tapering towards the apex. They are found in the market green, greenish yellow or yellow with red. They are mild and are basic to the *sofrito,* v.*, for which purpose you might substitute bell peppers. They can be stuffed.* For this, they can be substituted by *gueros.*

Bell peppers - *pimientos de asar (Capsicum grossum),* sweet peppers. Thick skinned, about 4 to 5" long, puffy with furrowed sides, and oblong. They are found green, yellow or red. A mild pepper, it is used roasted,* in salads, or stuffed. For certain purposes you may substitute pimientos.

Pimientos - *pimientos morrones.* A variety of the bell pepper that is tapered. It is usually sold in jars or cans packed in water and salt. Red in color, they can be substituted by roasted fresh red bell peppers.

Sweet chili peppers - *ajíes dulces,* (possibly *Capsicum chinense* var. *rocotillo*). A small pepper, usualy turban shaped, about 1" in diameter, thin skinned, green, yellow or red. A mild pepper, but highly aromatic. It is a basic ingredient in Puerto Rican food, particularly in the *sofrito,* v.* Because of its strong flavor and aroma, it determines much of the country's cooking flavor. It is found in Latin American markets, but unfortunately, even under refrigeration, it does not keep well. It loses most of its pungency soon after being taken off the plant. As there is no substitute, if unavailable, it should be simply omitted.

Hot chili peppers - *ajíes bravos, ajíes picantes.* There are many varieties of different pungency, but all are hot. Puerto Rican cooking is not particularly hot, if at all, so these peppers are used selectively. They are used in *pique,* v.*, a hot sauce that is placed on the table to use to taste. Most of the hot chilis used in the Island are of the small varieties, thin and tapering, such as the cayennes or tabascos. Seed before using, and be very careful to wash your hands after handling. They are highly irritating, particularly to the eyes.

Pergamino de cocina - v. parchment paper

Perejil - v. parsley

Picadillo - A dish of ground beef or pork, sauteed with vegetables, herbs and spices. It can be eaten as such, but it is also used as a stuffing for poultry, fritters and turnovers.*

Pigeon peas - *gandules (Cajanus cajan),* Congo peas. The seeds growing in pods of a tropical shrub of probable African origin. In Puerto Rico they are shelled just before maturity, when their color is still green. They are stewed and used in rice dishes and other recipes.* They can be bought dried, but also boiled and canned in salted water.

Pig's feet - *patitas de cerdo.* These are found packed in dry-salt. They are the ones to be used for recipes in this book. Do not use those brined or pickled.

Pimenton - *pimentón,* Spanish paprika. A seasoning spice, deep orange-red made from ground sweet to hot red peppers. Substitute a Hungarian paprika that is not too sweet.

Pimiento - v. peppers

Pimiento de asar - idem.

Pimiento de cocinar - idem.

Pimiento de freir - idem.

Pimientos morrones - idem.

Piña - v. pineapple

Pineapple - *Piña (Ananas comosus),* ananas. The fruit of an herb native to tropical America. This fruit is properly the thickened stem in which the berries are imbeded. About one foot long, it is ripe when greenish yellow tinged with red, and with a strong sweet aroma. It is peeled, cored, eaten raw, juiced, or cooked.* It is very sweet, fleshy and juicy. The Porto Rico variety is very large.

Pink beans - v. beans and peas

Pinto beans - idem.

Pique - A hot sauce made by steeping hot chili peppers in vinegar and water or sour orange juice, v.* It is kept in a jar to use as an ingredient or directly at the table to taste.

Plantain - *plátano (Musa paradisíaca),* cooking banana. The tropical fruit of a perennial herb with a trunk-like structure, probably native in India. It is a fleshy fruit with thick skin, 6 to 12" long, edible only when cooked either at its green or at its mature stage. It is cooked and eaten as a vegetable, although it is also used in compotes.* In its immature state it is called *plátano verde*, or green plantain. There are two degrees of ripeness: when greenish-yellow, it is called *pintón*, or mottled. When it is fully ripe, bright yellow and mottled with black, it is known as *plátano maduro* or *amarillo*. A ripe plantain should yield to the pressure of the fingers without feeling unduly soft. They can be kept in the refrigerator to hold them at the green or ripe stage you want them to be. They will ripen at room temperature kept in a brown paper bag. They are a staple of Puerto Rican cookery and are used more often than potatoes. *Plátano* in Castillian Spanish does not mean the plantain, but the common banana, v.

Plátano - v. plantain

Plátano maduro - idem.

Plátano pintón - idem.

Plátano verde - idem.

Plum tomato - v. tomato

Portorican coriander - v. *culantro*

Pulpo - v. octopus

Q

Queso de la tierra - Literally, cheese from the homeland, or native cheese, also called *queso del país*. This is a Puerto Rican white, lightly salty, pressed cheese which is used mainly to accompany compotes, pastes or preserves. Substitute any mild, crumbly cheese, or a cheddar.

Queso del país - v. *queso de la tierra*

R

Recao - From *recado*, the daily provision or marketing. In past times this was a combination of equal amounts of fresh cilantro and *culantro* leaves, v., sweet chili peppers, v., one cookinq tomato, v., and one frying pepper, v., to be used in the *sofrito**, v. The amount was stated in terms of the price, i.e., 5 cents or 10 cents of *recao*. Sometimes the term also is used to refer only to the leaves of *culantro*.

Red kidney beans - v. beans and peas

Rice - *arroz (Oryza sativa).* The grain of a marshy grass cultivated extensively in warm regions. The rice that is used daily in Puerto Rico is the white, polished, short-grain rice. Contrary to the usage of some of the other Caribbean islands, long-grain rice is used only in special recipes or occasions. *Arroz guisado*, which would literally mean stewed rice, refers to a rice cooked with other ingredients and of a yellow color, such as rice with chicken*, rice with sausages*, and so forth.

Rice and beans - *arroz con habichuelas.* A staple of the Puerto Rican meal, highly nutritious for it is almost a complete protein. It usually means simmered white rice* served with stewed beans or peas.* It is used as a side dish, but in the case of *arroces guisados*, v. rice, it is considered as a main dish, for these many times contain meat.

Roast pig - *lechón asado.* This is also called *lechón a la varita*, or spit-roast pig. Whole pork roasted over a charcoal pit, it is seasoned with salt, pepper, garlic and oregano. There are roadside stands or restaurants that specialize on this typical dish. Called *lechoneras*, they usually sell cooked tropical vegetables to accompany the pork, plus other pork dishes such as *morcillas*, v., or pork-offal ragout.*

S

Salchichas - v. sausages

Salsa de tomate - v. tomato sauce

Salt codfish - *bacalao* (Family: *Gadidae*), *bacalao seco, bacalao salado.* A fish from a family that includes some 22 genera. It is dry-salted, a custom that stems from pre-refrigeration times when the fish had to survive the long trips from the sea inland. It must be reconstituted and de-salted before cooking.* Even then, it retains a characteristic and pleasant chewy texture and light saltiness. As a Puerto Rican food staple it goes back to the 17th Century when it was imported from Seville. It is found in two forms: either the whole fillet of a small fish, with some bones and skin, or as a small piece of bone fillet from a larger fish.

Salt-pork - v. fatback

Sapodilla - *níspero (Manilkara zapota).* The fruit of a native tropical-American evergreen. It measures about 2½" diameter. Its skin is rough and brown; its flesh, sweet and translucent yellow-brown.

Sausages - *salchichas*. These are some of the most commonly used sausages in Puerto Rico:

Butifarras - A white pork sausage prepared in 3 to 4" x 1 to 1½" links. They are seasoned with garlic, pepper, salt, anisse, and sometimes cinnamon and spice cloves. They are served as a main dish fried until golden brown.

Chorizos - A Spanish pork sausage, lightly smoked and seasoned essentially with garlic and pimenton, v. The meat is coarsely chopped and stuffed in 3 to 4" links about 1" thick. They are sold fresh or packed in lard in tin cans. They can be kept for several weeks under refrigeration. They are used in dishes of Spanish origin brought to the Island. Substitute for any lightly smoked and spiced uncooked Italian, French or Polish sausage.

Longaniza - Literally, long sausage, this is another pork sausage colored with annatto, v. They are linkless and about ¾" in diameter. These are seasoned with garlic, pepper, oregano, cilantro and bay leaves. Used in rice* and other dishes.

Morcillas - Blood sausage. A black sausage, linkless, varying in thickness, made from the fresh blood of the pork, pieces of fat, and sometimes, cooked rice. It is seasoned with onions, salt, pepper, and sometimes hot chili peppers. Served fried as an hors d'oeuvre.

Seville orange - v. sour orange

Sierra - *(Scombero morus)*, Spanish mackerel. A milder fish than the Atlantic mackerel. It is found in the Gulf Coast and off the coast of Florida. It is fried in slices or made into escabeche.* Substitute with any mild, dark-fleshed fish.

Snap beans, string beans - v. beans and peas

Soda crackers - *galletas de soda*. Another staple of the Puerto Rican larder, they are used for eating, but also coarsely crushed for breading. Substitute bread crumbs.

Sofrito - A cooked condiment.* Literally, it means something lightly fried. The *sofrito* in Puerto Rico is a sauce composed of fatback, v., cooking ham, v., annatto lard, v., garlic, onion, cooking tomatoes, v., peppers, v., *culantro*, v., cilantro, v., oregano, pepper, salt and tomato sauce, v. These are all cooked together until the flavors blend well. It is the starting point of most dishes, not unlike the Italian *battuto*. It is used in stews, braises, and of course, in the stewed beans.* It can be cooked beforehand and kept in a tightly closed jar in the refrigerator for up to 2 weeks, or frozen in small quantities to use as needed. This book uses a different procedure, though. Instead of having *sofrito* around, an uncooked condiment* made of fresh vegetables, herbs and oregano is prepared and kept in the refrigerator or freezer. This allows the flexibility of adjusting the rest of the ingredients to the needs of each particular recipe.

Sour orange - *naranja agria (Citrus aurantium), naranja amarga,* bitter orange. The fruit of a semi-tropical tree of the Citrus genus. It is used commercially in the preparation of marmalade, and is also used in the tropics for the confection of compotes, pastes and other candies.* In Cuba its juice is used in marinades for pork and poultry. When ripe, the skin keeps its green color. This skin is thick and rough. The juice is sour, unlike that of the edible common orange —called in Puerto Rico *china*. There is a hybrid with sweet juice called Seville orange.

Soursop - *guanábana (Annona muricata),* guanábana, *corossol.* The fruit of a tropical American evergreen. It is of an ovoidal shape and measures up to 8" long. The skin is dark green and is covered by short fleshy spines. The pulp is white and sweet with a tinge of acid. It is used in the preparation of drinks and ice cream.* Other fruits from the Annonaceae family are:

Cherimoya *(Annona cherimola)*

Custard apple *(Annona reticulata),* bullock's heart, *corazón, mamón,* anona

Sweetsop *(Annona squamosa),* sugar apple, anon

Spanish mackerel - v. sierra

Spanish paprika - v. pimenton

Spiny coriander - v. *culantro*

Spiny lobster - *langosta* (Family: *Palinuridae).* A crustacean with no pincers, unlike the true lobster, and with thorny protuberances in the carapace and at the base of the second antennae, thus its name. It can measure up to 15" long and weigh as much as 4 pounds. Three of the species, the European *(Palinurus vulgaris)*, the American *(Palinurus argus)*, and the South African *(Janus Lalandi)* are highly prized for their tail meat. It can be substituted by the true lobster, either the European *(Homarus gammarus)* or the American *(Homarus americanus)*.

Star apple - caimito *(Chrysophyllum cainito)*. The fruit of an evergreen found in the West Indies and Central America. The globular fruit is about 3 to 4" in diameter with a smooth skin which is either white, greenish, or purple. These are the same colors of its sweet flesh. Cut in cross-section it shows its seeds in a star pattern, thus its name. It is exported very little, if at all, for the fruit must ripen on the tree. Caimitos can be kept in the refrigerator for a few days.

Star-gooseberry - *grosella (Phillantus acidus)*, jimbling, otaheite-gooseberry, West Indian gooseberry. The angled fruit, ¾" in diameter of a South Asian tree naturalized in South Florida and the West Indies. The skin is a pale yellow which turns bright red when cooked. The single stone of the berry remains in it, so be forewarned if you find it in compote for the first time. The fruit has to be chewed and the stone discarded, not unlike an olive. The fruit can be eaten raw when ripe, but it is very acid. It is an acquired taste, very much as eating raw tamarind, v. The common name in Spanish might create a confusion with currants (Genus: *Ribes*), the English name a confusion with the true goose-berry (Genus: *Grossularia*). it is neither of these.

Sugar aple - v. soursop

Sweet chili pepper - v. peppers

Sweet-corn roots - *lerenes (Calathea allouia)*. The edible tubers of a tropical American herb. About 1½" in diameter. They have light brown, thin skin with white firm flesh. They are boiled until tender to eat as a vegetable.

Sweet peppers - v. peppers

Sweet potato - batata *(Ipomoea batatas), boniato*. Tuberous vegetable grown in both of the Americas. Its skin color varies from white to pink to purple to brown. The flesh can also be white, yellow-orange or purple. The yellow-orange fleshed varieties are incorrectly called yam, v., altogether a different tuber. In spite of its name, it is not a potato either. Sweet potatoes can be boiled, baked, or roasted.* The white-flesh variety is the one called for in the recipes of this book. It can be found mostly in Latin American markets by the name of *batata blanca* (white sweet potato).

Sweetsop - v. soursop

T

Tabasco pepper - v. peppers

Tamarind - tamarindo *(Tamarindus indica).* The fruit of a tropical evergreen which is also grown for ornament. The pods are brittle, about 8" long and cinnamon brown in color. They enclose the black seeds which are surrounded by the brownish pulp which is edible, but very tart. It is eaten raw, made into drinks* or candy, into condiments, and also used for medicinal purposes.

Tanier - v. *Araceae*

Tapioca plant - v. yuca

Taro - v. *Araceae*

Tasajo - v. jerked beef

Tocino - v. fatback

Tomate - v. tomato

Tomate de cocinar - idem.

Tomate italiano - idem.

Tomato - *tomate* (Genus: *Lycopersicon*). The fruit of annual and perennial herbs native in South America. There are many varieties. In Puerto Rico, besides the salad tomatoes, the so-called *tomate de cocinar*, or cooking tomato *(Lycopersicon lycopersicum)* is widely used, particularly in the *sofrito.** This is the old-time tomato, smaller than the hybrids, brilliant red, with grooved sides and a more acid taste. A good substitute is the Italian or plum tomato *(L. esculentum pyriforme)*.

Tomato sauce - *salsa de tomate.* This book includes several tomato sauce recipes made from fresh tomatoes. They are used mainly in pasta dishes.* For cooking purposes, as in the *sofrito**, v., stews, beans, and so forth, the tomate sauce called for is the one sold in 8-ounce cans, which is always found in the Puerto Rican larder.

Tourlourou - v. great land crab

Turtle beans - v. beans and peas

U

Uncooked condiment - *condimento crudo*.* A combination of tomatoes, peppers, onions, *culantro*, v., cilantro, v., and oregano, all ground in a food processor or blender to be used as the basis for the *sofrito*., v.* Can be kept in the refrigerator or freezer in ½ cup quantities to be used as needed.

W

West-Indian gooseberry - v. star goose-berry

West-Indian lime - v. acid lime

West-Indian pumpkin - calabaza (Family: *Cucurbitaceae)*, green pumpkin, *zapallo*. A member of the gourd family, large, round or oval, with green or green-orange skin. Its firm and yellow flesh is similar to that of the winter squashes. It is not the American pumpkin, but it can be substituted by it or by any of the other winter squashes. It is usually boiled and used as an ingredient for many dishes, and as a thickener for the sauce of the stewed beans.*

Y

Yam - *ñame* (Family: *Dioscoraceae*). The tuberous root of plants of the warm regions of both hemispheres. Some of the species are cultivated for their mealy roots, eaten as a vegetable after peeling and boiling. The brown skin is thick and slightly bristly in some varieties such as Dioscorea alata or D. rotundata. D. sativa has flesh that can be white or yellow. This is the true yam, a name incorrectly applied to the sweet potato *(Ipoema batatas)*, v. When buying make sure that they are firm and fresh. They can be kept in the refrigerator for several days.

Yautía - v. *Araceae*

Yuca - *(Manihot esculenta)*, cassava, manioc, tapioca plant, *mandioca*. The tuberous edible root of a tropical American shrub widely used for food. The common name of yuca should not lead to confusion with the ornamental plants of the *Yucca* genus. The long starchy roots of the *Manihot esculenta* have a dark brown, bark-like skin. The flesh is white and firm. One variety is poisonous until cooked, but it is seldom found in the markets nowadays. Sweet yuca is peeled, cut into pieces and boiled to be served as a vegetable. Its grated flesh is used in *yuca pasteles* and in the flat bread of the Puerto Rican Taino indians, the *casabe*. Buy when fresh and firm, and refrigerate if not used within a few days.

Z

zapallo - v. West-Indian pumpkin

SOURCES:

Bailey, L.H. The Standard Cyclopedia of Horticulture. The McMillan Company, New York, 1930

Bailey, L.H. and Ethel Zoe Bailey. Hortus Second —A Concise Dictionary of Gardening, General Horticulture and Cultivated Plants in North America. The McMillan Company. New York, 1941.

Grzimek, Bernard, Dr. h. c., Ed. in Chief. Animal Life Encyclopedia. Van Nostrand Reinhold Co. 1974.

Little, Elbert L., Frank H. Wadsworth, and José Marrero. Arboles comunes de Puerto Rico y las Islas Vírgenes. Editorial Universidad de Puerto Rico. Río Piedras, 1967.

Martorell, Luis, Alain H. Liogier, and Roy O. Woodbury. Catálogo de los nombres vulgares y científicos de las plantas de Puerto Rico. Universidad de Puerto Rico, Recinto de Mayagüez y Estación Experimental Agrícola. Río Piedras, 1981.

Webster's Third New International Dictionary of the English Language. Ed. in Chief: Philip Babcock Gove. G & C Merriam Co. Springfield, 1976.

CHAPTER I: THE CORNERSTONES

ANNATTO OIL OR LARD

(Aceite o manteca de achiote)

1/2 cup annatto seeds
1 cup vegetable oil or lard

1. Sift the seeds in a colander to get rid of any dust or leaf particles.

2. Heat the oil or lard in a small saucepan over medium heat. Add the annatto seeds and reduce the heat to low. Cook for some 5 minutes, stirring occasionally, until the oil or lard is tinged a deep orange annatto color. Do not use high heat as this makes it bitter.

3. Strain and let cool. Refrigerate covered and use as needed in recipes. It lasts indefinitely in the icebox.

NOTES: If the seeds are of high quality, and only low heat was used, they can be cooked once more. Annatto oil or lard can be bought in jars at Latin American specialty stores or at some supermarkets.

UNCOOKED CONDIMENT

(Condimento crudo)

1 large seeded green frying pepper
1 peeled medium onion
4 large seeded sweet chili peppers
5 *culantro* leaves
3 cilantro sprigs
1/4 teaspoon ground oregano
1 large tomato

1. Chop coarsely all the vegetables and *culantro* leaves. Pull off the cilantro leaves and discard the stems.

2. In a food processor fitted with the steel blade or in a blender, grind the onion, frying pepper, sweet chili peppers, *culantro*

and cilantro leaves and the oregano. With the motor running add the tomato pieces a few at a time and process until all is finely ground.

3. Refrigerate or freeze by half cups in covered containers to be used as required in recipes.

NOTES: The condiment keeps for about 2 weeks in the refrigerator, about six months in the freezer. If *culantro* leaves are unavailable, substitute the leaves of one cilantro sprig per each *culantro* leaf.

Yield: about 1 cup

COOKED CONDIMENT

(Sofrito)

- 1 ounce finely diced fatback (1/4 cup)
- 1 tablespoon annatto oil or lard, p. 47
- 2 large minced garlic cloves
- 1 cup uncooked condiment, p. 47
- 1/8 teaspoon ground pepper
- 2 ounces diced cooking ham (1/2 cup)

1. In a heavy skillet sauté the fatback over moderate heat until it has rendered the fat.

2. Add the annatto oil, garlic and uncooked condiment. Lower the heat and cook, stirring, for 10 minutes, or until the vegetables are soft.

3. Add the pepper and ham. Cook an additional 10 minutes, stirring occasionally.

4. Refrigerate or freeze by the half cup in covered containers to use as needed. In the refrigerator it keeps for about 2 weeks; in the freezer, about 6 months.

Yield: about 1 cup

MARINADE

(Adobo)

Per pound of pork, beef or fowl:

3/4 teaspoon salt
1/8 teaspoon ground pepper
1/4 teaspoon ground oregano
1 pressed medium garlic clove or 1/4 teaspoon garlic powder
1 tablespoon olive oil (optional)
1 teaspoon vinegar (optional)

1. Rub the meat well with the salt.

2. Mix the rest of the ingredients except the oil and vinegar and rub well over the surface of the meat. Do not put inside the cavities of fowl.

3. Blend the optional olive oil and vinegar and dribble over the meat.

4. Cover and let stand for one half to one hour. Otherwise refrigerate for a few hours or overnight until ready to cook. Remove from the refrigerator about one hour before cooking.

NOTE: A dry marinade may be prepared in advance in larger quantities and kept in a tightly covered spice jar. Omit the olive oil and vinegar and use garlic powder instead of fresh garlic. Use 1 1/4 teaspoon of this dry marinade per pound of meat. Rub over the surface, then dribble the optional olive oil and vinegar over it.

CHAPTER II:
SAUCES, DRESSINGS AND DIPS

TOMATO SAUCE

(Salsa de Tomate)

- 6 cups chopped fresh or canned tomatoes (3 pounds fresh tomatoes)
- 2 tablespoons olive oil
- 1 chopped medium onion
- 1 small frying green pepper, seeded and chopped
- 2 large pressed garlic cloves
- 2 medium sweet chili peppers, seeded and chopped
- 1/4 teaspoon salt
- 1/4 teaspoon sugar
- 1/8 teaspoon ground oregano
- 2 chopped medium *culantro* leaves
- 1/2 teaspoon *pimentón*
- 1/4 cup dry vermouth
- 1/4 cup beef, chicken or vegetable stock, water, or the juice of the canned tomatoes

1. Sauté the onion, green pepper, garlic and chili peppers in the olive oil over medium-low heat for 5-10 minutes without browning in a heavy bottomed saucepan.

2. Add the rest of the ingredients and bring to a boil.

3. Cover, reduce the heat to low, and simmer for 1 1/2 hours.

4. Puree in a food processor or mill, then strain in a colander pressing the sauce out of the ingredients with a spoon.

5. Return the sauce to the pan and bring to a boil. Reduce the heat to a slow boil and cook uncovered for 1 to 1 1/2 hours or until it reaches the desired thickness. Stir often to prevent scorching the bottom.

6. Adjust the seasonings to taste.

7. Serve over hot pasta or continue with your recipe.

Yield: about 3 cups

CHUNKY TOMATO SAUCE

(Salsa de tomate en trozos)

4 cups plum or salad tomatoes, peeled, seeded and coarsely chopped, p.132, or chopped canned tomatoes (2 1/2 pounds fresh tomatoes)
2 tablespoons olive oil
1/4 cup finely minced onion
2 large minced garlic cloves
1 medium sweet chili pepper, seeded and minced
1 minced *culantro* leaf
1/4 teaspoon salt
1/4 teaspoon sugar
1/8 teaspoon ground oregano

1. In a heavy bottomed saucepan cook the onion, garlic, sweet chili pepper and *culantro* in the olive oil over medium-low heat for 5-10 minutes without browning.

2. Add the tomatoes, salt, sugar and oregano. Simmer covered for 5-10 minutes.

3. Uncover and simmer for 20 minutes.

4. Raise the heat to a slow boil and cook for 10-15 minutes or until the sauce thickens to taste. Stir frequently to prevent scorching.

5. Adjust seasonings to taste.

Yield: about 1 1/2 cups

DORA ROMANO'S SPAGUETTI SAUCE

(Salsa para espaguetis a la Dora Romano)

1 1/2 cup tomato sauce, p.53, or canned tomato sauce
6 bacon strips cut into 1/2" pieces
3/4 cup finely chopped onion
3/4 cup green frying pepper, seeded and finely diced
1 large minced garlic clove
12 pimiento-stuffed green olives, cut into 1/4" slices
2 ounces crumbled cheddar cheese

1. Fry the bacon pieces until crisp in a heavy frying pan. Drain on paper towels and save.

2. Remove all but 3 tablespoons of the bacon fat and cook the onion, pepper and garlic over medium-low heat for 5-10 minutes. Do not brown.

3. Add the tomato sauce and olives. Cover and simmer for 10 minutes.

4. Add the cheese and stir until it melts well into the sauce.

5. Serve over cooked spaghetti sprinkled with the crumbled crisp bacon.

Yield: about 3 cups

PASTA SAUCE WITH CHICKEN WINGS

(Salsa para pastas con alas de pollo)

2 pounds chicken wings
2 1/2 teaspoons salt
2 pressed medium garlic cloves
1/4 teaspoon ground oregano
1/8 teaspoon ground pepper
1/3 cup vegetable oil
1/2 cup uncooked condiment, p. 47
1 tablespoon capers, minced after measuring
1 1/2 cup tomato sauce, p.53, chunky tomato sauce, p.54 or canned tomato sauce
10 medium green or ripe pitted olives
1/2 teaspoon sugar (optional)
1 1/2 cup stock or water

1. Remove the tips of the wings.

2. Divide at the joints. Rub with the salt, then with the garlic, oregano and pepper. Let stand for at least 30 minutes.

3. In a *caldero* or chicken fryer heat the oil over medium-high heat. Brown the wings, remove and set apart.

4. Drain all but 2 tablespoons of the browning oil.

5. Set on low heat and cook the uncooked condiment and capers for 5 minutes.

6. Add the tomato sauce, olives and optional sugar. Cook for 5 more minutes.

7. Add the chicken wings and stock or water. Bring to a boil, cover, lower the heat and simmer for 45 minutes.

8. Uncover and raise the heat to thicken the sauce, if necessary, to the desired consistency.

9. Serve over hot pasta with parmesan cheese.

Serves: 6

SPAGUETTI SAUCE WITH MEATBALLS AND SPARERIBS

(Salsa para espaguetis con albóndigas y costillas)

Tomato Sauce

14 1/2-ounce can Italian style peeled tomatoes, coarsely chopped
10 1/2-ounce can tomato puree
1/2 cup tomato sauce
6 tablespoons tomato paste
2 tablespoons olive oil
1 medium minced onion (3/4 cup)
1 large minced garlic clove
1 1/2 cup water or stock
1 3/4 teaspoons salt
1/4 teaspoon Italian seasoning
1/4 teaspoon dried basil
1 small bay leaf
3 tablespoons chopped parsley
2 or 3 teaspoons sugar, depending on the acidity of the tomatoes and puree
1/4 teaspoon hot sauce or 1/8 teaspoon ground pepper

Spareribs

1 1/2 pounds country style spareribs, cut into 1-rib segments
1 1/4 teaspoon salt
1/2 cup vegetable oil
1 large pressed garlic clove
4 crushed peppercorns

Meatballs

3/4 pound ground beef
3/4 teaspoon salt
2 pressed garlic cloves
1 tablespoon chopped parsley
1/4 teaspoon ground pepper
1/4 cup parmesan cheese
3 white bread slices, crust removed
1/2 cup water
1 lightly beaten egg
flour

1. In a large heavy-bottomed saucepan cook the onion and minced garlic in the two tablespoons of olive oil over medium low heat for 5 minutes.

2. Add the rest of the tomato sauce ingredients and mix well. Bring to a simmer and cook covered for 3 hours. Stir occasionally.

3. In the meantime, prepare the spareribs and meatballs.

4. Rinse the spareribs and pat dry. Season with the 1 1/4 teaspoon salt and set apart.

5. Mix the ground beef with the 3/4 teaspoon salt, garlic, tablespoon of parsley, pepper and parmesan cheese.

6. Soak the bread slices in the water, mash and mix well with the ground beef.

7. Blend in the beaten egg.

8. Make about 20 meatballs with this mixture, each one about 1 1/2" in diameter. Set apart.

9. In a large skillet set over medium high heat, cook briefly and without browning the garlic clove and crushed peppercorns in the 1/2 cup of vegetable oil. Remove the garlic.

10. Brown the spareribs in this oil and add them to the simmering sauce.

11. Dredge the meatballs in flour and shake off the excess. Brown in the same oil where you browned the spareribs, then add to the simmering sauce.

12. Continue cooking the sauce for the full three hours.

13. Adjust the seasonings to taste.

Yield: about 9 1/2 cups, enough for 10 people

UNCOOKED TOMATO AND AVOCADO SAUCE FOR PASTA

(Salsa cruda de tomate y aguacate para pastas)

1 1/2 pound ripe, but firm, salad tomatoes, peeled, seeded and coarsely chopped, p. 132
1 ripe, but firm, large avocado
1/2 cup olive oil
1 small garlic clove, finely minced or slivered
2 teaspoons finely chopped fresh basil
1/4 teaspoon salt
1/8 teaspoon ground pepper

1. Blend well the oil, garlic, basil, salt and pepper.

2. Add the tomatoes and mix well.

3. Peel the avocado, and cut the meat into 3/4" cubes. Fold gently into the other ingredients.

4. Marinade at room temperature for two hours before serving over hot pasta.

Serves: 6

MEXICAN STYLE SAUCE

(Salsa a la mexicana)

2 tablespoons olive oil
1 large minced garlic clove
1 cup tomatoes, peeled, seeded and finely chopped, p.132 or 1/2 cup canned tomato puree
1/4 teaspoon salt
1/8 teaspoon ground oregano
1 tablespoon minced cilantro leaves
2 small hot chili peppers, seeded and minced
1/4 cup beef or chicken stock

1. In a heavy bottomed skillet sauté the garlic without browning in the olive oil over low heat.

2. Add the rest of the ingredients and simmer uncovered until it thickens. Stir occasionally to prevent scorching.

3. Use warm on egg dishes or tacos

NOTE: You may use more chilis if you want a hotter sauce. For a milder one, just halve the chilis lengthwise and remove the seeds. You may use bottled hot sauce instead of the chilis —up to 4 teaspoons according to preference.

Yield: about 3/4 cup

GRAVY FOR ROAST POULTRY, BEEF OR PORK

(Salsa para asados de ave, res o cerdo)

- 2 cups pan juices rendered by the roast, stock, water or a combination of any of these
- 4 tablespoons all-purpose flour
- 4 tablespoons butter

1. Remove the roast from the pan.

2. If the pan juices have not burned, add 1/2 cup of water or stock to the pan and cook over moderate heat, scraping the brown bits off the bottom.

3. Remove from the pan and degrease.

4. Measure 2 cups, put in a heavy saucepan and bring to a simmer.

5. Prepare a *beurre manié* by kneading together the butter and flour and forming little balls about 3/8" diameter.

6. Stir the balls into the simmering sauce, a few at a time, until they blend in and thicken the sauce to the desired consistency. You may not have to use all of the *beurre manié*.

7. Adjust the seasonings and strain the gravy before serving with the roast.

NOTE: You may omit the *beurre manié* thickening. Simply follow the recipe up to step 3 and enrich the sauce by adding a tablespoon of butter and 2 tablespoons of chopped parsley.

Yield: 2 cups

SAUCE FOR BROILED LOBSTER

(Salsa para langosta a la parrilla)

1/4 pound sweet butter, cut into pieces
1 tablespoon brandy
1 teaspoon lemon juice
1/8 teaspoon salt
1/8 teaspoon ground pepper

1. Melt the butter over very low heat.

2. Add the rest of the ingredients and blend well.

3. Serve warm over broiled lobster meat.

NOTE: For a more refined sauce, you may clarify the butter.

Yield: 1/2 cup

CHIMICHURRI

1/2 cup olive oil
10 medium whole garlic cloves, peeled
2 tablespoons vinegar
1/4 teaspoon salt
1/2 teaspoon ground oregano or 1 teaspoon rosemary leaves
1/8 teaspoon ground black or cayenne pepper
3/4 teaspoon *pimentón* or paprika

1. Cook the garlic cloves in the olive oil in a small skillet over low heat until tender but not brown.

2. Mash the cloves with a fork into the oil.

3. Blend in the rest of the ingredients and continue cooking at very low heat for 10-12 minutes.

4. Serve over charcoal-broiled or grilled steaks. You may also brush over steaks while grilling, broiling, or barbecueing.

Yield: 2/3 cup

VINEGAR AND HOT CHILI PEPPERS SAUCE

(Pique de vinagre y ajíes bravos)

- 1 cup cider vinegar
- 12 medium-size hot chili peppers, halved lengthwise, seeds left in
- 4 medium garlic cloves, peeled and halved lengthwise
- 12 black peppercorns
- 1/8 teaspoon salt

1. Put all the ingredients in a glass jar or bottle with a non-reactive cap.

2. Keep in a cool place, or refrigerate to use sprinkled to taste over food. Use also for cooking in the same manner as you would use any commercial hot sauce.

NOTES: The longer it stands, the hotter the sauce gets. You may use any empty bottle with an inner plastic cap that controls the amounts poured, such as a soy sauce or Worcestershire sauce bottle.

Yield: 1 cup

SOUR ORANGE AND HOT CHILI PEPPER SAUCE

(Pique de naranjas agrias y ajíes bravos)

1/2 cup sour orange juice
8 small hot chili peppers, halved lengthwise and seeded
1/8 teaspoon salt

1. Put all the ingredients in a food processor or blender and process until well mixed.

2. Keep in a glass jar or bottle with a non-reactive cap.

3. Refrigerate or keep in a cool place to use to taste over foods.

NOTE: Strain after processing if you want to prevent the sauce from getting hotter.

Yield: 1/2 cup

GREEN SAUCE

(Salsa verde)

2 cups strained warm fish stock, p.73
3 tablespoons butter
3 tablespoons flour
1/4 cup finely diced green bell pepper
1/8 teaspoon ground pepper
2 tablespoons finely chopped parsley

1. Melt the butter over low heat in a heavy bottomed saucepan. Cook the flour in it, stirring, for 2-3 minutes to make a roux.

2. Remove from the heat and with a wire whisk stir in the hot stock until well blended with the roux.

3. Add the bell pepper, salt and ground pepper.

4. Return to the heat and simmer uncovered until it thickens to gravy consistency. Stir frequently to prevent scorching.

5. Remove from the heat and stir in the parsley.

6. Serve warm over broiled or poached fish.

Yield: 2 1/2 cups

GUAVA JELLY GLAZE

(Glaceado de jalea de guayabas)

4 tablespoons butter or margarine
4 tablespoons guava jelly
4 teaspoons Worcestershire Sauce
1 teaspoon lemon juice

1. Melt the butter or margarine and the guava jelly in a small heavy saucepan over very low heat. Blend well.

2. Add the Worcestershire Sauce and lemon juice. Cook over very low heat, stirring, for 3 minutes.

3. Brush over baking, broiling or barbecueing chicken pieces.

Yield: 1/2 cup

VINAIGRETTE

(Vinagreta)

8 tablespoons olive oil
2-3 tablespoons wine vinegar or lemon juice
1/4 teaspoon salt
1/8 teaspoon ground pepper

1. Put all the ingredients in a covered jar and shake until they are well blended.

NOTE: You may add 1 tablespoon of fresh minced herbs such as parsley, tarragon, etc.

Yield: 2/3 cup

Variation:

CAPERS AND PEPPERS VINAIGRETTE

(Vinagreta de alcaparras y pimientos)

1 cup vinaigrette —see above
1 very thinly sliced medium onion
1 teaspoon minced capers
2 tablespoons finely diced green bell pepper or red pimiento
1 tablespoon chopped parsley

1. Blend well all the ingredients and serve over cold fish, shellfish or salads.

Yield: 1 1/4 cup

AJILIMÓJILI

1/2 cup olive oil
2 tablespoons vinegar
2 tablespoons lemon juice
2 peeled medium garlic cloves
2 peppercorns
1/2 teaspoon salt

1. Put all the ingredients in a food processor or blender and process until well mixed and smooth.

2. Use to taste over fried fish or other cooked foods.

Yield: 3/4 cup

Variation:

HOT *AJILIMÓJILI*

(Ajilimójili picante)

Follow the recipe for *Ajilimójili*, but add 6 small hot chili peppers halved lengthwise and seeded. Let stand for 10 minutes after processing, then strain before serving.

Yield: 3/4 cup

AVOCADO SALAD DRESSING

(Aderezo de aguacate para ensalada)

1/2 medium ripe avocado, pitted and coarsely chopped
1/3 cup olive oil
2 tablespoons vinegar or 2 teaspoons lemon juice
1/4 teaspoon salt
1/8 teaspoon pepper

1. Put all the ingredients, except the avocado, in a food processor or blender and process for some 30 seconds.

2. Add the avocado and process until well blended and smooth.

Yield: about 1 cup

FOOD PROCESSOR MAYONNAISE

(Mayonesa en procesador de alimentos)

1 whole extra-large egg
1/4 teaspoon dried mustard or 1/2 teaspoon prepared mustard
1/2 teaspoon salt
1 tablespoon lemon juice or vinegar
1 1/2 cup olive oil or a blend of vegetable oils

1. Bring all the ingredients to room temperature.

2. Process the egg, mustard, salt and lemon juice or vinegar with the metal blade for 3-4 seconds.

3. With the machine running, pour the oil slowly and gradually through the feed tube until the mayonnaise begins to thicken. Add the additional oil more quickly.

4. Process only until the mayonnaise is thick and smooth.

5. Put in a covered container and refrigerate.

Yield: 1 3/4 cup

TARTAR SAUCE

(Salsa tártara)

- 1 cup mayonnaise made with lemon juice, p.66, or commercial mayonnaise mixed with 1 tablespoon lemon juice
- 2 tablespoons minced sour pickles
- 1 tablespoon minced capers
- 1 tablespoon finely minced onion
- 1 tablespoon chopped parsley

1. Blend well all the ingredients. Put in a covered container and refrigerate.

Yield: 1 1/4 cup

AVOCADO DIP

(Unto de aguacate)

- 1 large ripe avocado
- 1/2 cup tomato, peeled, seeded and finely chopped, p.132
- 1/2 teaspoon salt
- 1 tablespoon wine vinegar
- 1 tablespoon mayonnaise
- 1 tablespoon finely minced onion
- 1/4 teaspoon pepper or 1/2 teaspoon hot sauce

1. Dissolve the salt in the vinegar. Add the mayonnaise, onion, pepper or hot sauce, and blend well.

2. Add the tomato.

3. Peel, seed and mash the avocado. Blend well with the rest of the ingredients.

4. Chill in a covered container before serving.

Yield: 2 cups

AVOCADO AND SOUR CREAM DIP

(Unto de aguacate y crema agria)

- 1 medium ripe avocado, peeled, pitted and cut into large chunks
- 1 teaspoon lemon juice
- 1 teaspoon hot sauce, or to taste
- 1 tablespoon mayonnaise
- 1/4 teaspoon salt
- 1/3 cup sour cream

1. Put all the ingredients, except the sour cream, in a food processor or blender. Process until smooth.

2. Add the sour cream and process only until well blended with the rest of the ingredients.

3. Put in a covered container and chill until ready to serve.

Yield: 1 1/3 cup

CHAPTER III: FIRST COURSE SOUPS, FULL MEAL SOUPS

BEEF BROTH

(Caldo de res)

1 pound boneless beef —brisket, round or chuck, in one piece
1 pound short ribs, cut into pieces
2 quarts cool water
1 medium onion, peeled and quartered
1 medium frying green pepper, seeded and quartered
2 peeled medium garlic cloves
2 large sweet chili peppers, seeded and quartered
4 large *culantro* leaves
1 medium tomato, seeded and quartered

1. Place the meats in a heavy-bottomed soup pot or kettle and add the cool water. Bring to a simmer over moderate heat. Remove the scum that rises to the surface for 5 minutes or so, or until it almost stops rising.

2. Add the rest of the ingredients and, if necessary, more water to cover all by at least one inch.

3. Bring again to a simmer and skim as necessary. Simmer with the pot lid slightly ajar for at least 1 1/2 hours. Do not let boil as this will incorporate the fats into the liquid.

4. Skim off any fat or scum periodically during the simmering period.

5. Strain the broth into a bowl and discard the vegetables, bones and gristle. Use the meat in other recipes that ask for cooked soup meat.

6. Degrease the broth by letting the fat rise to the surface and ladling it out, or by refrigerating and scraping off the solidified fat.

7. Proceed with your recipe.

NOTES: Instead of step 1, you may put the meats in another pan and cover them with cool water. Bring to a slow boil for 5 minutes or so. Drain and rinse under running cold water. Place in the soup pot, add fresh cool water, and continue with the recipe.

This broth may be served as is, garnished with the meats cut into cubes, plus rice, potatoes, or vermicelli. Cook them until tender in the broth salted to taste.

Yield: about 6 cups

CHICKEN BROTH

(Caldo de pollo)

2 1/2 pounds stewing chicken pieces, chicken giblets excluding the liver), and carcasses, or a combination of these
2 quarts cool water
1 medium onion, peeled and quartered
2 peeled medium garlic cloves
2 large sweet chili peppers, seeded and chopped
4 large *culantro* leaves

1. Place the chicken meat and bones in a heavy-bottomed pot or kettle and add the cool water. Bring to a simmer over moderate heat. Remove the scum that comes to the surface for 5 minutes or so, or until it almost stops rising.

2. Add the rest of the ingredients and cover everything by at least one inch of water.

3. Bring again to a simmer, and skim if necessary. Simmer with the pot lid slightly ajar for at least 1 1/2 hours. Do not let boil as this will incorporate the fats into the liquid.

4. Skim off any fat or scum periodically during the simmering.

5. Strain the broth into a bowl and discard the vegetables and bones. Save the meat for other recipes that ask for cooked chicken.

6. Degrease the broth by letting the fat rise to the surface and ladling it out, or by refrigerating and scraping off the solidified fat.

7. Proceed with your recipe.

NOTES: If you want to use the meat of the stewing chicken pieces, you may have to cook the broth for more than the 1 1/2 hours until the chicken is tender —as much as 3 hours.

Instead of step 1 you may put the chicken meat and bones in another pot and cover them with cool water. Bring to a slow boil for 5 minutes or so. Drain and rinse under running cold water. Place in the soup pot, add fresh water, and proceed with the recipe.

This broth may be served as is, garnished with the shredded chicken meat plus rice, potatoes, or vermicelli. Cook them in the broth salted to taste until tender.

Yield: about 6 cups

FISH BROTH

(Caldo de pescado)

1 1/2 pounds fish heads, bones and trimmings, rinsed and cut into pieces
2 quarts cool water
1 medium onion, peeled and quartered
1 quartered medium tomato
1 medium green frying pepper, quartered and seeded (optional)
3 peeled medium garlic cloves
3 large *culantro* leaves

1. Place the fish pieces in the soup pot and add the cool water. Bring to a simmer over moderate heat. Remove the scum that comes to the surface until it almost stops rising.

2. Add the rest of the ingredients and more water, if necessary, to cover all by at least one inch.

3. Bring again to a simmer and skim if necessary. Simmer with

the pot lid slightly ajar for some 30-45 minutes, or more according to the strength desired.

4. Strain the broth through a fine sieve and discard the solid ingredients.

5. Proceed with your recipe.

NOTE: This broth may be served as is, garnished with pieces of fish meats plus rice, potatoes or vermicelli. Cook them until tender in the strained broth salted to taste.

Yield: about 5 cups

VEGETABLE BROTH

(Caldo de vegetales)

- 2 medium onions, peeled and thinly sliced
- 3 chopped medium carrots
- 1 chopped small celery rib
- 2 chopped medium tomatoes
- 1 medium frying green pepper, seeded and chopped
- 3 peeled large garlic cloves
- 3 large sweet chili peppers, seeded and minced
- 4 large *culantro* leaves
- 2 quarts water

1. Place all the ingredients in a heavy-bottomed soup pot, making sure that the water covers the ingredients by at least one inch.

2. Bring slowly to a boil and skim off the surface until it is clear.

3. Simmer, undisturbed, with the lid slightly ajar for 45 minutes to an hour.

4. Strain through a fine sieve or a colander lined with a double layer of cheesecloth.

Yield: about 6 cups

GARLIC SOUP

(Sopa de ajos)

6 tablespoons olive oil
9 peeled large garlic cloves
6 cups beef broth, p. 71
salt and pepper
6 eggs
6 slices of toasted French bread, 1/2" thick

1. Heat the oil in the soup pot over low heat. Add the garlic cloves and stir fry until lightly golden. Do not let the garlic burn for it will turn bitter.

2. Add the beef broth, cover and simmer for 20 minutes. Remove the garlic cloves, and keep the soup warm. Season to taste.

3. In a large skillet containing 1 to 1 1/2" of simmering salted water poach the eggs, 3 at a time, for 2-3 minutes. Remove with a slotted spoon and trim any ragged edges.

4. Place a piece of toast on each soup plate and one egg on top of each toast. Ladle one cup of soup on each plate and serve warm.

Serves: 6

BREAD AND EGGS SOUP

(Sopa de pan con huevos)

2 tablespoons olive oil
1 thinly sliced medium onion
6 cups beef, chicken or vegetable broth, pp.71, 72, 74
salt and pepper
12 slices toasted French bread, 1/2" thick
12 eggs
1/2 cup freshly grated parmesan cheese

1. Heat the olive oil in a soup pot over medium-low heat and cook the onions for some 5 minutes, until tender but not browned.

2. Add the broth and simmer covered for 10 minutes. Season to taste and keep warm.

3. In a large skillet with 1 to 1 1/2" of simmering salted water poach the eggs three at a time for 2 to 3 minutes. Remove with a slotted spoon and trim off any ragged edges.

4. In each soup plate place two slices of bread and an egg on top of each slice. Sprinkle with the parmesan cheese.

5. Ladle one cup of hot broth on each plate and serve warm.

Serves: 6

GREEN PLANTAIN SOUP

(Sopa de plátano verde)

6 cups cool chicken or vegetable broth, pp. 72, 74
1 large green plantain
2 cups water
1 1/2 teaspoons salt
salt and pepper

1. Peel the plantain by cutting off its tips, making three lengthwise slits on its skin and pulling it off helping with the knife.

2. Cut the plantain into four pieces and soak in the water and 1 1/2 teaspoons of the salt for 10 minutes. Drain.

3. Grate the plantain on a food processor or hand grater. Measure 3/4 cup and add to the cool broth. Stir well.

4. Bring the broth and grated plantain to a simmer. Cover and cook for 15 minutes.

5. Strain through a fine sieve, or a colander lined with a double layer of cheesecloth. Press the plantain with a spoon to extract the liquid.

6. Season the soup to taste.

NOTE: This soup may be served garnished with small *mofongos*, p.

Serves: 6

YAUTIA AND OKRA SOUP

(Sopa de yautía y guingambós)

6 cups beef, chicken, or vegetable broth, pp. 71, 72, 74
2 tablespoons tomato sauce
1 teaspoon salt
1 teaspoon vinegar
1 1/2 pound white yautia root, peeled and cut into 1" cubes
3/4 pound fresh okra, rinsed, dried, trimmed of tips and stems, and cut into 1/2" slices
1/2 cup freshly grated parmesan cheese

1. Bring the broth, tomato sauce and salt to a boil.

2. Add the yautia cubes and vinegar. Bring again to a boil.

3. Stir in the okra.

4. Lower the heat, cover and simmer for 20 minutes or more until the yautia is tender.

5. Serve warm sprinkled with the cheese.

Serves: 6

VEGETABLE SOUP

(Sopa de Vegetales)

6 cups beef, chicken, or vegetable broth, pp. 71,72,74
1 large green plantain
3 cups salted water
3/4 cup white yautia, peeled and diced into 1" pieces
3/4 pound green string beans, trimmed and sliced into 1" pieces
2 small carrots, trimmed and cut into 1/2" slices
2 medium tomatoes, peeled, seeded and coarsely chopped, p.132
2 minced medium garlic cloves (optional)
salt and pepper

1. Cut off the tips of the plantain, make three lengthwise slits in its skin and pull it off helping with the knife.

2. Cut the plantain into 1" slices and boil until tender in the three cups of salted water.

3. In a soup pot bring the broth to a boil. Stir in the yautia, green beans, carrots, tomatoes and optional garlic, plus salt to taste. Cover, lower the heat to a simmer.

4. Mash the plantain in a mortar and form into 1 to 1 1/2" balls with your hands. Add to the simmering soup.

5. Cook for 20 minutes or until all the vegetables are tender.

6. Adjust the salt and season with pepper to taste.

Serves: 6

FISH SOUP

(Sopa de pescado)

1 1/2 pounds firm white fish, boned and cut into 1½" pieces
2 tablespoons olive oil
1 small frying green pepper, seeded and diced
1 diced small onion
3 tablespoons tomato sauce
2 medium tomatoes, peeled, seeded and chopped, p.132
2 chopped large *culantro* leaves
8 cups warm fish broth, p. 73
1/3 cup white rice, rinsed under cold running water and drained
3 small potatoes, peeled and quartered
salt and pepper

1. Sauté the frying pepper and onion over medium-low heat for 5 minutes in a soup pot.

2. Add the tomato sauce, tomatoes, and *culantro*. Sauté for 5 more minutes.

3. Add the broth and bring to a boil.

4. Stir in the rice and potatoes. Lower the heat, cover and simmer for 20 minutes.

5. Add the fish pieces and simmer for 10 more minutes.

6. Season to taste.

Serves: 6

CHICKEN SOUP

(Sopa de pollo)

3 pounds chicken pieces
4 teaspoons salt
2 quarts cool water
1 small onion, peeled and halved
2 peeled large garlic cloves
2 large sweet chili peppers, seeded and halved
4 large *culantro* leaves
2 ounces vermicelli, cut to desired length
4 medium potatoes, peeled and quartered

1. Salt the chicken pieces with 3 teaspoons of the salt. Let stand for at least 15 minutes.

2. Place the chicken pieces in a heavy-bottomed pot or kettle with the cool water and bring to a simmer over medium-high heat. Remove the scum that comes to the surface for about 5 minutes, or until the liquid is almost clear.

3. Add the onion, garlic, sweet chili peppers, *culantro* and remaining salt.

4. Lower the heat and simmer covered for 50 minutes.

5. With a slotted spoon remove the onion, garlic, sweet chili peppers and *culantro* leaves.

6. Add the potatoes and simmer covered for 10 minutes.

7. Add the vermicelli and simmer for 10 additional minutes, or until they are cooked and the potatoes are tender.

NOTES: Instead of vermicelli you may use 1/3 cup rice, rinsed under running cold water and drained. Add with the potatoes. You may use a stewing chicken, but it must be simmered for 2 to 3 hours or until the chicken is tender; then proceed with steps 6 and 7.

Serves: 6

BEEF SOUP

(Sopa de res)

2 pounds lean beef or a combination of lean beef and short ribs, cut into 2" cubes
2 1/2 quarts cool water
5 teaspoons salt
1 halved small onion
1 quartered medium tomato
4 large *culantro* leaves
3 large sweet chili peppers, seeded and quartered
1/2 pound West-Indian pumpkin, peeled and cut into 6 pieces
3 medium potatoes, peeled and quartered
1/2 pound green cabbage, cut into 6 pieces
2 husked corn ears, cut into 3 pieces each
1 ounce vermicelli, cut to desired length
1 medium green frying pepper, seeded and quartered

1. Rinse the meat and put it in a heavy-bottomed soup pot or kettle with the cool water.

2. Bring to a simmer over medium-high heat and remove the scum that comes to the surface for some 5 minutes or until it stops rising.

3. Add the salt, onion, tomato, green frying pepper, sweet chili peppers and *culantro*.

4. Lower the heat and simmer covered for 1 1/2 to 1 3/4 hours.

5. Strain through a colander. Discard the vegetables but return the liquid and meat to the soup pot.

6. Bring again to a simmer. Add the pumpkin, potatoes, cabbage and corn. Cover and simmer for 10 minutes.

7. Add the vermicelli and simmer for 10 more minutes or until they are cooked and the vegetables are tender.

NOTES: You may mash some of the pumpkin into the soup just before serving.

For a quicker soup you may start with 8 cups beef broth, p. 71, and substitute 6 ounces diced cooked ham for the beef cubes. Reduce or eliminate the salt accordingly, and start your recipe at step 6.

Serves: 6

HAM SOUP

(Sopa de jamón)

6 ounces diced cooked ham
1/2 pound ham bone with some meat attached
6 cups water
1 quartered medium tomato
1 halved medium onion
1 medium frying pepper, halved and seeded
2 large sweet chili peppers, halved and seeded
4 large *culantro* leaves
2 ounces vermicelli, cut to desired length
3 medium potatoes, peeled and halved
salt as needed, if at all

1. Place all the ingredients except the diced ham, vermicelli and potatoes in the soup pot. Bring to a simmer over moderate-high heat and skim off the scum that rises to the surface until the liquid is almost clear.

2. Cover, lower the heat and simmer for 1 hour.

3. Strain the soup and return to the pot.

4. Bring to a slow boil and add the potatoes and diced ham. Cover and simmer for 15 minutes.

5. Stir in the vermicelli and simmer covered for 15 more minutes or until they are cooked and the potatoes are tender.

6. Adjust the salt to taste.

Serves: 6

FRESH BEANS AND SPARERIBS SOUP

(Sopón de habichuelas frescas y costillas)

3/4 pound shelled fresh white or red beans —not dried
1 1/2 pound pork spareribs divided into 2-rib sections
2 tablespoons annatto oil or lard
1 diced small onion
1 green frying pepper, seeded and diced
1 medium tomato, peeled, seeded and chopped, p.132
2 large sweet chili peppers, seeded and minced
2 minced medium garlic cloves
1/3 cup tomato sauce
1/4 teaspoon ground oregano
6 large *culantro* leaves, chopped
4 teaspoons salt
10 cups water
1/2 cup rice, rinsed under cool running water and drained

1. In a heavy-bottomed soup pot or kettle saute the onion, frying pepper, tomato, sweet chili peppers and garlic in the annatto oil or lard over medium-low heat for 5 minutes.

2. Add the tomato sauce, oregano, *culantro* and salt. Cook for 5 more minutes.

3. Raise the heat to medium-high, add the spareribs and sauté, stirring for 2-3 minutes.

4. Add 5 cups of the water. Bring to a simmer. Cover and simmer over low heat for 45 minutes or until the ribs are tender. Skim off any excess fat from the soup.

5. In the meantime, in another pot, boil the beans in the additional 5 cups of water until almost tender. Save the boiling liquid.

6. When the ribs are tender, add the beans and 2 cups of their boiling liquid.

7. Bring to a slow boil, and stir in the rice.

8. Lower the heat to moderate and cook uncovered for 20-25 minutes, or until the rice is tender.

Serves: 6

SPANISH SOUP

(Cocido español)

3 pounds beef brisket, in one piece
1/4 pound piece of cooked ham
3 quarts cool water
2 whole medium onions, peeled
1 green frying pepper, halved and seeded
2 medium tomatoes, peeled, seeded and chopped, p.132
2 minced medium garlic cloves
1 tablespoon tomato sauce
2 tablespoons olive oil
5 teaspoons salt
4 medium chorizos, halved
4 large potatoes, peeled and halved
1 pound green cabbage, cut into 4 pieces or 2 small cabbage heads, quartered
1 pound dried chick peas, boiled until tender, or 2 one-pound cans of boiled chick peas, drained

1. Put the brisket and ham in the water in a heavy-bottomed soup pot or kettle and bring to a simmer over medium-high heat. Skim off the scum that comes to the surface for 5 minutes or until it almost stops rising.

2. Add the onions, pepper, tomatoes, garlic, tomato sauce, olive oil and salt. Cover and simmer for 2 hours or until the meat is tender.

3. Add the chorizos and potatoes. Simmer covered for 10 minutes.

4. Add the chick peas and cabbage and simmer uncovered for 10-20 minutes or until the potatoes are tender. Skim off the fat from the soup.

5. Remove the meats and vegetables and arrange on a warm platter. Keep warm.

6. Strain the soup and serve warm, as is, or garnished with cooked rice or pasta.

Serves: 8

GALICIAN SOUP

(Caldo gallego)

1 pound lean beef cut into 2" cubes
1 pound lean pork cut into 2" cubes
1 1/2 pound stewing chicken pieces
1/4 pound cured or country ham
1/2 pound dried white beans, soaked in water overnight, rinsed and drained
1 quartered medium onion
2 1/2 quarts cool water
4 teaspoons salt
2 large chorizos cut into 4 pieces each
1/2 pound apio, peeled and cut into 1 1/2" pieces
2 medium turnips, peeled and quartered
2 medium potatoes, peeled and quartered
1 cup chopped turnip greens
3 cups chopped Swiss chard or fresh spinach

1. Place the beef, pork, chicken, ham, beans and onion in the water in a heavy-bottomed soup pot or kettle. Bring to a simmer over medium-high heat and remove the scum that rises to the surface for 5 minutes or so.

2. When the liquid is clear of scum, add the salt. Lower the heat and simmer covered for 2 hours.

3. Add the chorizos and simmer for 30 more minutes.

4. Add the apio, turnips, potatoes, turnip greens and chard or spinach.

5. Simmer with the lid ajar for 30 minutes or until the vegetables are tender and the soup is thickened to taste.

Serves: 8

SANCOCHO

1 pound brisket in one piece
1 pound spareribs cut into 2-rib pieces
2 ounces ham or a ham bone
2 1/2 quarts cool water
2 tablespoons olive oil
1 diced medium onion
1 medium green frying pepper, seeded and diced
1 large tomato, peeled, seeded and chopped, p. 132
3 large sweet chili peppers, seeded and minced
1 minced large garlic clove
1/4 cup tomato sauce
6 chopped large *culantro* leaves
4 1/2 teaspoons salt
1 pound white yautia root, peeled and cut into 1 1/2" cubes
1 pound white sweet potato, peeled and cut into 1 1/2" cubes
1/2 pound yam, peeled and cut into 2" cubes v. Glossary
1/2 pound medium potatoes, peeled and quartered
1 green plantain, peeled and cut into 8 segments, p. 91
1 ripe plantain, peeled and cut into 8 pieces, p. 91
1/2 pound West-Indian pumpkin, peeled and quartered
2 fresh husked corn ears, cut into 4 segments each

1. Bring the brisket, spareribs, ham and water to a simmer over medium-high heat in a heavy-bottomed soup pot or kettle. Skim off the scum that rises to the surface for about 5 minutes or so.

2. Cover, lower the heat and simmer for one hour.

3. In the meantime, sauté the onion, pepper, tomato, chili peppers and garlic in the olive oil over medium-low heat in a skillet for 5 minutes.

4. Add the tomato sauce, *culantro*, and salt. Cook for 5 more minutes, then add to the simmering meats.

5. In the meantime, peel and cut the vegetables.

6. After the hour of simmering is over, bring the soup to a slow boil and add the yautia, sweet potato, yam, potatoes, green and ripe plantains. Lower the heat and simmer covered for 15 minutes.

7. Add the corn and pumpkin. Simmer uncovered for 15 more minutes or until all the vegetables are tender.

8. Remove the green plantain pieces. Mash with a mortar and pestle and form them into small balls with your hands. Return to the soup and continue cooking until this thickens to taste.

NOTE: For a thicker soup mash some of the vegetables and stir them well into it.

Serves: 8

TRIPE SOUP

(Mondongo)

2 pounds blanket and honeycomb tripe, cut into 2" pieces
3 unsalted pig's or veal feet, cleaned and split lengthwise
1 1/2 quart hot water
1/3 cup sour orange juice, lemon juice, or vinegar
3 quarts cool water
4 1/2 teaspoons salt
2 tablespoons annatto oil or lard
1 diced medium onion
1 medium green frying pepper, seeded and diced
1 large tomato, peeled, seeded and chopped, p. 132
2 large sweet chili peppers, seeded and minced
2 minced medium garlic cloves
6 tablespoons tomato sauce
4 large chopped *culantro* leaves
3 medium potatoes, peeled and halved
1 1/2 pound yautia, peeled and cut into 1 1/2" cubes
1 pound West-Indian pumpkin, peeled and cut into 2" pieces
1 one-pound can boiled chick peas, drained

1. Soak the tripe and pig's or veal feet in the hot water and sour orange juice, lemon juice or vinegar for 15 minutes, stirring every five.

2. Rinse well under running cold water and drain.

3. Place in a heavy-bottomed soup pot or kettle with the cool water and three teaspoons of salt. Bring slowly to a simmer over medium-high heat and remove the scum that comes to the surface for 5 minutes or so.

4. Lower the heat and simmer covered for 3 hours or until the tripe is tender.

5. In the meantime, heat the oil or lard in a skillet and sauté the onion, frying pepper, tomato, sweet chilis and garlic for 5 minutes over medium-low heat.

6. Add the tomato sauce and *culantro*. Cook for 5 more minutes, then add to the simmering tripe.

7. Once the tripe is tender, add the potatoes, yautia and additional salt. Simmer covered for 15 minutes.

8. Add the pumpkin and chick peas. Simmer uncovered for 15 minutes or until all the vegetables are tender and the soup thickens to taste.

NOTE: If you are using parboiled tripe —ask your butcher—, check every hour for tenderness as this takes shorter to cook.

Serves: 6

CHAPTER IV: THE PLANTAIN, THE GREEN BANANA, THE BREADFRUIT AND OTHER VEGETABLES

HOW TO PEEL GREEN AND RIPE PLANTAINS AND GREEN BANANAS

(Manera de pelar plátanos verdes y maduros y guineos verdes)

1. Cut off the tips of the plantains or bananas.

2. With the tip of a sharp knife, make 2 or 4 lengthwise slits at opposite sides of the skin.

3. Helping yourself with the knife peel the skin by pulling off in a crosswise direction.

4. Soak green plantains or bananas in salted water for 10-15 minutes. Drain and proceed with your recipe.

NOTES: If your recipe does not ask for whole plantains or bananas, it is easier to cut them in half before peeling. Ripe plantains are easier to peel, as the skin does not adhere as fast to the pulp as green ones do. Sometimes just one lengthwise slit will suffice.

Green plantains and bananas can stain your hands while peeling, you can avoid this by peeling under running cool water.

BOILED GREEN PLANTAINS AND GREEN BANANAS

(Plátanos verdes y guineos verdes hervidos)

Green plantains or green bananas, peeled, soaked, in salted water and drained, V. above
Salted water for boiling —2 teaspoons salt per quart of water

1. Boil in the salted water to cover by at least two inches. Plantains should cook for 15-20 minutes: bananas, 10-15. Boil just until tender at the core, but not mushy. Drain.

2. Serve warm or proceed with your recipe.

NOTE: If using in any recipe that asks for cool plantains or bananas, rinse under running cold water to stop their cooking.

STEWED GREEN PLANTAIN BALLS

(Albóndigas de plátano verde guisadas)

1 1/2 cup ground meat stuffing, p. 236
3 large green plantains, halved crosswise, peeled and soaked in salted water, p. 91
1/2 pound yautia root
1 1/2 teaspoon salt
1 tablespoon vegetable oil
2 large chorizos cut into 1/4" slices
1 thinly sliced medium onion
1 thinly sliced and seeded medium frying pepper
2 seeded and minced sweet chili peppers
1 large tomato, peeled, seeded and chopped, p. 132
2 pressed medium garlic cloves
1/2 cup tomato sauce
1/8 teaspoon ground oregano
3 cups warm beef stock, p.71

1. Peel the yautia and grate by hand or in a food processor with the metal blade.

2. Drain the plantains and grate.

3. Mix 3/4 cup of the grated yautia with 3 cups of the grated plantain. Add the salt, mix well and set aside.

4. Heat the oil over moderate heat in a *caldero* or heavy-bottomed pot. Sauté the chorizo slices for 3-4 minutes.

5. Add the onion, pepper, sweet chilis. Lower the heat and cook for 5 minutes.

6. Add the tomato, garlic, tomato sauce and oregano. Cook for 5 more minutes.

7. Add the stock and bring to a boil. Cover, lower the heat and simmer for 15 minutes.

8. In the meantime, prepare the balls; divide the mash into 12 equal portions. Cup each portion in one hand, make a depression and stuff with 2 teaspoons of the ground meat stuffing. Roll in your hands to make a ball.

9. Bring the stock to a gentle boil. Add the balls one at a time, cover, return the heat to simmer and cook for 30 minutes. Turn the balls once.

NOTE: For a smoother texture, pound the grated plantain and yautia with a mortar and pestle.

Serves: 6

GREEN PLANTAIN *TOSTONES*

(Tostones)

3 peeled large green plantains, p. 91
1 1/2 quarts of water seasoned with 2 tablespoons of salt, divided into two containers
shortening

1. Slice the plantains into 1" rings and soak for 10 minutes in one of the containers with salted water. Drain.

2. In a *caldero* or deep skillet over moderate heat, fry the rings in one layer in shortening to cover for 8 minutes or until tender. Turn once.

3. Remove from the pan and flatten to about 1/4" thick between double layers of waxed or kraft paper.

4. Raise the shortening's heat to medium high.

5. Drop the flattened rings in the second container of salted

water and remove immediately. Soak only as many rings as you can refry in one layer.

6. Refry in the shortening for 5 more minutes or until golden crisp.

7. Drain on paper towels and serve warm. Sprinkle, if at all, with salt to taste.

NOTE: There is a kitchen gadget called a *tostonera* for flattening the rings. It is essentially two pieces of hinged wood with depressed or carved inner sides. It is available in Latin American specialty stores.

Serves: 6

Variation:

GARLIC *TOSTONES*

(Tostones con ajo)

Follow the recipe for Green Plantain *Tostones*, but after the second frying, dip briefly in a mixture of

1/4 cup olive oil
2 pressed medium garlic cloves

Serve warm.

NOTE: You may sautée the garlic lightly in the oil beforehand, or warm them together in a butter warmer.

Serves: 6

GREEN PLANTAIN CHIPS

(Platanutre)

3 large green plantains, peeled but not soaked in salted water, p. 91
shortening
salt

1. Slice the plantains very thinly with a sharp knife or with the very thin serrated slicing disk of a food processor —1 mm. blade.
2. Bring the shortening to 350°F in a *caldero* or deep chicken fryer.

3. Fry the chips by small batches until crisp and golden. As you drop them into the hot shortening separate the chips from each other as much as possible as they have a tendency to stick together while raw. This will prevent uneven cooking.

4. Drain from the shortening, lay on papel towels and salt to taste. Let cool before serving.

5. Keep in a covered container until ready to use.

Yield: 12 ounces

GREEN PLANTAIN *MOFONGOS* WITH PORK CRACKLINGS

(Mofongos con chicharrón de cerdo)

3 large peeled green plantains, p. 91
3 cups water seasoned with 1 tablespoon salt
1/4 pound finely crushed pork crackling, p. 265
1/4 cup olive oil
3 pressed medium garlic cloves
1/2 cup seasoned stock, or 1/2 cup water seasoned with 1/2 teaspoon salt
shortening

1. Cut each plantain into 10-12 rings and soak in the salted water for 15 minutes. Drain.

2. In a small skillet sauté the garlic in the olive oil lightly without browning or crisping it; or heat both in a butter warmer.

3. In a *caldero* or chicken fryer set over medium heat, cook the plantain rings in shortening to cover until tender, but not crisp. Cook in small uncrowded batches. Turn once.

4. With a mortar and pestle mash 6 plantain slices at a time, adding gradually 2 tablespoons of the crushed crackling.

5. Add one tablespoon of the stock or salted water and one or two teaspoons of the garlic oil. Continue mashing with the pestle until well blended.

6. Remove from the mortar and form into a ball with your hands.

7. Keep warm until ready to serve as a side dish or in a bowl of clear broth.

Yield: 6 *mofongos*

Variation:

GREEN PLANTAIN *MOFONGOS* WITH GARLIC OIL

(Mofongos con ajo y aceite)

Follow the recipe for the Green Plantain *Mofongos* with Pork Crackling, but:

1. substitute medium plantains for the large ones

2. omit the crackling and stock

Yield: 6 *mofongos*

PICKLED GREEN BANANAS

(Guineos verdes en escabeche)

12 boiled medium-size green bananas, p. 91
1 1/4 cup olive oil
1/3 cup vinegar
3/4 teaspoon salt
30 black peppercorns
1 1/2 large bay leaves
3 pressed large garlic cloves
3 small onions, peeled and thinly sliced

1. Combine the olive oil, vinegar, salt, peppercorns, bay leaves and garlic cloves in an enameled or other non-reactive saucepan. Stir well and simmer uncovered for 20 minutes.

2. Add the onion slices and cook for an additional 10 minutes. Let cool.

3. In the meantime, boil the bananas, p.91. Drain.

4. Slice the boiled bananas in slanted 3/4"-thick rings.

5. Fold well into the pickling sauce and refrigerate covered if not serving soon.

6. Remove from the refrigerator one hour before serving.

Serves: 6

CABBAGE, PINEAPPLE AND GREEN BANANA SALAD

(Ensalada de col, piña y guineos verdes)

3 cups shredded green or red cabbage
1 cup fresh or canned pineapple chunks
1 cup boiled green bananas, cooled and cut into 1/4" —thick slices— 2 medium bananas, p. 91
3/4 cup mayonnaise
2 teaspoons vinegar
1 tablespoon pineapple syrup (if using canned pineapple) or 1 teaspoon sugar (optional)
1/2 teaspoon salt
pepper

1. Mix together the cabbage, pineapple and bananas.

2. Blend well the mayonnaise, vinegar, optional pineapple syrup or sugar, salt and pepper.

3. Mix all the ingredients well and chill before serving.

Serves: 6

FRICASEED GREEN BANANAS

(Guineos verdes en fricasé)

12 medium-size green bananas, boiled, p. 91
1/4 cup olive oil
1 sliced medium onion
3 peeled and minced garlic cloves
1 cup tomato sauce
3/4 teaspoon salt
1/2 teaspoon sugar
7 ounces sliced pimiento
12 medium pimiento-stuffed green olives or pitted ripe olives
1 tablespoon small capers (optional)
1/4 teaspoon peppercorns, hot sauce to taste or 1 tablespoon *pique*, p. 62
1/4 cup water

1. Cook the onion and garlic in a heavy-bottomed pan in the olive oil over low heat until tender but not browned —about 10 minutes.

2. Add the tomato sauce, salt, sugar, pimiento slices, olives and optional capers. Simmer for 5 minutes.

3. Add the peppercorns or hot sauce or *pique* and the water. Bring to a simmer and cook covered for 15 minutes, stirring occasionally.

4. Cut the bananas into slanted slices 3/4" thick. Add to the finished sauce and cook just until reheated.

5. Serve either warm or at room temperature.

Serves: 6

BOILED RIPE PLANTAINS

(Plátanos maduros hervidos)

Ripe plantains
Lightly salted water —1/2 teaspoon salt per quart of water

1. Rinse the plantains and cut off their tips. Leave the skin on.

2. Cut crosswise into 2 or 3 segments and boil for 15 minutes or until tender in salted water to cover by at least 2 inches.

3. Drain, peel and serve warm with butter, or proceed with your recipe.

RIPE PLANTAIN BALLS

(Albóndigas de plátano maduro)

3 medium-size ripe plantains, boiled and peeled, v. above
1 tablespoon softened butter
1 teaspoon sugar
1/2 teaspoon ground cinnamon
2 large eggs beaten with a pinch of salt
1 cup soda cracker or bread crumbs
shortening
flour

1. Mash or puree the plantains while still warm.

2. Add the butter, sugar and cinnamon. Blend well. If the mixture is not thick enough add 2 or 3 teaspoons of the crumbs.

3. Dust your hands with flour. Take the mixture by tablespoonfuls and roll into balls or ovals.

4. Roll in the crumbs, dip in the beaten egg, and roll in the crumbs again.

5. Fry them in hot shortening —375°F— in a *caldero* or chicken fryer over medium high heat until golden crisp.

6. Drain on paper towels and serve hot.

Yield: 18 balls

STUFFED RIPE PLANTAIN FRITTERS

(Rellenos de plátano maduro)

1 1/2 cups ground meat stuffing, p. 236
4 large ripe plantains, boiled and peeled, p. 99
1 1/2 tablespoon softened butter
1 teaspoon sugar (optional)
flour
shortening

1. Mash or puree the plantains in a food processor.

2. Blend well with the butter and optional sugar, and divide into 12 equal portions.

3. Sift flour over a square piece of waxed paper and spread a portion of mashed plantain on the center to about 4" in diameter.

4. Spread about one tablespoon of the stuffing in the center of the mashed plantain circle without coming out to the edges.

5. Fold the wax paper over itself to form a semi-circle with the mashed plantain. Press the borders together.

6. Sift flour lightly over it and transfer to a floured platter.

7. Proceed as above until all the portions are shaped. They may be refrigerated covered until ready to fry.

8. Heat a 1/2"-deep layer of shortening in a large skillet over medium-high heat until it begins to form a haze over the surface.

9. Transfer the fritters into the hot oil with a slotted spatula. Fry, turning once, 3 minutes on each side or until golden brown. Fry only one layer at a time without crowding. Adjust the heat to prevent burning of the shortening.

10. Drain on paper towels and keep warm until all the fritters are done.

NOTE: Instead of stuffing, you may use diced cheddar cheese.

Yield: 12 fritters

RIPE PLANTAIN PIE

(Pastelón de plátano maduro)

2 1/2 cups ground meat stuffing, p.236
4 large ripe plantains, boiled and peeled, p.99
3 tablespoons softened butter
1/2 teaspoon sugar
melted butter

1. Mash the plantains or puree in a food processor.

2. Blend well with the butter and sugar.

3. Line the bottom and sides of a buttered 9" x 1 1/2" pie dish with half of the mashed plantain.

4. Spread the stuffing over this and cover with the rest of the plantain.

5. Bake in a preheated 375°F oven for 15 minutes.

6. Brush the top with melted butter and bake for 10 more minutes or until golden.

7. Remove from the oven and let rest for 10-15 minutes before slicing.

NOTE: If you are using an electric oven with a top heating element, before brushing with the melted butter change the setting to broil but leave at 375°F.

Serves: 6

FRIED RIPE PLANTAINS

(Amarillos fritos)

3 large ripe plantains, peeled, p. 91
shortening

1. Slice the plantains into 3/4" to 1"-thick rings either straight or slanted: or cut them first into 2 or 3 crosswise segments, then lengthwise into 4 slices each.

2. Fry in a skillet in shortening over medium-high heat, turning once, until golden and tender.

3. Drain on paper towels and serve warm as a side dish.

Serves: 6

PIONONOS

1 3/4 cups ground meat stuffing, p. 236
3 very large ripe, but firm, plantains, peeled, p.91
2 large eggs beaten with a pinch of salt
1/3 cup soda cracker or bread crumbs
1/4 pound diced cheddar cheese (optional)

1. Slice the peeled plantains lengthwise into four segments.

2. Bake the plantain slices on a slightly buttered cookie sheet at 350°F for 15 minutes or until tender but still firm.

3. Roll the slices into rings, overlapping the ends about 1/2". Hold securely together with wood toothpicks.

4. Fill the rings to the rim with the stuffing, patting it in firmly.

5. Put the beaten eggs in a shallow bowl and spread the crumbs in a platter.

6. One at a time, dip the bottom of the rings in the beaten egg and lay on the crumbs. Place on the buttered cookie sheet.

7. Spoon beaten egg over the top of the rings and pat crumbs over them.

8. Bake in a preheated 375° oven for 10 minutes.

9. Put under the broiler for a few minutes until the tops are golden.

NOTE: You may stuff the *piononos* with just the cheese, or you may mix the stuffing with cheese. The tradition is to serve some stuffed with cheese, some with meat. If you stuff some with cheese, reduce the amount of ground meat stuffing accordingly.

Yield: 12 *piononos*

DEEP-FRIED RIPE PLANTAIN SANDWICHES

(Emparedados fritos de plátano maduro)

6 medium plantains, ripe but firm, peeled, p. 91
vegetable oil
12 slices cooked ham, 4" x 1 1/2"
24 slices swiss or american cheese, 3 1/2" x 1/2"
flour
3 large eggs beaten with a pinch of salt
1 1/2 cups soda cracker or bread crumbs

1. Halve the plantains crosswise, then halve again lengthwise.

2. Bake the plantain slices on a lightly buttered cookie sheet in a 350°F oven for 15 minutes or until tender but still firm. Let cool.

3. Flatten out the plantain slices lightly to make them wider.

4. Sandwich a ham slice between 2 slices of cheese and two slices of plantain. Secure with segments of wood toothpicks.

5. Dredge in flour, shake off excess. Dip in beaten egg and cover completely with crumbs, patting in. Follow this process only for as many sandwiches as you can fry at a time.

6. Deep fry the sandwiches without crowding in hot vegetable oil in a large skillet until golden brown.

7. Drain on paper towels and keep warm untill all are fried.

8. Remove the toothpicks before serving.

Serves: 6

BAKED RIPE PLANTAINS

(Plátanos maduros asados)

Ripe plantains
butter (optional)
sugar (optional)
cinammon (optional)

1. Cut the tips off the plantains, but leave the skin on.

2. Bake in a preheated 350°F oven for 20-30 minutes, or until tender at the core. Turn once.

3. Peel, spread with optional butter and serve as a side dish.

Variation:

1. Cut the tips off the plantains, and with the tip of a sharp knife make lengthwise slits in the skin and peel off.

2. Rub with butter, sugar and cinammon and wrap in tin foil.

3. Bake for 20 to 30 minutes in a preheated 350°F oven until tender at core. Turn once.

4. Unwrap and serve warm.

GROUND MEAT, RIPE PLANTAIN, AND STRING BEANS *PIÑÓN* 1

(Piñón de plátano maduro, carne y habichuelas tiernas I)

2 1/2 cups ground meat stuffing, p.236
3 large ripe plantains, peeled, p. 91
1 tablespoon butter
5 large eggs, separated
1/4 teaspoon salt
1/2 pound string beans, boiled until tender but crunchy, cut lengthwise

1. Preheat the oven to 350°F.

2. Halve the plantains crosswise, then slice each section lengthwise in four.

3. Bake the plantain slices on a lightly buttered cookie sheet for 15 minutes or until tender, but still firm. Remove from cookie sheet and let cool.

4. Grease a 9" x 1 3/4" heavy skillet or range-and-ovenproof dish with a tablespoon of oil.

5. Beat the egg whites with the salt until they form soft peaks. Beat in the yolks just enough to mix them with the whites.

6. Set the skillet or dish on top of the range over very low heat.

7. Pour about 2/5 of the beaten eggs on the bottom of the skillet and immediately layer it with plantain slices, covering the whole bottom.

8. On top of these, lay the meat stuffing and the string beans.

9. Cover with a layer of plantain slices and pour another fifth of the beaten eggs around the sides of the skillet to come up to the rim.

10. Continue cooking at a very low heat for 4 minutes.

11. Pour the rest of the beaten eggs on top of all and transfer immediately to the oven. Bake for 15 minutes.

12. Remove from the oven, separate from the sides of the skillet or dish with a sharp knife or spatula.

13. Drain off any fat from the pan by tilting it carefully and holding the *piñón* with a plate.

14. Turn the *piñón* over on a serving platter.

15. Let stand for 10-15 minutes before slicing.

Serves: 6-8

GROUND MEAT, RIPE PLANTAIN, AND STRING BEANS *PIÑÓN* II

(Piñón de plátano maduro, carne y habichuelas tiernas II)

- 2 1/2 cups ground meat stuffing, p. 236
- 4 large ripe plantains, peeled, p. 91
- 1 teaspoon butter or margarine
- 5 large eggs, 3 of them separated
- 1/4 teaspoon salt
- 1/2 pound string beans, boiled until tender but crunchy, cut lengthwise

1. Preheat the oven to 350°F.

2. Halve the plantains crosswise, then slice each section lengthwise in four.

3. Bake the plantain slices on a lightly buttered cookie sheet for 15 minutes or until tender, but firm. Remove from cookie sheet and let cool.

4. Grease with the butter or margarine an 11 3/4" x 7 1/2;" x 1 3/4" oven-proof mold.

5. Beat two of the eggs with half of the salt and pour into the mold.

6. Line the bottom of the mold with a layer of plantain slices.

7. Lay the meat stuffing and then the string beans over these and cover with the rest of the plantain slices.

8. Beat three whites of the separated eggs with the rest of the

salt to form soft peaks. Beat lightly two of the yolks and mix with the beaten whites.

9. Pour over the *piñón* and place immediately in the oven.

10. Bake for 15 minutes or until the eggs set to a golden color.

11. Remove from the oven and let rest for 10 minutes before serving directly in the mold.

Serves: 6-8

GROUND MEAT, RIPE PLANTAIN AND MOZZARELLA *PIÑÓN*

(Piñón de plátano maduro, carne y queso mozzarella)

- 3 cups ground meat stuffing, p. 236
- 4 large ripe plantains, peeled, p. 91
- 1 tablespoon butter
- 1/2 pound sliced mozzarella cheese
- 1/2 pound shredded mozzarella cheese
- 1/3 cup freshly grated parmesan cheese
- 3 tablespoons tomato sauce

1. Preheat the oven to 350°F.

2. Halve the plantains crosswise, then slice each section in four lengthwise.

3. Bake the plantain slices in a lightly buttered cookie sheet for 15 minutes or until tender, but still firm.

4. Butter an oven-proof dish 11 3/4" x 7 1/2" x 1 3/4".

5. Lay half of the plantain slices in one layer in the bottom of the dish. Lay half of the sliced mozzarella on top.

6. Spread the meat stuffing on top of the cheese and sprinkle with half of the parmesan.

7. Lay the other half of the mozzarella slices on top of the meat and cover with the additional plantain slices.

8. Spread the shredded mozzarella on top of the plantain,

dribble with the tomato sauce and sprinkle with the rest of the parmesan.

9. Bake uncovered for 20 minutes.

Serves: 6-8

FRIED LADYFINGER BANANAS

(Guineítos niños fritos)

24 ladyfinger bananas
shortening or butter

1. Peel the bananas.

2. Fry in one layer in a skillet set over moderate to medium-high heat either in shortening or butter until tender and golden. Turn to cook all sides evenly.

3. Drain on kraft paper and serve warm as a side dish. Do not use paper towels for draining as they will stick.

Serves: 6

BREADED LADYFINGER BANANAS

(Guineítos niños empanados)

18 ladyfinger bananas
3/4 cup flour
4 large eggs beaten with a pinch of salt
2 cups soda crackers or bread crumbs
shortening

1. Peel the bananas, dredge with flour and shake off the excess.

2. Dip in the beaten egg, then roll in the crumbs, patting them into the bananas.

3. Deep fry in one layer in shortening to cover in a skillet set over medium-high heat until golden brown.

4. Drain on paper towels and serve warm as a side dish.

Serves: 6

LADYFINGER BANANAS OMELET

(Tortilla de guineítos niños)

12 medium or 8 large ripe ladyfinger bananas
4 large eggs beaten with 1/4 teaspoon salt
vegetable oil

1. Peel the bananas and fry in vegetable oil until tender and golden. Turn frequently.

2. Chop or mash the bananas and mix well with the beaten eggs.

3. Heat 1 1/2 teaspoon oil in a 6 1/2" diameter heavy skillet over low heat.

4. Pour in the banana and egg mixture and cook for 7 minutes, separating the edges of the omelet from the sides of the skillet with a spatula or knife blade.

5. Turn the omelet over onto a greased plate placed over the skillet.

6. Add one more teaspoon of oil to the skillet and slide in the omelet.

7. Cook for 5 more minutes or until a cake tester or knife blade inserted in the center comes out clean.

8. Turn over onto a clean plate and let rest 5 minutes before slicing.

Serves: 6

BOILED BREADFRUIT

(Panapén hervido)

1 medium size breadfruit —about 3 pounds— neither too green nor ripe
2 1/2 quarts water
2 tablespoons salt

1. Cut off the top and bottom of the breadfruit.

2. Cut lengthwise into 6 slices and peel with a knife.

3. Cut off the spongy core.

4. Boil in the water and salt for 25-35 minutes or until tender.

5. Drain and serve warm or cool with butter or olive oil as a side dish, or proceed with your recipe if you are making one that asks for boiled breadfruit.

Serves: 6

BAKED BREADFRUIT PUREE

(Puré de panapén horneado)

3 cups boiled breadfruit, pureed, p. 109
3 tablespoons butter
3 teaspoons flour
1 cup warm milk
1/4 teaspoon salt
3 beaten egg yolks
1/3 cup freshly grated parmesan cheese

1. Preheat the oven to 350°F.

2. Make a roux by cooking the flour in the butter over low heat for 3-4 minutes in a saucepan that can hold all the ingredients.

3. Remove the pan from the heat and stir in the milk and salt with a wire whisk.

4. Return to the range and cook over moderate heat until it thickens to a medium-thick consistency.

5. Remove the saucepan again from the heat and stir in the egg yolks.

6. Add the pureed breadfruit and the cheese. Blend well.

7. Bake in a buttered oven-proof dish —8" x 6" x 2"— for 40 minutes.

8. Raise the temperature to 375°F and bake for 5 more minutes or until golden on top.

Serves: 6

BREADFRUIT FRITTERS

(Frituras de panapén)

1 1/2 cup warm boiled breadfruit, p.109, pureed (3/4 pound breadfruit)
1 tablespoon butter
1 large egg beaten with a pinch of salt
shortening

1. Add the butter to the warm pureed breadfruit. Blend well.

2. Add the egg and mix well.

3. Deep fry by tablespoonfuls in a *caldero* or deep skillet in shortening heated to 350°F until golden brown.

4. Drain on paper towels and serve warm as a side dish.

Yield: 12 fritters about 1 1/2" diameter

BREADFRUIT *TOSTONES*

(Tostones de panapén)

1 medium breadfruit —about 3 pounds— neither too green nor ripe
salted water
1/3 cup olive oil or 2 tablespoons melted butter
1 pressed large garlic clove
shortening
salt

1. Cut off the top and bottom of the breadfruit. Slice lengthwise into 8-10 segments. Peel with a knife and cut off the spongy core.

2. Cut the segments crosswise into 1"-thick pieces and soak in the salted water for 10 minutes.

3. Drain and fry in the shortening, in a *caldero* or deep skillet set over medium heat, until tender —about 10 minutes.

4. Raise the heat to medium-high.

5. Flatten the breadfruit pieces slightly and fry again for 5 minutes until golden crisp.

6. Drain and toss with the olive oil and garlic.

7. Remove with a slotted spoon, place in a platter, and salt to taste. Serve warm as a side dish.

Yield: 40-50 *tostones*

STUFFED BREADFRUIT

(Panapén relleno)

3 cups ground meat stuffing, p. 236
3 small breadfruits —neither too green nor ripe
butter
3 large eggs beaten with a pinch of salt
1 cup soda cracker or bread crumbs

1. Peel the breadfruits and halve crosswise.

2. Cut off a sliver from the side of both halves to make them stand flat.

3. Scrape a hollow in the center of each halve to make a pocket for stuffing.

4. Boil gently until tender in salted water to cover.

5. Preheat the oven to 400°F.

6. Drain the breadfruit, rub with butter and set on a cookie sheet or baking dish.

7. Fill each pocket with 1/2 cup of stuffing. Spoon beaten egg over this and sprinkle with crumbs.

8. Bake in the oven until golden brown.

Serves: 6

BREADFRUIT CHIPS

(Hojuelas de panapén)

1 3-pound green breadfruit
1 1/2 quart water
2 tablespoons salt
4 cups shortening

1. Cut off the top and bottom of the breadfruit. Slice lengthwise into 6 segments.

2. Peel with a knife and remove the spongy core.

3. Slice the wedges very thinly with a sharp knife or the very thin serrated slicing disk of a food processor.

4. Soak the slices in the salted water for 15 minutes. Drain well.

5. Fry until golden crisp in the shortening heated to 350°F in a *caldero* or deep chicken fryer set over medium-high heat —about 15-20 minutes. Stir once.

6. Drain and lay on paper towels.

7. Sprinkle with salt to taste, if at all.

NOTE: After the chips cool, they will keep crisp for several days in a closed container.

Yield: 6 cups

BOILED BREADFRUIT SEEDS

(Pepitas de panapén hervidas)

1 1/2 pound breadfruit seeds
1 1/2 quart water
2 1/2 tablespoons salt

1. Rinse the seeds and cut off a small piece at either end of their shells, so that they can absorb the salt.

2. Bring the water and salt to a boil in a large pot. Add the seeds and bring back to a boil.

3. Cook covered at moderate to moderate-low heat, keeping them at a steady boil, for 30 minutes or until tender.

4. Drain and serve hot to be shelled and eaten as an appetizer, very much like roasted chestnuts.

Serves: 6

BOILED SWEET-CORN ROOTS

(Lerenes hervidos)

1 pound sweet-corn roots
6 cups water
2 tablespoons salt

1. Rinse. Boil in the water and salt over moderate heat for 50-60 minutes until tender.

2. Serve as an appetizer to be peeled before eating.

Serves: 6

CHAYOTE HASH

(Boronía de chayote)

3 medium chayotes
2 1/2 quarts water
5 teaspoons salt
2 tablespoons annatto oil or lard, or olive oil
3 ounces diced ham
1 diced medium onion
1 medium frying pepper, seeded and diced
2 large sweet chili peppers, seeded and minced
2 pressed medium garlic cloves
1 large tomato, peeled, seeded and chopped, p. 132
3 tablespoons tomato sauce
4 large eggs beaten with 1/4 teaspoon salt

1. Quarter the chayotes and boil in the water and salt for 15-20 minutes or until tender but not mushy. Some varieties of chayotes may take longer.

2. In the meantime, sauté the ham in the annatto oil or lard, or olive oil, for 3 minutes.

3. Add the onion, pepper, chili peppers, garlic and cook over low heat for 5 minutes.

4. Add the tomato and tomato sauce. Cook for 5 more minutes.

5. Peel the chayote quarters, remove the seed and fibers. Dice.

6. Add to the cooking sauce and stir well.

7. Add the beaten eggs and cook over medium heat, stirring occasionally, until the eggs are done.

Serves: 6

CREAMED CHAYOTES

(Chayotes a la crema)

3 large chayotes
2 1/2 quarts water
1 tablespoon salt
3/4 cup milk
7 teaspoons cornstarch
7 tablespoons sugar
1/4 teaspoon salt
2 egg yolks
1 1/2 tablespoon seedless raisins
ground cinnamon

1. Boil the chayotes in the water and tablespoon of salt for about 30 minutes, or until tender. Some varieties of chayotes take longer to cook.

2. Cut in half, remove the seed and fibers attached to it.

3. Scoop out the pulp being careful not to tear the skin. Save the shells.

4. Puree the pulp and drain in a colander or sieve to remove excess water.

5. Mix well the milk, cornstarch, sugar, 1/4 teaspoon salt and egg yolks.

6. Preheat the oven to 400°F.

7. Cook the milk mixture over medium-low heat, stirring continually, until it thickens —about ten minutes.

8. Fold in the chayote puree and raisins.

9. Stuff the shells with the mixture. Sprinkle with cinnamon and bake in the oven for 15 minutes on a buttered cookie sheet.

Serves: 6

STUFFED CHAYOTES

(Chayotes rellenos)

2 1/2 cups ground meat stuffing, p. 236
3 large chayotes, about 3/4 pound each
2 quarts water
5 teaspoons salt
2 large eggs beaten with a pinch of salt
1 1/2 tablespoons grated parmesan cheese

1. Halve the chayotes lengthwise and boil gently in the salted water for 30 minutes, or until tender. Start checking after 15 minutes for the different varieties of chayotes take different cooking times.

2. Drain the chayotes and let cool. Remove their seed and the fibers attached to it.

3. Scoop out the pulp carefully so as not to pierce or tear the skin. Save the shells.

4. Mash the pulp and drain in a colander to get rid of any excess water.

5. Mix the ground meat with 2 1/2 cups of mashed chayote and the cheese. Sauté in a skillet over moderate heat until most of the liquid evaporates — about 5-10 minutes.

6. Preheat the oven to 400°F.

7. Put the shells on a buttered baking sheet and stuff with the meat and chayote mixture.

8. Spoon beaten egg over the chayotes. Bake for 10-15 minutes, or until the egg sets to a golden brown.

Serves: 6

PUMPKIN FRITTERS

(Frituras de calabaza)

1 1/2 pounds West-Indian pumpkin or any other winter squash
1 quart water
1 teaspoon salt
6 tablespoons flour
4 tablespoons sugar
1/4 teaspoon ground cinnamon
1/8 teaspoon ground cloves
1/4 teaspoon salt
1 egg yolk
shortening

1. Cut the pumpkin into 6 pieces, peel and seed. Boil in the water and teaspoon of salt for 10-15 minutes, or until tender.

2. Puree or mash the pumpkin and drain in a sieve or colander to remove excess liquid.

3. Measure 1 1/2 cups of the puree.

4. Sift together the flour, sugar, cinnamon, cloves and salt. Mix well with the pumpkin puree.

5. Blend in the egg yolk. If the mixture is too runny, add up to 4 teaspoons of additional flour, testing after every teaspoon.

6. Bring enough shortening to cover the fritters in an uncrowded single layer to 350°F in a *caldero* or deep skillet set over medium-high heat.

7. Fry the mixture by tablespoonfuls until golden brown.

8. Drain on paper towels and serve warm as a side dish.

Yield: 18-20 fritters

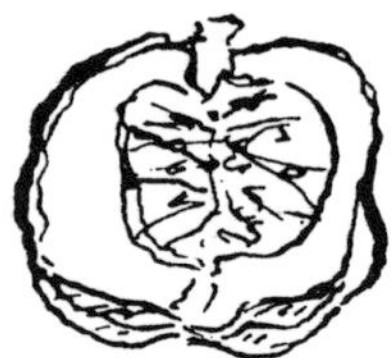

ROASTED BELL PEPPERS

(Pimientos asados)

1. Preheat the oven to 400°F

2. Rinse the peppers and dry with a kitchen towel.

3. Roast in the middle rack of the oven, turning once, for 20-25 minutes.

4. Put inside a paper bag or wrap in a clean kitchen towel. Let stand for 10 minutes. This loosens the skin.

5. Peel, halve and seed.

6. Proceed with your recipe.

NOTES: You may use frying peppers, but roast only for 10-12 minutes.

If you have a gas range, you may roast them directly over the flame, turning frequently until the skin blackens and blisters. Then proceed to step 4.

STUFFED FRYING PEPPERS

(Pimientos rellenos)

2 1/2 cups ground meat stuffing, p. 236
6 large green frying peppers, as uncrooked as possible to facilitate stuffing

1. Cut the stems off the peppers, cutting as close as possible to the stem to prevent breaking the flesh that tapers in. This rim helps to keep the stuffing inside the peppers.

2. Remove the seeds carefully.

3. Stuff the peppers tightly with the ground meat up to the rim.

4. Place in a lightly greased baking dish.

5. Bake in a preheated oven at 375°F for 30 minutes, turning once at mid cooking.

NOTE: You may peel the peppers once baked just before serving.

Serves: 6-8

EGGPLANT SALAD

(Ensalada de berenjenas)

- 3 eggplants, 1/2 pound each
- 2 quarts water
- juice of one lemon
- 2 teaspoons salt
- 3 green frying peppers, roasted, peeled, seeded and sliced lengthwise into 1/2" strips, p.119
- 3 salad tomatoes, peeled, and cut lengthwise into 6-8 wedges each
- 1 medium onion, sliced 1/4" thick
- 1 peeled garlic clove
- 2 tablespoons olive oil
- vinaigrette dressing, p. 64

1. Trim off the ends of the eggplants and cut crosswise into 1/2" slices.

2. Boil in the water, lemon juice and salt in a non-reactive large saucepan for 5-10 minutes or until tender.

3. Drain and dip into cool water to stop the cooking. Drain, pat dry, and cut each slice in half.

4. In the meantime, cook the onion slices and garlic clove in the oil over very low heat until tender but not browned. Discard the garlic clove.

5. On a serving dish arrange th e eggplant slices, skin-side up,

overlapping each other. Spread the pepper strips and onions over them. Arrange the tomatoes all around.

6. Sprinkle all with the oil in which you cooked the onions and garlic.

7. Serve at room temperature with vinaigrette sauce.

Serves: 6

EGGPLANT FRITTERS

(Frituras de berenjena)

1 1/2 pounds eggplant
1 cup all-purpose flour
1 cup water
1/2 teaspoon salt
2 tablespoons vegetable oil or melted butter
1 quart water
2 teaspoons salt
shortening
sugar (optional)

1. Blend well the flour, cup of water, 1/2 teaspoon salt and the two tablespoons of oil or butter for the batter. Let stand for 30-60 minutes.

2. Trim off the ends of the eggplants and peel. Cut into 1/4"-thick slices.

3. Soak the eggplant in the quart of water and 2 teaspoons salt for 15 minutes. Drain and dry with paper towels.

4. When ready to fry, test the batter. It should not be runny, but thick enough to coat the slices. If too thick, blend in 1-2 teaspoon of water.

5. Pour enough shortening in a *caldero* or deep skillet to cover the slices in one layer at a time without crowding. Bring to 350°F over medium-high heat.

6. Dip the eggplant slices in the batter as you are ready to fry them, and cook for 2 minutes on each side.

7. Drain on paper towels and serve warm, sprinkled with the optional sugar, as a side dish.

NOTE: If you are not using the sugar, you may add a pinch of oregano or your favorite herb to the batter.

Serves: 6

EGGPLANT WITH PORK

(Berenjenas con cerdo)

1 1/2 pounds eggplant
1 pound lean boneless pork, preferably fresh ham butt end, cut into 3/4" cubes
1 1/4 teaspoon salt
2 tablespoons olive oil
1/2 cup uncooked condiment, p.47, or 1 small onion,
1 tomato, 1 frying pepper, 2 sweet chili peppers, minced
1 pressed large garlic clove
1/2 cup tomato sauce
1 1/2 cup hot water
1 1/2 quart water
1 tablespoon salt
1 tablespoon chopped parsley
1/3 cup freshly grated parmesan cheese

1. Trim off any membranes or fat from the pork. Pat dry.

2. Heat the oil in a *caldero* or deep chicken fryer over medium-high heat. Brown the pork cubes. Remove and season with 3/4 teaspoon salt.

3. Reduce the heat to moderate-low and add the uncooked condiment or minced vegetables. Sauté por 5 minutes.

4. Add the garlic and tomato sauce. Cook for 5 minutes.

5. Add the hot water and bring to a boil. Return the meat to the pot, cover, and simmer gently for some 50 minutes, or until almost tender.

6. Thirty minutes into the cooking of the pork, peel and cube the eggplant 1" thick.

7. Soak the eggplant cubes in the 1 1/2 quart of water seasoned with the tablespoon of salt for 15 minutes. Drain, rinse and pat dry.

8. Add the eggplant cubes to the meat, the additional 1/2 teaspoon salt and the parsley. Cover and simmer gently for 25-30 minutes, or until tender. Stir once or twice.

9. Sprinkle the parmesan cheese over it before serving.

NOTE: You may mash some of the eggplant into the stew after cooking to thicken the sauce.

Serves: 6

OKRA WITH PORK

(Guingambós con cerdo)

1 pound tender okra
1/2 pound lean boneless pork, preferably fresh ham butt end, cut into 1/2" cubes
2 tablespoons olive oil
1 1/4 teaspoon salt
1/4 cup frying pepper, seeded and diced
1/4 cup diced onion
2 large sweet chili peppers, seeded and minced
1 pressed medium garlic clove
1 small tomato, peeled, seeded and chopped, p. 132
1/3 cup tomato sauce
1/8 teaspoon ground oregano
1 3/4 cup stock or water
1 teaspoon vinegar
1 tablespoon chopped parsley

1. Heat the oil in a *caldero* or deep chicken fryer over medium-high heat. Brown the pork cubes. Remove and season with 1/2 teaspoon of the salt.

2. Lower the heat to medium-low. Add the onion, pepper and sweet chili peppers. Sauté 5 minutes.

3. Add the garlic, tomato, tomato sauce and oregano. Cook for 5 minutes.

4. Add the stock or water, 3/4 teaspoon additional salt and bring to a boil.

5. Return the meat to the pot with any rendered juices. Cover, lower the heat and simmer gently for 50 minutes, or until almost tender.

6. Forty minutes into the cooking of the pork, rinse and pat dry the okra. If they are very small and tender, merely trim off the stem; if they are larger, trim off the stem, the point, and slice into 1" rings.

7. Add the okra to the pot with the vinegar and parsley. Cover and simmer gently for 15 minutes. Uncover and cook for 5 additional minutes, or until the sauce thickens.

Serves: 6

Variation:

OKRA WITH GROUND PORK

(Guingambós còn cerdo molido)

1/2 pound ground pork instead of the cubed pork

1. Follow the above recipe thru step 4.

2. Have the okra trimmed and ready, as on step 6.

3. Add the meat and okra, vinegar and parsley to the pot.

4. Bring to a boil, cover, reduce the heat and simmer for 20 minutes. Uncover and cook for 5 more minutes, or until the sauce thickens.

Serves: 6

ALCAPURRIAS

1 1/2 cup ground meat stuffing, p.236
1 pound yautia roots
1 medium size green plantain, peeled, p. 91
salted water
1 1/4 teaspoon salt
2 tablespoons annatto lard or annatto oil
vegetable oil or lard

1. Peel the yautias and soak with the peeled plantain in the salted water for 2-3 minutes. Drain.

2. Grate the yautia and plantain, separately, either by hand or in a food processor fitted with the metal blade.

3. Mix 2 cups grated yautia to one of grated plantain.

4. Add the salt and annatto lard or oil and blend well.

5. Put 3 tablespoons of the mash on a square piece of greased wax paper laid on a flat surface. Spread the mash into a 1/4"-thick oval.

6. Put 2 teaspoons of meat stuffing in the center of the oval, and spread it lengthwise without reaching the edges.

7. Fold the wax paper over itself to cover the stuffing with the mash. Holding the paper by the edges, roll the mash to form an oval shape —about 2 1/2-3" long by 1 1/2" wide.

8. In a *caldero* or deep skillet heat a 3"-deep layer of vegetable oil or lard to 350°F over medium-high heat.

9. Deep fry the fritters a few at a time, without crowding, for 8 to 10 minutes or until golden brown.

10. Drain on paper towels and keep warm until all are fried.

11. Serve as an appetizer.

Yield: 12-14 fritters

YAUTIA AND PARMESAN CHEESE FRITTERS

(Frituras de yautía y queso parmesano)

1 1/2 pounds white yautia, peeled, rinsed and grated —about 3 cups
1 1/4 teaspoon salt
1/3 cup freshly grated parmesan cheese
2 tablespoons annatto lard or oil
shortening

1. Blend well all the ingredients.

2. On a piece of greased wax paper put two tablespoons of the mixture and shape with a spatula or knife into a croquette-like shape.

3. Deep fry in the shortening in a *caldero* or deep skillet in one uncrowded layer, 4 minutes on each side or until golden brown.

4. Drain on paper towels and serve warm either as an appetizer or side dish.

Yield: 16 fritters

FRIED WHITE SWEET POTATOES

(Batata blanca frita)

2 1/2 pounds white sweet potatoes
salted water
shortening
melted butter

1. Peel the potatoes and cut into 1/2"-thick slices. Soak in the salted water for 15 minutes.

2. Drain and dry on paper towels.

3. Pour enough shortening in a *caldero* or deep skillet to cover the slices in one uncrowded layer. Heat the shortening over medium heat and fry the slices for 5 minutes.

4. Raise the heat to medium-high and cook for 5 more minutes or until golden brown.

5. Drain on paper towels and serve warm dribbled with melted butter as a side dish.

Serves: 6

APIO PIE

(Pastelón de apio)

3 pounds apio
3 cups ground meat stuffing, p. 236
1 quart water with 1 tablespoon salt
2 tablespoons butter
1/4 cup annatto oil
1 large egg beaten with 1/4 teaspoon salt
melted butter
buttered deep pie mold —10" x 1 1/2"

1. Peel the apio and cut into 2" pieces. Rinse.

2. Blanch in water to cover for 5 minutes and drain.

3. Bring to a boil in the salted water and cook covered at moderate heat for 10 to 15 minutes or until very tender.

4. Mash and measure 5 1/2 cups.

5. Preheat the oven to 375°F.

6. Mix well the mashed apio with the 2 tablespoons butter, the annatto oil and the beaten egg.

7. Line the bottom and sides of the mold with half of the apio.

8. Spread the ground meat stuffing over this and cover with the rest of the mashed apio.

9. Bake in the oven for 15 minutes.

10. Brush the top with the melted butter and bake for 10 more minutes or until golden.

11. Remove from the oven and let rest for 10-15 minutes before slicing.

NOTE: If you are using an electric oven with a top heating element, change the setting to broil, but leave at 375°F before brushing with the melted butter.

Serves: 6

GROUND MEAT AND POTATO BALLS

(Rellenos de papas)

1 1/2 cups ground meat stuffing, p. 236
6 cups mashed potatoes —2 1/2 pounds potatoes
6 tablespoons flour or 3 tablespoons cornstarch
1/4 teaspoon salt
1 tablespoon melted butter (optional)
vegetable oil or lard

1. Blend well the flour, salt and the mashed potatoes. If the mixture is too dry, add the optional butter.

2. Divide into 12 equal portions.

3. Dust your hands with flour and cup a portion of the potato mixture in one hand. Make a hollow in the center and fill with one heaping tablespoon of stuffing. Close the hollow and roll the potato mixture in your hands to form a ball.

4. Repeat the process until all portions are used.

5. Dredge the balls in flour and shake off the excess.

6. Deep fry the balls —a few at a time—, in a *caldero* or deep fryer, in hot vegetable oil or lard (375°F), until golden brown. Make sure that the temperature is right otherwise they might either get soaked with fat, disintegrate or burst.

7. Drain on paper towels and keep warm until all the balls are fried.

NOTE: You may also bread the balls. Dredge in flour, shake off excess, dip in beaten egg and roll over soda cracker or bread crumbs.

Serves: 6

POTATO PIE

(Pastelón de papas)

2 1/2 cups ground meat stuffing, p. 236
5 1/2 cups mashed potatoes —2 1/2 pounds potatoes
2 tablespoons butter
2 large eggs beaten with 1/4 teaspoon salt
melted butter
deep pie dish, buttered —9" x 1 1/2"

1. Mix well the potatoes and butter. Add the beaten eggs and blend.

2. Line the bottom and sides of the dish with half of the potato mixture.

3. Put the stuffing on top of this and cover with the rest of the potatoes.

4. Bake in a preheated 375°F oven for 20 minutes.

5. Brush the top with melted butter and bake for 5-10 more minutes or until golden.

6. Remove from the oven and let rest 10-15 minutes before serving.

NOTE: If you are using an electric oven with a top heating element, before brushing with the melted butter change the setting to broil, but leave it at 375°F.

Serves: 6

BREADED POTATO AND HAM SANDWICHES

(Emparedados de papa y jamón empanados)

1/2 pound cooked ham in slices or an 8-ounce can of deviled ham
6 large potatoes, boiled in salted water, peeled and sliced 1/4" thick after cooling
flour
3 large eggs beaten with a pinch of salt
1 cup soda cracker or bread crumbs
vegetable oil

1. Trim the slices of ham to fit the potato slices.

2. Select the best 24 potato slices and put 2 or 3 slices of the ham in between 2 of the potatoes' —or spread with deviled ham. Fasten with wood toothpicks.

3. Dredge in flour and shake off the excess. Dip in beaten egg and cover completely with crumbs, patting them onto the surface. Follow this process only for as many sandwiches as you can fry at a time.

4. Heat a 1/2"-deep layer of vegetable oil in a large skillet over medium-high heat. Fry the sandwiches, turning once, until golden.

5. Drain on paper towels and keep warm until all are fried. Remove the toothpicks before serving.

Serves: 6

FRENCH FRIES WITH PEPPERS

(Papas fritas con pimientos)

2 pounds mealy baking potatoes
2 large green frying peppers
shortening

1. Peel the potatoes and cut into the desired french fry shape and thickness.

2. Rinse under running cool water, drain and dry on paper towels.

3. Halve the peppers lengthwise, seed and cut into 1/2"-thick strips or half-rings.

4. Bring enough shortening to cover the potatoes by at least 2 inches to deep fry temperature —350°F.

5. Add the potatoes and fry until almost golden —about 5 minutes.

6. Add the peppers and continue frying until the potatoes are crisp —about 5 more minutes. Do not let the pepper burn.

7. Drain on paper towels, and salt to taste.

Serves: 6

SPANISH OMELET

(Tortilla española)

1 1/2 pounds potatoes, peeled and sliced about 1/8" thick
1/2 pound onions, peeled and thinly sliced
1 quart water
4 teaspoons salt
3/4 cup olive oil
5 extra-large eggs, beaten —1/2 cup of egg whites and 1/3, yolks

1. Soak the potatoes in the water with 3 teaspoons of the salt for 5 minutes. Drain well.

2. In a *caldero* or deep skillet heat the oil over medium heat. Add the potatoes, onions, and the rest of the salt.

3. Cook uncovered, stirring often, for 20 minutes.

4. Drain the onions and potatoes in a strainer. Save the oil.

5. Pour 2 teaspoons of the frying oil in a heavy 8" skillet and set over low heat.

6. Mix the onions and potatoes with the beaten eggs and pour into the skillet. Cook for 10 minutes, separating the edges of the omelet from the sides of the pan with a spatula or knife blade.

7. Grease a flat dish, put over the skillet and turn the omelet into the plate.

8. Add another teaspoon of oil to the skillet and slide the omelet back into it.

9. Cook over low heat for 5 more minutes, or until a cake tester or knife blade inserted in the center comes out clean.

10. Separate the sides of the omelet from the skillet and turn it over onto a clean plate.

NOTES: Instead of turning the omelet over, as in step 7, turn your electric oven's upper heating element to 375°F, and set the skillet in the center rack for 8 minutes. This omelet may be served either warm or at room temperature as a main dish. If serving warm, wait 5 minutes before slicing. It can be served also as an appetizer, either at room temperature or cold, cut into cubes.

Serves: 6

PEELED AND SEEDED TOMATOES

(Tomates pelados y sin semillas)

ripe but firm tomatoes
boiling water

1. Put the tomatoes in the boiling water for one minute.

2. Peel off the skin with a paring knife.

3. Halve crosswise and squeeze with your hand to extract the seeds. Scoop out any additional seeds with your finger or the handle of a small spoon.

4. Cut off the stem end.

5. Proceed with your recipe.

NOTE: If the tomatoes are firm enough they can be peeled successfully with a swivel-type potato peeler, without having to use the boiling water.

POLENTA WITH MILK

(Funche con leche)

1 1/2 cup cornmeal
1 1/2 cup milk
1 1/2 cup water
3/4 teaspoon salt
2 tablespoons butter

1. Put all the ingredients, except the cornmeal, in a saucepan and bring to a boil.

2. Remove from the heat and add the cornmeal gradually, stirring all the time with a wire whisk.

3. Return the saucepan to the heat.

4. Lower the heat to medium-low and cook, stirring, until it thickens to taste.

5. Serve warm as a side dish. Add sugar and more milk to taste, if so desired.

Serves: 6

SURULLITOS

1 1/4 cup coarse ground yellow cornmeal
1 cup water
1 teaspoon salt
2 teaspoons butter
1/4 cup freshly grated parmesan or 1/3 cup grated Edam cheese
shortening

1. Bring the water, salt and butter to a boil.

2. Mix the cornmeal and cheese. Remove the pan from the heat and stir these in rapidly with a wooden spoon or whisk. If the mixture is too dry, add one more tablespoon of water.

3. Take one tablespoonful of the mixture and shape into a cylinder about 2 1/2" long. Place on wax paper as you shape each.

4. Heat shortening to 350°F in a *caldero* or deep skillet.

5. Fry the "surullitos" in one uncrowded layer until golden crisp.

6. Remove and drain on paper towels. Keep warm until serving either as a side dish or an appetizer.

Yield: 36 *surullitos*

FLUFFY CORNMEAL AND CHEESE CRULLERS

(Almojábanas de harina de maíz y queso)

1 1/4 cup fine ground yellow cornmeal
1 cup water
2 tablespoons butter
3/4 teaspoon salt
2 slightly beaten large eggs
1/2 cup grated mild crumbly white cheese or parmesan

1. Bring to a boil the water, butter and salt.

2. Remove the pan from the heat and beat in the cornmeal gradually with a wooden spoon or wire whisk. Let cool.

3. Beat in the eggs.

4. Add the cheese and mix well. If the mixture is too thick add 1-2 tablespoons of water or milk.

5. Deep fry by tablespoonfuls in shortening heated to 350°F over medium high heat in a *caldero* or deep skillet until golden crisp.

6. Drain on paper towels and serve warm either as a side dish or appetizer.

NOTES: These may be served with a cinnamon-flavored syrup, but then reduce the salt to 1/4 teaspoon.

The mixture may be prepared beforehand and re-stirred before frying.

Yield: 40 crullers

FLUFFY CORNMEAL FRITTERS

(Frituras de maíz esponjosas)

1 1/3 cup fine ground yellow cornmeal
3/4 cup water
3/4 teaspoon salt
2 tablespoons butter
2 lightly beaten large eggs
shortening

1. Bring the water, salt and butter to a boil.

2. Remove the pan from the heat and stir in the cornmeal gradually with a wooden spoon or wire whisk until well mixed. Let cool.

3. Add the beaten eggs gradually, mixing well.

4. Bring enough shortening to frying temperature —350°F— over medium-high heat in a *caldero* or deep skillet.

5. Fry the mixture by tablespoonfuls in single uncrowded layers until golden crisp —2-3 minutes on each side.

6. Drain on paper towels and serve warm either as a side dish or appetizer.

NOTE: You may use 2 1/2 tablespoons sugar in the mixture, but reduce the salt to 1/4 teaspoon.

Yield: 30 fritters

CORNMEAL TURNOVERS

(Empanadillas de harina de maíz)

12 tablespoons ground meat stuffing, p. 236
2 cups fine ground cornmeal
1/4 cup all-purpose flour
3/4 teaspoon salt
2 cups water
4 teaspoons butter
shortening

1. Mix the cornmeal, flour, salt and water together and cook over moderate heat, stirring continuously, for 7 minutes or until the mixture forms a soft, but fairly stiff dough that separates from the bottom of the pan.

2. Remove from the heat, add the butter and blend well.

3. On a greased piece of waxed paper spread 1/4 cup of the dough into a 5" diameter circle. If the dough sticks to the spatula used to spread it, it is too moist. Scrape it off, add a little more flour to the dough and start over.

4. Lay a tablespoon of the stuffing in the center of the dough circle and spread it out without coming to the edge.

5. Fold the paper over and press the edges of the turnover together. Place on waxed paper.

6. Deep fry in shortening in a *caldero* or deep skillet at medium-high heat —350°F— for 6 or 7 minutes on each side or until golden crisp.

7. Drain on paper towels and serve warm as an appetizer.

Yield: 12 turnovers

CHAPTER V: PASTELES *AND PASTA*

HOW TO PREPARE BANANA LEAVES FOR WRAPPING *PASTELES* AND OTHER FOODS

(Método para preparar hojas de guineo o plátano para pasteles y otros platos)

If using freshly picked banana or plantain leaves, cut off the central rib and trim off the edges. Cut into the desired sizes. To make them flexible for folding wilt in single layers, or slightly overlapping, in a 200°F oven for 5-15 minutes. An alternative method of wilting is to place them directly over the coils of an electric range on low heat, or pass them carefully over the low flame of a gas range. Be careful not to burn them unduly. Wipe with a damp kitchen cloth or paper towel.

Commercial banana leaves usually come in packages which are sold either by the package or by pound. They may or may not be already wilted.

The alternative to banana leaves, if these are unavailable, is parchment paper cut into the sizes indicated in your recipe. In the case of recipes that ask for an outer and an inner leaf, you need use only pieces of parchment paper cut to the size of the larger leaf piece.

You may combine leaf and parchment paper, using this latter for the outer wrapping.

PASTELES

Stuffing

10 cups pork meat, trimmed of connective tissues and excessive fat, and diced into 1/2" cubes —fresh ham, picnic or shoulder butt (about 7 pounds of boneless meat)
5 teaspoons salt
1/2 cup annatto lard or oil, p. 47
1 1/4 cup uncooked condiment, p. 47
6 large pressed garlic cloves
12 large sweet chili peppers, seeded and minced
12 minced large *culantro* leaves
12 cilantro sprigs, finely chopped
1 1/2 cup tomato sauce
1 teaspoon ground oregano
1 cup water
1 cup seedless raisins
2 16-ounce cans boiled chick peas, drained
14 ounces pimientos, sliced into 1/2" strips
48-96 small pimiento-stuffed olives (optional)
6 hot chili peppers, pureed in a mortar, mixed with 4-5 tablespoons of the meat stew sauce, then strained (optional)

Mash

4 pounds medium size green bananas, peeled, p.91, and cut into 1 1/2" rings
1 large green plantain, peeled, p.91, and cut into 1" segments
salted water
7 pounds white yautia, peeled and cut into 1 1/2" cubes
3 cups annatto lard, p. 47
4 1/2 tablespoons salt
1 cup sauce from the meat stew (see above)
2 cups warm milk

Wrapping

48 pieces of banana or plantain leaves, 12" x 12", p. 141

48 pieces of banana or plantain leaves, 7" x 10", p. 141
or
48 pieces parchment paper, 12" x 12"
48 pieces banana or plantain leaves 7" x 10"
kitchen twine

Meat stew

1. Season the meat cubes with 3 teaspoons of the salt and let stand while you prepare the condiments and the annatto lard for the meat and the mash.

2. In a *caldero* or a chicken fryer large enough to hold the meat, heat 1/2 cup of annatto lard over moderate heat and add the uncooked condiment. Cook for 5 minutes.

3. Add the garlic, sweet chili peppers, *culantro* leaves, cilantro, tomato sauce, oregano and the remaining 2 teaspoons of salt. Cook for 5 more minutes.

4. Raise the heat to medium-high, add the meat and cook stirring for 5 minutes.

5. Add the water and bring to a boil. Cover, lower the heat and simmer for 30-45 minutes or until the meat is tender. Set apart or refrigerate covered if not continuing with the recipe on the same day.

Mash

6. Peel the bananas and plantain.

7. Cut the bananas into 1 1/2" rings and the plantain into 1" segments. Soak in salted water to cover.

8. Peel the white yautia and cut into 1 1/2" cubes.

9. Rinse and drain the bananas and plantain.

10. Process the bananas, plantain and yautia in a food processor fitted with the steel blade only until finely grated but not mushy. Do not overprocess.

11. Put all in a large bowl and mix well.

12. Add the 3 cups annatto lard and the 4 1/2 tablespoons of salt. Blend well.

13. Add the milk and 1 cup of sauce from the meat stew. Blend well and set apart, or refrigerate covered if not continuining with the recipe on the same day. Do not refrigerate longer than overnight, as it might ferment.

Assembly

14. If making some of the *pasteles* with the hot chili sauce, divide the meat stew into two parts and add to one part one tablespoon of the hot sauce per 12 pasteles, or more to taste.
15. Lay a 12" x 12" banana leaf on a table. Ribs paralell to you on top place one of the 7" x 10" leaves, long side parallel to you, the edges of both leaves nearer you flush with each other.
16. In the center of the small leaf spread 6 tablespoons of the mash in a rectangle slightly smaller than 4" x 6".

17. Put 2 tablespoonfuls of the meat in a narrow rectangle along the center of the mash, add one or two pimiento strips.

18. Add some raisins, chick peas to taste, and one or two of the optional olives.

19. Dribble with some of the meat sauce.

20. Fold over the edges nearer you of both leaves to cover the mash and stuffing.

21. Continue folding until you reach the edge of the outer leaf. The *pastel* should be about 3" wide.

22. Fold the ends of the leaves over the seam, for a length of about 6".

23. Pat lightly to flatten out to no less than 1/2".

24. Put two *pasteles* together, seam sides facing each other.

25. Tie with twine, package like: two lengths of twine lengthwise; two, crosswise. Do not tie too tightly as they swell when cooking.

26. Add an additional bow or piece of string to identify those *pasteles* which have hot sauce.

27. If not cooking immediately, refrigerate for up to 5 days, or freeze for up to a year.

Cooking

28. Bring to a boil 6 quarts of water per 12 *pasteles.*

29. Add the *pasteles,* bring again to a boil. Cover, lower the heat to medium low and cook for 45 minutes, turning once. If frozen, boil for an hour.

30. Drain the *pasteles,* unwrap and serve warm, two per person. Serve two *pasteles* on one of the inner leaves placed on a dinner plate.

NOTES: 1. If using a food processor, you may first slice the plantain, bananas and yautia with the serrated slicing disk, and then grate with the steel blade.

2. If grating by hand, leave the vegetables whole after peeling.

3. You may use any bottled hot sauce to taste instead of the hot chili pepper sauce.

4. You may combine parchment paper and leaves, if available. Use the leaf for the inner wrapping, as this imparts a distinctive flavor and aroma to the *pasteles.*

5. If using only parchment paper, spread the mash about 3" from the edge nearest from you. Bring this edge over to cover the mash and stuffing. Fold the side of the paper nearest you over this, and continue folding until you reach the edge of the paper. Fold the ends over the seam side and tie two *pasteles* together, seam sides facing, with kitchen twine.

Yield: 48 *pasteles*

YUCA *PASTELES*

(Pasteles de yuca)

Follow the recipe for *Pasteles*, p. 142 but add an additional 1/4 cup of water to the meat stew and prepare instead the following mash:

10 1/2 pounds yuca
1 cup water
3 1/2 tablespoons salt
1 3/4 cup annatto lard, p. 47
1 1/4 cup warm milk
3/4 cup sauce from the stewed meat

1. Peel the yuca and grate by hand, being careful not to grate the central fiber of the tuber; or, cut the tuber lengthwise, remove the core fiber, cut into appropriate pieces and grate in a food processor.

2. Add one cup of water to the grated yuca and press through a potato ricer or a sieve with a spoon to remove the starchy liquid. This would make the *pasteles* gummy. You should remove from 1 1/2 to 2 cups of liquid, which is then discarded.

3. Add the salt and annatto lard and blend well.

4. Add the warm milk and the meat sauce. Mix well.

5. Proceed to step 14 of the *pasteles* recipe —assembly and cooking.

Yield: 48 *pasteles*

GREAT LAND CRAB TURNOVERS

(Empanadillas de jueyes)

2 cups grated yuca, either fresh or frozen (1 1/4 pounds fresh yuca roots)
2 1/2 cups boiled land crab meat, p.179
1/2 cup plus two tablespoons of annatto oil or lard, p. 47
1/2 cup uncooked condiment, p.47, or a small tomato, small onion, small frying pepper, and two sweet chili peppers, well minced
1 pressed medium garlic clove
1/8 teaspoon dried oregano
1/8 teaspoon ground pepper
2 tablespoon tomato sauce
2 1/8 teaspoons salt
8 12-inch square pieces of banana leaf, p.141
8 10-inch square pieces of aluminum foil

1. Prepare the stuffing first. Sauté the uncooked condiment —or minced vegetables— garlic clove, oregano, pepper and tomato sauce in two tablespoons of the annatto oil or lard for 5 minutes over medium-low heat.

2. Add the crab meat and 1 teaspoon of the salt. Sauté, stirring, for some 5 minutes. Set apart.

3. If using fresh yuca to prepare the mash, peel it and grate on the fine side of a metal grater, being careful not to grate the central fiber of the tuber. If you are using a food processor, cut the peeled yuca into lengthwise quarters and remove the fiber. Cut into appropriate pieces, then grate using the metal blade. Do not overprocess.

4. Measure two cups and add 1/4 cup of water. Squeeze the starchy liquid out of the yuca by pressing through a ricer or with a spoon and fine-mesh strainer. Discard this liquid.

5. If using frozen yuca, defrost according to the package instructions.

6. Add the milk to the grated yuca and blend well.

7. Add the 1/2 cup of annatto oil or lard and the remaining 1 1/8 teaspoons salt. Blend well until the mash is smooth and uniform in color. It should drop easily from a spoon without being too runny.

8. Assemble the turnovers. On the top edge of a banana leaf piece spread 1/4 cup of the mash into a 6" x 5" rectangle.

9. Along the lower half of this rectangle spread three tablespoons of the stuffing.

10. Wrap the turnovers by folding towards you so that the upper half of the mash covers the stuffing.

11. Continue folding until the leaf piece is used up. Then fold the ends of the leaf over the seam. Pat lightly with your hand.

12. Wrap in an aluminium foil piece. Follow the same process for all of the turnovers.

13. Preheat the oven to 375°F.

14. Place the turnovers in one layer on a baking sheet and bake for 30 minutes, turning once.

15. Serve warm on a trimmed piece of the banana leaf square as an appetizer.

NOTES: They may be frozen after folding, but they should be baked then at 400°F for the first 10 minutes and at 375° for the rest of the time.

The milk for the mash may be substituted by fresh coconut milk.

Yield: 8 turnovers

GREEN PLANTAIN *GUANIMES*

(Guanimes de plátano verde)

3 large green plantains, peeled and soaked in salted water, p. 91
1/2 teaspoon salt
1/2 cup plus 2 tablespoons of sugar
1 cup coconut milk, p.416
1/2 teaspoon anise seeds
12 pieces of banana leaf, 10" x 10", p.141
kitchen twine

1. Drain the plantains from the salted water, grate either by hand or in a food processor fitted with the steel blade. Measure 3 densely packed cups.

2. Mix well the salt, sugar, coconut milk and anise seeds.

3. Blend with the grated plantain.

4. One inch off the edge of the leaf farthest away from you, spread a narrow 4" rectangle of the mash.

5. Bring that edge over the mash and start rolling until you reach the edge of the leaf nearest you.

6. Tie the ends securely with kitchen twine.

7. Bring to a boil 3 quarts of water with 1 tablespoon salt. Put in the *guanimes*, cover and lower the heat. Simmer for 30 minutes.

8. Unwrap and serve warm as an appetizer.

Yield: 12 *guanimes*

CANNELLONI STUFFED WITH PORK

(Canelones rellenos con cerdo)

30 large cannelloni (Tufoli Núm. 82)
3 1/2 cups ground meat stuffing, p.236, made with ground pork
1/2 pound fresh mushrooms
2 tablespoons butter
1 tablespoon oil
1 1/2 cups tomato sauce, p.53, chunky tomato sauce, p.54 or commercial tomato sauce (see note below)
1/2 teaspoon sugar (optional)
1/2 pound shredded mozzarella cheese, a combination of shredded mild cheddar and Colby, or slices of pasteurized processed cheese spread

1. Trim off the base of the mushroom stems, and wipe with a moist kitchen cloth. Slice.

2. Heat the butter and oil in a frying pan over medium-high heat and sauté the sliced mushrooms for 6-8 minutes or until lightly browned.

3. Mix the tomato sauce, optional sugar, and sauteed mushrooms and simmer for 5-10 minutes. Adjust seasonings to taste.

4. In the meantime, cook the cannelloni following the package instructions. Drain and dip into cool water to stop their cooking. Drain again and separate to prevent their sticking to each other.

5. Preheat the oven to 350°F.

6. Stuff 24 of the cannelloni with the ground meat stuffing and place in one layer in a buttered oven-proof dish measuring 14" x 10" x 2".

7. Pour the tomato sauce with the mushrooms over the cannelloni and sprinkle with the mozzarella or cheese combination, or lay the slices of processed cheese over all.

8. Cover with aluminum foil and bake for 30 minutes.

9. Uncover and bake for 5 more minutes or until crisp at the top.

NOTES: If you are using commercial tomato sauce, sauté 1/2 chopped onion and one minced garlic clove for 5 minutes in oil or butter. Add the sauce, some basil, oregano, or your favorite herbs. Simmer covered over low heat 20-30 minutes. Pass through a sieve, add the sauteed mushrooms and simmer for 10 more minutes. Proceed to step 4.

Instead of the fresh tomato sauces, or the flavored commercial one, you may use your favorite commercial spaguetti sauce with mushrooms.

Cook 30 cannelloni to get 24, since some break during the boiling.

You may use manicotti, boiling and timing them according to the package instructions. Count on 2-3 per person.

Variation:

CANNELLONI STUFFED WITH CHICKEN

(Canelones rellenos con pollo)

Follow the recipe for Cannelloni Stuffed with Pork but substitute for the ground meat stuffing, 3 1/2 cups shredded fricaseed chicken. Use the recipe on p. 193 for the fricassee, omit the potatoes and bone and shred the meat after cooking and cooling.

LASAGNA

(Lasaña)

9 pieces of lasagna pasta
7 cups ground meat stuffing, p.236, made with ground beef, but omiting the olives, capers and raisins
1/2 pound fresh mushrooms
2 tablespoons butter
1 tablespoon oil
2 - 2 1/2 cups tomato sauce, p.53, chunky tomato sauce, p.54, or commercial tomato sauce (see note below)
1/2 teaspoon sugar (optional)
1 can 14 1/2 ounces peeled tomatoes, drained and coarsely chopped
1/2 pound ricotta cheese
1/2 cup grated parmesan cheese
3/4 pound sliced or shredded mozzarella cheese

1. Trim off the base of the mushroom stems, wipe clean with a damp kitchen cloth and slice.
2. Heat the butter and oil in a frying pan over medium-high heat and sauté the sliced mushrooms for 6-8 minutes, or until lightly browned.
3. Add the tomato sauce and optional sugar to the frying pan, and simmer for 5-10 minutes. Adjust seasonings to taste.

4. Cook the lasagna pieces following the instructions on the package. Drain and dip into cold water to stop the cooking. Drain again and separate to prevent the pieces from sticking to each other while assembling the dish.

5. Butter or oil a 13" x 9" x 2" ovenproof dish.

6. Preheat the oven to 350°F.

7. Spread some tablespoons of the tomato sauce on the bottom of the dish.

8. Line the bottom of the dish with 3 pieces of lasagna. Spread over these half of the meat stuffing, half of the tomatoes, half of the ricotta, 1/3 of the sauce, 1/3 of the mozzarella and 1/3 of the parmesan, in that order.

9. Lay over all three more pieces of the lasagna and layer with the ingredients stated above in the same proportions and order.

10. Lay over these the remaining lasagna pieces, top with the remaining 1/3 of mozzarella, 1/3 sauce and sprinkle with the remaining 1/3 parmesan cheese.

11. Bake uncovered for 20 minutes.

12. Let rest for 10-15 minutes before serving to firm it up.

NOTES: If you are using canned tomato sauce, sauté 1/2 chopped onion, 1 minced garlic clove for 5 minutes. Add the sauce, some basil, oregano, or your favorite herbs. Simmer covered over low heat for 20-30 minutes. Pass through a sieve, add the sauteed mushrooms and simmer for 10 more minutes. Continue with step 4.

You may substitute your favorite commercial spaghetti sauce with mushrooms for the home-made one.

Serves: 6-9

MACARONI WITH CHICKEN

(Macarrones con pollo)

- 3/4 pound ziti tagliati, mostaccioli, or penne macaroni
- 2 pounds chicken, cut into small pieces, preferably boned
- 2 1/2 teaspoons salt
- 2 pressed garlic cloves
- 1/4 teaspoon ground oregano
- 1/8 teaspoon ground pepper
- 1 tablespoon olive oil
- 1 teaspoon vinegar
- 1/3 cup vegetable oil
- 1/2 cup uncooked condiment, p.47, or 1 small tomato, seeded, 1 small frying pepper, seeded, 1 small onion, all finely minced

1 1/2 cup canned tomato sauce, or tomato sauce, p.53, if not too thick
1/4 teaspoon dried basil leaves
1 1/2 cup water
1/2 cup grated parmesan cheese

1. Season the chicken with the salt, garlic, oregano and pepper.

2. Mix the olive oil with the vinegar, dribble over the chicken and let stand for at least 30 minutes.

3. In a large skillet set over medium-high heat, brown the chicken pieces and set aside.

4. Take 3 tablespoons of the browning oil and put in a *caldero* or deep chicken fryer. Set over medium heat.

5. Sauté the uncooked condiment or minced vegetables for 5 minutes.

6. Add the tomato sauce and basil. Simmer for 5 minutes.

7. Add the chicken pieces and the water, bring to a boil, cover, lower the heat and simmer for 45 minutes or until the sauce thickens.

8. Once the chicken is done, cook the macaroni following the instructions on the package. Drain and add to the chicken.

9. Cook uncovered over moderate heat for 5 minutes, stirring occasionally.

10. Remove from the heat. Stir in the parmesan cheese and serve warm.

NOTE: You may bone and skin the chicken after it is cooked.

Serves: 6

Variation:

MACARONI WITH SPARERIBS

(Macarrones con costillas)

Follow the instructions for Macaroni with Chicken, but substitute: 2 pounds spareribs for the chicken.

Serves: 6

ELBOW MACARONI WITH GROUND BEEF

(Macarrones en coditos con carne de res molida)

1/2 pound elbow macaroni
1/2 pound lean ground beef
6 bacon slices
1/2 cup diced onion
1/2 cup green pepper, seeded and diced
1 medium tomato, peeled, seeded and coarsely chopped, p.132
2 pressed medium garlic cloves
3 cups tomato sauce, p.53, chunky tomato sauce, p.54, or commercial tomato sauce for spaghetti
1/4 teaspoon ground oregano
1/2 teaspoon salt
1 teaspoon sugar (optional)
1/2 cup water
1/3 cup grated parmesan cheese or 2 ounces crumbled cheddar cheese
2 tablespoons minced capers

1. Fry the bacon slices and remove. Crumble and save.

2. In 2 tablespoons of the bacon fat cook the onion and pepper for 5 minutes over low heat.

3. Add the tomatoes, garlic, capers, tomato sauce, oregano, salt and optional sugar. Cook for 5 more minutes.

4. Raise the heat to medium high, add the meat and stir-fry for 5-7 minutes.

5. Add the water and bring to a boil, lower the heat, cover and simmer for 15 minutes, stirring once or twice.

6. In the meantime, cook the elbow macaroni following the package instructions. Drain and add to the meat after this is done. Stir well and cook for 5 minutes.

7. Off heat, stir in the cheese and the crumbled bacon.

Serves: 6

Variation:

ELBOW MACARONI WITH GROUND BEEF AND BEANS

(Macarrones en coditos con carnè de res molida y habichuelas)

Follow the recipe for Elbow Macaroni with Ground Beef, but:

Add one 11-ounce can of boiled pink beans, drained, along with the cooked pasta.

Serves: 6

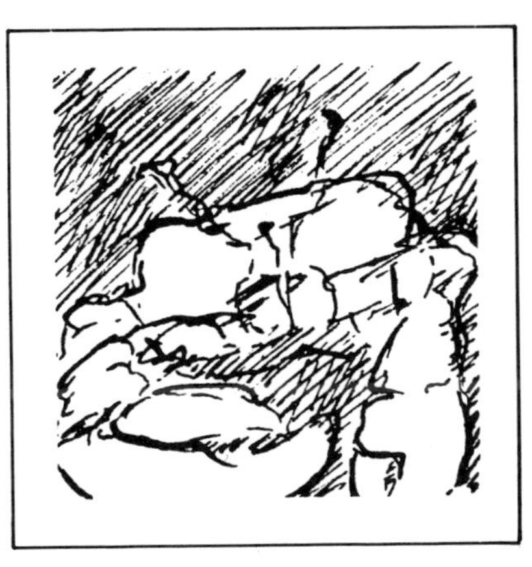

CHAPTER VI: FISH, SHELLFISH, AND THE GREAT LAND CRAB

BREADED FISH FILLETS

(Filetes de pescado empanados)

3 pounds firm white-flesh fish fillets, 1/2" thick
1 1/2 teaspoons salt
1/4 teaspoon ground pepper
4 large eggs beaten with a pinch of salt
2 cups soda-cracker or bread crumbs
vegetable oil

1. Pat dry the fillets. Salt and pepper.

2. Heat a 1" layer of vegetable oil in a heavy frying pan over moderate heat.

3. Dip the fillets in beaten eggs, then cover with crumbs patting them lightly onto the fish. Dip only as many as you can fry in one uncrowded layer.

4. Fry, turning once, until golden crisp.

5. Skim out any burnt crumbs from the oil as you fry, or change the oil if necessary.

6. Drain on paper towels.

Serves: 6

Variation:

MINUTE FISH

(Pescado a la minuta)

Follow the recipe for breaded fish fillets, but use fillets 1/4" thick.

FRIED FISH WITH *MOJITO*

(Pescado frito con mojito isleño)

3 pounds firm white-flesh fish steaks, 1" thick
2 teaspoons salt
vegetable oil

Mojito
1/4 cup olive oil
2 sliced medium onions
3/4 cup tomato sauce
1/3 cup water
1 small bay leaf
2 sliced pimientos
12 pitted green olives
1/2 teaspoon salt

1. Pat dry and salt the fish steaks. Let stand for at least 30 minutes.

2. Sauté the onion slices in the olive oil for 5 minutes in a saucepan set over medium heat.

3. Add the rest of the ingredients for the *mojito*. Cover and simmer for 20 minutes.

4. In a heavy frying pan set over moderate heat, fry the fish steaks in a half-inch layer of vegetable oil for 6 minutes on each side.

5. Place the steaks on a serving platter and pour the *mojito* over them.

Serves: 6

POACHED FISH

(Pescado escalfado)

3 pounds firm white-flesh fish steaks, 1" thick
1 minced small onion
1 chopped small tomato
1 small frying pepper, seeded and minced
2 medium garlic cloves, peeled and quartered
2 minced large sweet chili peppers
3 large *culantro* leaves or 2 sprigs of cilantro
2 1/2 teaspoons salt
1/8 teaspoon ground pepper
1 1/2 quarts water
fish head and trimmings (optional)
2 tablespoons butter

1. Combine all the ingredients in a saucepan except the fish steaks and butter. Bring to a boil, cover and simmer for at least half hour.

2. Melt the butter in a pan where the steaks will fit in an uncrowded layer.

3. Put the steaks in the pan, and strain the simmered stock to cover them.

4. Bring to a slow simmer and cook for 10 minutes, or until the fish flakes easily.

5. Proceed with your recipe, or serve with melted butter or tartar sauce.

Serves: 6

FISH CROQUETTES

(Croquetas de pescado)

2 1/2 cups poached fish, p.161, flaked small
6 tablespoons butter
1/2 cup all-purpose flour
1 1/2 cups hot milk
1/2 teaspoon salt
1/4 teaspoon ground pepper
3 large eggs beaten with a pinch of salt
1 1/3 cup soda-cracker or bread crumbs
vegetable oil

1. To prepare the roux melt the butter in a medium saucepan over low heat. Blend in the flour with a wooden spoon and cook, stirring, for 2 minutes.

2. Remove the pan from the heat. Pour in the hot milk, salt and pepper and whip rapidly with a wire whisk until smooth and blended.

3. Return the pan to moderate heat and boil slowly, stirring occasionally, until the sauce thickens to a creamy consistency.

4. Add the fish flakes and continue stirring until the mixture is thick enough to separate from the sides and bottom of the pan.

5. Pour onto a platter and let cool.

6. Flour your hands and form oval croquettes with the fish mixture by tablespoonful measures.

7. Roll the croquettes in soda-cracker or bread crumbs, dip in the beaten eggs and roll again in crumbs.

8. Let stand for 15 minutes, or refrigerate covered overnight.

9. Fry in an uncrowded layer in oil to cover over medium-high heat until golden crisp on the outside. Adjust the heat to prevent over-browning.

10. Drain on paper towels and serve warm.

NOTE: The croquettes can be frozen, but remove from the freezer 20 minutes before frying.

Yield: 18 croquettes

FISH BALLS

(Albóndigas de pescado)

1 1/2 cups poached fish, p.161, flaked
2 1/2 cups potatoes mashed with 1/4 cup milk and 1 tablespoon butter —about 1 pound potatoes
3 large eggs beaten with a pinch of salt and 1/8 teaspoon ground pepper
1 1/3 cups fine bread or soda-cracker crumbs
vegetable oil

1. Mix the fish flakes with the mashed potatoes. If the mixture is too soft, add 2 or 3 teaspoons bread crumbs.

2. Flour your hands and form balls using tablespoonful measures.

3. Roll the balls in the crumbs. Dip in the beaten eggs and roll again over the crumbs.

4. Let stand for 15 minutes, or refrigerate covered overnight.

5. Fry the balls in vegetable oil to cover in a deep skillet set over medium-high heat until golden crisp on the outside. Regulate the heat to prevent overbrowning.

7. Drain on paper towels and serve warm.

Yield: 22 balls

Variation:

SALT-CODFISH BALLS

(Albóndigas de bacalao)

Follow the recipe for Fish Balls, but substitute for the fish:

1 cup salt-codfish, de-salted, poached, skinned, boned and shredded into small flakes, p.165 —about 1/2 pound codfish fillet.

Yield: 22 balls

PICKLED FISH

(Pescado en escabeche)

3 pounds sierra fish steaks, 1" thick
1 tablespoon salt
vegetable oil

Sauce
1 3/4 cup olive oil
3/4 cup white wine vinegar
1/4 teaspoon salt
1/2 teaspoon peppercorns
2 small bay leaves
3 medium garlic cloves, peeled
3 sliced medium onions

1. Pat dry and salt the fish steaks. Let stand for 30 minutes.

2. In a 3 quart non-reactive pan, simmer the sauce ingredients for 20 minutes except the onions.

3. Add the onions and simmer an additional 10 minutes. Remove from the heat and allow to cool completely.

4. In a frying pan set over moderate heat, sauté the fish steaks in a 1/2" deep layer of vegetable oil for 8 minutes on each side. Shake the pan frequently to prevent sticking.

5. As soon as the fish and sauce cool completely, put the steaks in a crock or glass jar with a cover. Pour the sauce over them and cover tightly.

6. Let stand in a cool place for 24 hours to allow the fish to absorb the flavor of the sauce.

7. Refrigerate and serve chilled as an appetizer.

Serves: 6

RECONSTITUTING AND DE-SALTING SALT-CODFISH

(Bacalao salado —cómo reconstituir y desalar)

1. Cut the salt-codfish into 2" square pieces.

2. Rinse and place in a bowl of cold water to cover for at least 4 hours, changing the water at least 3 times.

3. For a less salty taste, extend this process overnight, but then refrigerate.

4. Drain.

5. Put the cod in a pan full of fresh water. Bring slowly to a simmer and poach gently some 15 minutes, removing the scum that comes to the surface of the water.

6. Drain the fish. Peel off any skin and remove any bones with your fingers.

7. Proceed with your recipe.

SALT-CODFISH FRITTERS

(Bacalaítos fritos)

1 1/2 cup salt-codfish, de-salted, skinned, boned and flaked, v. above —1/2 pound salt-codfish
1 1/2 cups all-purpose flour
1/2 teaspoon baking powder
1/4 teaspoon salt, if needed
2 cups water
3 pressed medium garlic cloves
1/4 teaspoon dried oregano
1/8 teaspoon pepper
2 large sweet chili peppers, seeded and mashed in a mortar or minced
vegetable oil or lard

1. Mix the flour with the baking powder. Add the water and blend well.

2. Add the garlic, oregano, pepper, sweet chili peppers and codfish flakes. Mix well and let stand for 15 minutes.

3. Stir the batter again before frying. Add the salt if needed.

4. Heat 2 or 3 inches of oil or lard in a deep fryer or *caldero* to 350°F.

5. To test the consistency of the batter, drop a tablespoonful of it into the hot oil or lard and fry until golden and crisp. If not crisp enough add 2 tablespoons of water to the batter.

6. Fry by tablespoonfuls, only a few at a time to prevent their sticking to each other.

7. Drain on paper towels and keep warm in a low temperature oven until all are done.

8. Serve warm as an appetizer.

Yield: 24 fritters

BISCAYAN SALT-CODFISH

(Bacalao a la vizcaína)

1 pound salt-codfish, de-salted, poached, skinned, boned and flaked into large pieces, p.165
1 1/2 pounds potatoes, peeled and thinly sliced
2 thinly sliced medium onions
3 sliced hard-boiled eggs
1 teaspoon minced capers
8 chopped green pitted olives
1 4-ounce jar sliced pimientos
1/3 cup seedless raisins
1 small bay leaf
3/4 cup tomato sauce
1/2 cup olive oil
1 cup water

1. In the bottom of a large *caldero*, stove-top casserole or deep chicken fryer, layer half of the potatoes, codfish flakes, onions and egg slices.

2. On top of these add half of the capers, olives, pimientos, raisins, and the bay leaf.

3. Add half the tomato sauce and half the oil.

4. Repeat the above process with the rest of the ingredients with the exception of the water.

5. Add the water and bring to a boil over medium-high heat.

6. Reduce the heat to low, cover and simmer for 30 minutes.

Serves: 6

SALT-CODFISH PIE

(Pastelón de bacalao)

1/2 pound salt-codfish fillet, de-salted, poached, skinned and flaked, p.165
1/4 cup olive oil
1 teaspoon vinegar
1/4 teaspoon salt
1 pressed medium garlic clove
1 medium frying pepper, seeded and diced
1 small diced onion
1 small peeled, seeded and chopped tomato, p. 132
1 large sweet chili pepper, minced
1/2 pound shredded green cabbage
5 cups mashed potatoes —2 pounds of potatoes, boiled and mashed with 4 tablespoons butter and 1/4 cup hot milk
2 sliced hard-boiled eggs
1 four-ounce jar sliced pimientos

1. Mix well the olive oil, vinegar, salt, garlic, frying pepper, onion, tomato and sweet chili peppers.

2. Add the cabbage and flaked cod and mix well. If necessary, add more oil, vinegar or salt.

3. Butter a deep-pie dish 9" x 1 1/2" and lay half of the mashed potatoes on its bottom.

4. Over them lay the codfish and cabbage mixture, and some of the hard-boiled egg slices.

5. Cover with the rest of the mashed potatoes and decorate with the remaining egg slices and pimientos.

6. Serve cool, but not chilled.

Serves: 6

SALT-CODFISH GAZPACHO

(Gazpacho de bacalao)

- 1 pound salt-codfish, de-salted, poached, skinned, boned and cut into 1" squares, p.165
- 1 thinly sliced medium Spanish onion
- 3/4 pound potatoes, boiled, peeled and diced
- 3 sliced hard-boiled eggs (save one of the yolks)
- 1 4-ounce jar sliced pimientos (save the liquid)
- 1/2 cup cooked small peas
- 1/2 pound salad tomatoes, peeled, seeded and cut into strips, p.132
- 1 minced dill pickle
- 1/3 cup slivered almonds
- 2 ounces pimiento-stuffed olives
- 1 ounce small capers
- 1/2 cup olive oil
- 1/4 cup white wine vinegar

1. In a crock, or any non-corrosive container, mix well all the ingredients except the oil, vinegar, pimiento liquid and saved egg yolk. If you have an attractive clear-glass jar or container, you may layer the ingredients in contrasting color combinations.

2. Prepare the sauce by mashing the saved egg yolk and gradually adding the oil, vinegar and pimiento liquid, in that order. Blend well.

3. Pour the sauce over the other ingredients.

4. Cover and chill well.

5. Toss well before serving. If you have layered the ingredients, spoon sauce over each serving, instead of tossing.

Serves: 6

SALT-CODFISH SERENADE

(Serenata de bacalao)

1 pound salt-codfish, de-salted, poached, skinned, boned and flaked, p.165
2 diced medium Spanish onions
2 diced large green peppers
2 large salad tomatoes, sliced into wedges
2 cups shredded green cabbage
a combination of boiled yautia, green bananas, breadfruit slices, yuca, green and ripe plantains (v. glossary and recipes)
olive oil and vinegar
avocado slices

1. Place the cooled codfish flakes on a serving platter. Surround with the onion, pepper, tomato wedges and green cabbage, plus the avocado slices.

2. On another platter serve any combination of the above-mentioned boiled roots and fruits.

3. Pour olive oil and vinegar to taste over the individual servings.

Serves: 6

AVOCADO-TUNA SALAD

(Ensalada de aguacate y atún)

3 large ripe, firm avocados, halved lengthwise and peeled
lettuce leaves
2 teaspoons lemon juice
2 seven-ounce cans white, chunk or solid, tuna fish, flaked
1 cup diced celery
1/2 cup mayonnaise
1/8 teaspoon salt
1/8 teaspoon ground pepper

1. Rub the peeled avocado halves with the lemon juice and place on the lettuce leaves.

2. Blend well the mayonnaise, salt and pepper. Add the flaked tuna and diced celery. Mix well.

3. Stuff the avocado halves with the tuna mixture.

4. Cover and chill before serving.

Serves: 6

BOILED SHRIMP

(Camarones hervidos)

1 pound fresh, raw, medium-size shrimp
2 quarts water
1 tablespoon salt
1 small onion, cut into 4 wedges
1 small bay leaf

1. Bring the water, salt, onion and bay leaf to a boil in a large pan.

2. Rinse the shrimp and add to the pot. Start timing as soon as the water returns to a boil.

3. Boil slowly, 3-4 minutes, or until they turn pink. Do not overcook.

4. Drain and plunge into cold water to stop cooking. Drain again, and let cool.

5. To shell, pull out the shells starting from the leg side. Remove the black vein running through the back with a sharp paring knife.

6. Proceed with your recipe.

NOTE: One pound of fresh, raw shrimp equals half a pound of cooked and shelled shrimp. You may also shell and devein before cooking.

BREADED SHRIMP

(Camarones empanados)

2 pounds shrimp, boiled, shelled and deveined, p. 170
—4 pounds fresh shrimp
3 large eggs
1 1/2 cups soda-cracker or bread crumbs

1. Beat the eggs with a pinch of salt.

2. Dip the shrimp in the beaten egg, then roll in cracker or bread crumbs.

3. Deep fry in vegetable oil over medium-high heat until golden crisp.

4. Drain on paper towels.

5. Serve hot with Tartar Sauce, or your favorite hot sauce.

Serves: 6

SHRIMP SALAD

(Ensalada de camarones)

1 1/2 pounds small shrimp, cooked, shelled and deveined, p.170 —3 pounds fresh shrimp
2 cups potatoes, boiled in salted water, peeled and diced
1/2 cup mayonnaise
1 tablespoon lemon juice
2 tablespoons olive oil
1/8 teaspoon ground pepper

1. Blend the mayonnaise, lemon juice, olive oil, and pepper in a glass or non-reactive bowl.

2. Toss the shrimp in the sauce.

3. Fold in gently the diced potatoes.

4. Cover and chill well before serving.

Serves: 6

KILLING A LIVE LOBSTER

(Cómo matar una langosta viva)

1. Bring water to a boil in a kettle large enough to hold the lobster or lobsters without crowding. Add 1 1/2 teaspoon salt per quart of water.

2. Plunge the lobster head-in first into the boiling water, which kills them instantly. Cover the kettle until the water starts boiling again.

3. Remove the cover and regulate the heat to a steady and gentle boil.

4. Boil for one minute, or until the lobster is limp. Remove unless your recipe calls for a longer boiling time.

5. Drain any water inside the lobster by cutting off a piece of shell from the head and holding up by the tail.

6. Proceed with your recipe.

BOILED SPINY LOBSTER

(Langosta hervida)

6 live spiny lobsters, 2 pounds each
1 1/2 teaspoon salt per quart of water
melted butter
lemon wedges

1. In a kettle large enough to hold the lobsters without crowding bring salted water to a boil. Use two kettles if a large one is not available.

2. Plunge the lobsters head-in first into the boiling water and cover the kettle immediately.

3. As soon as the water returns to a boil, regulate the heat to a steady gentle boil.

4. Start timing, and boil uncovered for 18 minutes.

5. Take out of the water and drain by cutting off a piece of shell from the head and holding up by the tail.

6. Serve hot either whole or split lengthwise with melted butter and lemon wedges.

7. It may be served cold with mayonnaise.

8. If serving split, discard the stomach sack, gills and intestinal vein before serving; but do leave the edible tomalley and corals.

9. If serving whole provide lobster shears or nutcrackers and picks.

Serves: 6

Timings for boiled lobster:
1 pound. . . . . 10 minutes
2 pounds. . . . . . . 18 minutes
3 pounds. . . . . . . 22 minutes
4 pounds. . . . . . . 24 minutes
5 pounds. . . . . . . 25 minutes

GETTING THE MEAT OUT OF BOILED LOBSTER

(Método para sacar la carne de la langosta hervida)

1. Remove the legs and feelers —and claws, if using American lobsters.

2. Split the lobster lengthwise and remove the stomach sack from behind the head, the intestinal vein that runs down the tail, and the grayish gills, or lungs. The green liver —tomalley— and the red roes —corals are edible. Pick out the chest meat.

3. To get the tail meat, simply pull out. Slice or dice according to your recipe.

4. If you want to cut the tail meat into medallions, do not split in haf. Twist off the tail, cut off its flaps and push out the meat from that end. Then split the chest in half lengthwise and proceed as in step 2.

5. If you are using American lobsters, crack the claws with a mallet or nutcracker and pull out the meat.

BAKED SPINY LOBSTER STUFFED WITH MASHED YAM

(Langosta al horno con ñame majado)

- 6 spiny lobsters, 2 pounds each, killed, p.172, and split lengthwise
- 3 pounds yam —see glossary
- 8 tablespoons butter
- 3 tablespoons mayonnaise
- 1 cup hot milk
- melted butter

1. Discard the stomach, intestinal vein and gills of the split lobsters.

2. Peel and boil the yams in salted water until tender. Mash

with the 6 tablespoons of butter, the mayonnaise, and milk.

3. Preheat the oven to 400°F.

4. Put the lobster halves meat side up on a broiler rack. Salt and pepper to taste and brush with the melted butter.

5. Stuff the chest cavity with the mashed yam.

6. Bake in the oven some 20 minutes brushing with melted butter once or twice.

7. Serve hot with additional melted butter.

NOTE: If yam is unavailable, substitute with white yautia or potatoes.

Serves: 6

SAUTEED LOBSTER

(Langosta a la sartén)

- 3 live spiny lobsters, 3 pounds each
- 1/2 pound butter
- 1 tablespoon oil
- 2 medium garlic cloves, crushed
- 1/4 teaspoon pimenton or 1/2 teaspoon paprika

1. Boil the lobsters for 20 minutes, p.173. Remove and drain.

2. Remove the legs and feelers —and claws if using American lobster. Crack with a mallet or nutcracker, pick out the meat and save.

3. Split the lobsters lengthwise and discard the stomach sack, gills and intestinal vein.

4. Pick out the chest meat, tomalley and roe and mix with the saved meat. Salt lightly and sprinkle with part of the pimenton or paprika.

5. Rub the tail meat with a little salt and the rest of the pimenton or paprika.

6. Melt the butter and oil in a frying pan —or two— where the lobster halves will fit without crowding.

7. Sauté the crushed garlic for one minute over medium heat, then discard. Do not let burn.

8. Put the lobster halves meat side down in the pan and sauté, shaking to prevent sticking, some 5-7 minutes, or until the meat is colored golden.

9. Remove and keep warm.

10. In the same butter and oil sauté the saved meat from the legs, chest and claws, roe and tomalley for one minute.

11. Fill the chest cavities of the lobsters with this meat and pour the pan butter over all.

Serves: 6

LOBSTER SALAD

(Ensalada de langosta)

2 pounds boiled lobster tail meat, cut into medallions and chilled, p. 173
1 thinly sliced medium Spanish onion
2 sliced medium tomatoes
2 sliced pimientos
large pitted green olives
lemon wedges
lettuce leaves
Ajilimójili, p.p.65-66

1. On a bed of lettuce arrange the lobster medallions alternating with the onion and tomato slices.

2. Decorate with the pimientos, lemon wedges and olives.

3. Serve the *Ajilimójili* separtely to be used to taste over the individual servings.

Serves: 6

DORA ROMANO'S LOBSTER SALAD

(Ensalada de langosta a la Dora Romano)

3 cups boiled lobster meat, cubed, p. 173
3 cups potatoes, boiled in salted water, peeled and diced
3/4 cup mayonnaise
1/3 cup olive oil
3/4 cup minced onion
4 teaspoons lemon juice
1/4 teaspoon salt
3 hard-boiled eggs

1. Blend the mayonnaise, olive oil, onion, lemon juice and salt in a mixing bowl.

2. Mash the egg yolks and whites with a fork and add to the bowl.

3. Fold in gently the lobster meat and potatoes.

4. Cover and chill thoroughly before serving.

Serves: 6

SAILOR LOBSTER SALAD

(Ensalada de langosta marinera)

4 cups boiled lobster meat, p.173

Sauce
1/2 cup mayonnaise
1/2 cup olive oil
4 teaspoons lemon juice
2 tablespoons grated green pepper
1/4 teaspoon salt
1/4 teaspoon ground pepper

1. Blend well the sauce ingredients in a non-reactive bowl.

2. Fold in the cubed lobster

3. Cover and chill well before serving.

Serves: 6

LOBSTER VINAIGRETTE

(Langosta a la vinagreta)

2 pounds boiled lobster meat, cubed, p. 173

Vinaigrette Sauce

1 cup olive oil
1/3 cup wine vinegar
2 thinly sliced medium onions
4 tablespoons finely chopped green pepper
2 teaspoons chopped parsley
1/2 teaspoon salt

1. Combine all the ingredients for the vinaigrette sauce until thoroughly blended.

2. Toss the lobster meat with the sauce in a non-reactive bowl.

3. Cover and chill before serving.

NOTE: This salad may also be prepared with boiled, shelled and deveined shrimp.

Serves: 6

BOILED GREAT LAND CRABS

(Jueyes hervidos)

12 great land crabs
water
1 tablespoon salt per quart of water

1. Bring water to a boil in a large kettle that will hold the 12 crabs. Add 1 tablespoon salt per quart of water.

2. In a second, smaller ketle of plain boiling water drop in the crabs, one at a time. Boil for one minute, or until limp.

3. Transfer the crabs to the larger kettle.

4. Boil small crabs 20 minutes, large crabs, 30.

5. Drain and serve with melted butter. Provide mallets, nut crackers and picks.

NOTE: If the crabs are to be cooked further in any other recipe, boil small crabs only 10 minutes, large ones, 15.

Serves: 6

GETTING THE MEAT OUT OF BOILED GREAT LAND CRABS

(Jueyes hervidos — cómo sacarles la carne)

1. Boil great land crabs according to the preceeding recipe.

2. Pull out the legs and claws from the chest section. Divide into segments by bending backward at the joints.

3. Crack the leg and claw shells with a wooden mallet or nut cracker. Pick out the meat and save.

4. Turn the carapace upside down. Pull out and twist off the flap or tail, which is broad in female crabs, narrow in males. Discard.

5. Pry open the crab by holding the carapace with one hand and pulling out the chest section with the fingers of the other hand or a spoon handle.

6. Discard the grey spongy gills. Scrape off the fat (greenish or orangey substance) in the chest section and save along with that sticking to the inside of the carapace.

7. Rinse and dry the carapaces if required for your recipe, otherwise discard.

8. Pull off the crab's mouth and stomach sack in one piece from the chest section. Discard.

9. Add the corals (the orange-red roe of female crabs) sticking to the chest section, to the fat saved. Keep all of this matter separate from the meat proper.

10. Remove the leg joints attached to the chest section with a paring knife.

11. Cut the chest section lengthwise, and the resultant two pieces crosswise. Pick out all the meat with the paring knife.

12. Proceed with your recipe.

NOTES: The meat can be frozen successfully. You may wish to freeze the three types of meat separately to use according to your recipe. The fat and corals can also be frozen apart.

Depending on how long the crabs have been kept in captivity to rid them of any muddy taste, and to the diet fed them —coconut, corn, etc.— the color of their fat might range from green to orange.

Yield: 12 medium great land crabs will yield approximately 1 1/2 cups fat, 1 1/2 cups claw meat, 1 1/2 cups leg meat, and 2 cups chest meat.

GREAT LAND CRAB SAUTEE I

(Jueyes fritos)

4 1/2 cups boiled crab meat, p. 179
4 tablespoons olive oil
2 large minced frying peppers
6 seeded and minced sweet chili peppers
1 tablespoon annatto oil or lard
3 pressed medium garlic cloves
1 1/2 teaspoon salt

1. Sauté the pepper and sweet chili peppers in the olive oil in a frying pan set over medium heat for one minute.

2. Add the annatto oil or lard, pressed garlic, crab meat and salt. Sauté for 10 minutes, shaking the pan often to prevent sticking.

3. Serve hot with boiled tropical roots or fruits —yautia, plantains, etc.

Serves: 6

GREAT LAND CRAB SAUTEE II

(Salmorejo de jueyes)

4 1/2 cups boiled crab meat, p.179
4 tablespoons olive oil
1 cup seeded and diced green frying pepper
4 tablespoons minced onion
6 sweet chili peppers, seeded and minced
5 tablespoons tomato sauce
1 1/4 teaspoon salt

1. Sauté the pepper, onion, sweet chili peppers in the oil in a large skillet set over medium heat for about one minute.

2. Add the tomato sauce and salt and cook for 3 minutes.

3. Add the crab meat and sauté for 10 minutes, stirring occasionally.

4. Serve hot with boiled tropical roots, such as yautia or yuca, and/or fruits such as green and ripe plantains or green bananas.

Serves: 6

GREAT LAND CRAB SAUTEE III

(Jueyes guisados)

4 1/2 cups boiled crab meat, p.179
4 tablespoons annatto oil or lard
2 medium tomatoes, peeled, seeded and chopped, p.132
2 medium frying peppers, seeded and minced
1 minced medium onion
5 large sweet chili peppers, seeded and minced
3 large pressed garlic cloves
1/8 teaspoon dried ground oregano
1/4 teaspoon ground pepper
3/4 cup crab fat, p.180
6 teaspoons tomato sauce
1 1/4 teaspoon salt

1. Sauté the tomato, frying pepper, onion, sweet chili peppers, garlic, oregano, ground pepper and crab fat in the annatto oil or lard in a *caldero* or frying pan set over medium heat for 3 minutes.

2. Add the tomato sauce and salt and cook for 3 minutes.

3. Add the crab meat and sauté, stirring, for 5 additional minutes.

4. Serve hot decorated with sliced pimientos along boiled tropical roots or fruits such as ripe or green plantains or green bananas.

Serves: 6

GREAT LAND CRAB IN THE SHELL

(Jueyes al carapacho)

6 great land crab carapaces, from boiled crabs, rinsed and dried
2 1/2 cups boiled crab meat, p.179
2 tablespoons lard or annatto oil or lard
1 medium tomato, peeled, seeded and chopped, p.132
1 frying pepper, seeded and minced
1 minced small onion
2 large sweet chili peppers, seeded and minced
1 medium garlic clove, pressed
1/8 teaspoon dried ground oregano
1/8 teaspoon ground pepper
1 tablespoon tomato sauce
1 teaspoon salt
1 sliced pimiento
1 large egg beaten with a pinch of salt

1. Preheat the oven to 400°F.

2. Sauté the tomato, frying pepper, onion, sweet chili peppers, garlic, oregano and pepper in the annatto oil or lard over medium heat for 3 minutes.

3. Add the tomato sauce and stir. Cook for 3 minutes.

4. Add the crab meat and salt. Sauté for 5 minutes, or until the meat has absorbed most of the sauce.

5. Stuff the carapaces with the meat tixture and decorate with pimiento slices.

6. Pour the beaten egg over the meat and place the carapaces on a baking sheet.

7. Bake in the preheated oven for 5 minutes or until the egg sets to a golden color.

8. Serve immediately.

Serves: 6

CONCH SALAD

(Carrucho en ensalada)

1 pound fresh conch meat or 2 ten-and-a-half-ounce cans of cooked meat, drained

Sauce:

4 teaspoons wine vinegar
1/2 teaspoon salt
4 teaspoons lemon juice
1/4 cup olive oil
1 pressed medium garlic clove
1 thinly sliced small onion
1/2 teaspoon hot sauce

1. If using fresh conch meat, clean well with a vegetable bristle brush under running cool water.

2. Peel off the outer dark skin with a paring knife.

3. Tenderize by beating with a pounder and cut into 1 1/2" square pieces.

4. Bring to a boil in a quart of water seasoned with 2 teaspoons salt. Lower the heat, cover and simmer the smaller pieces about 45 minutes, the larger as much as 75, or until tender.

5. Drain and let cool. Slice into thin strips.

6. In a non-reactive bowl, dissolve the salt in the vinegar.

7. Add the rest of the sauce ingredients and mix well.

8. Toss in the conch meat, blending well.

9. Serve cool, but not chilled.

Serves: 6

OCTOPUS SALAD

(Ensalada de pulpo)

Follow the recipe for conch salad, but substitute for the conch:

1 pound fresh boiled octopus meat

NOTE: To clean an octopus turn it inside out and remove the eyes, beak-like mouth, and the translucent pen. Remove, but do not pierce the ink sac. With a paring knife remove the skin if it does not pull off easily. Clean and rinse well under running cool water and proceed as for conch salad. Octopi under two pounds will be more tender, yet they still need pounding, and no less than 45 minutes of boiling.

CHAPTER VII: THE CHICKEN, THE TURKEY, AND THE GUINEA HEN

FRIED CHICKEN

(Pollo frito)

3 pounds chicken pieces
2 1/2 teaspoons salt
4 pressed medium garlic cloves
1/4 teaspoon ground oregano
1/4 teaspoon ground pepper
2 teaspoons olive oil
4 cups lard or oil
3/4 cup flour

1. Rinse and pat dry the chicken.

2. Rub well with the salt.

3. Mix the garlic, oregano, pepper and olive oil. Rub the chicken all over with them. Cover and let stand for at least one hour.

4. Heat the shortening over medium-high heat in a large *caldero* or deep chicken fryer until it forms a haze over its surface (375°F).

5. In the meantime, dredge the chicken pieces with the flour, shaking off the excess.

6. Fry the chicken pieces at medium-high heat for 5 minutes on each side.

7. Reduce the heat to moderate, cover the pot and fry for an additional 10 minutes.

8. Uncover the pot, raise the heat to high and keep frying for some 5 minutes, or until the chicken is golden brown.

9. Drain on paper towels and serve warm.

Serves: 6

CHICKEN CRACKLINGS

(Chicharrones de pollo)

3 pounds chicken pieces
2 1/2 teaspoons salt
4 pressed medium garlic cloves
1/4 teaspoon ground pepper
vegetable oil or shortening

1. Cut the chicken into 2" pieces. Rub well with the salt, then with the garlic and pepper. Let stand for at least 30 minutes.

2. Heat enough vegetable oil or shortening to cover the chicken pieces in a *caldero* or deep chicken fryer over medium-high heat until a haze forms on the surface —350°F.

3. Put in the chicken pieces and stir to prevent their sticking to the pan. Fry for 5 minutes on each side.

4. Reduce heat to moderate, put the cover on slightly ajar, and fry for 10 additional minutes.

5. Uncover. Raise the heat to high and fry for 5 more minutes or until the chicken is golden brown.

6. Drain on paper towels and serve immediately.

Serves: 6

CHICKEN SMOTHERED IN ONIONS

(Pollo encebollado)

3 pounds chicken pieces
2 1/2 teaspoons salt
4 pressed medium garlic cloves
1/4 teaspoon ground pepper
3 tablespoons olive oil
vegetable oil
4 sliced medium onions
1/3 cup tomato sauce
8-12 pitted green olives
1 small bay leaf
1/2 cup dry sherry

1. Rinse the chicken, pat dry and rub well with the salt, then with the garlic and pepper. Dribble 1 tablespoon of the olive oil over it. Let stand for at least 30 minutes.

2. Heat a 1/4"-deep layer of vegetable oil in a frying pan over medium-high heat. Brown the chicken, set aside and discard the oil.

3. In another skillet, where the chicken pieces will fit in one layer, heat the remaining 2 tablespoons of olive oil over medium heat. Cook the onions for 5 minutes until tender but not browned.

4. Add the tomato sauce, olives and bay leaf. Cook for 5 more minutes.

5. Add the sherry and blend well.

6. Add the chicken to the pot and cover with part of the onions.

7. Bring to a simmer, cover and cook for 40 minutes or until the chicken is tender.

8. Remove the chicken and onions, place on a warm platter.

9. Degrease the sauce and pour over the chicken.

Serves: 6

CHICKEN IN SHERRY

(Pollo al jerez)

3 pounds chicken pieces
2 teaspoons salt
1/4 teaspoon ground pepper
1/4 teaspoon thyme
3 tablespoons butter or margarine
3 tablespoons oil
1 thinly sliced large onion
1/2 cup warm chicken stock
1 cup dry sherry
1 1/2 teaspoon cornstarch blended with 1 tablespoon water

1. Rinse the chicken, pat dry and rub with the salt, pepper and thyme. Let stand for at least 30 minutes.

2. Heat the butter, or margarine, and oil in a frying pan over medium-high heat. Brown the chicken pieces about 5 minutes on each side. Set aside.

3. Strain about 3 tablespoons of the browning fat into a clean frying pan. Sauté the onion slices over medium heat for 5 minutes, until tender but not browned.

4. Add the stock and sherry and lay the chicken pieces over the onion.

5. Bring to a simmer, cover and cook for 30 minutes.

6. Turn the chicken over and cover with the lid slightly ajar. Cook for 15 additional minutes or until the chicken is tender and thoroughly cooked.

7. Remove the chicken pieces and onion. Keep warm.

8. Degrease the sauce. Return to the pan over low heat and whisk in the cornstarch. Keep stirring until the sauce thickens, about 2 to 3 minutes. Pour over the chicken.

Serves: 6

CHICKEN FRICASSEE

(Fricasé de pollo)

3 pounds chicken pieces
2 1/2 teaspoons salt
4 pressed medium garlic cloves
1/8 teaspoon ground pepper
1/4 teaspoon ground oregano
1 tablespoon olive oil
1 teaspoon vinegar
vegetable oil
1/2 cup diced ham
1/2 cup uncooked condiment, p.47, or 1 small onion, 1 small tomato, 1 small frying green pepper, seeded, and 2 sweet chili peppers, seeded, all finely diced
1/2 cup tomato sauce
6 pitted green olives
1 teaspoon minced capers
1 1/4 cup water
3 medium potatoes, peeled and quartered
1/2 cup frozen sweet peas or petit pois, defrosted

1. Rinse the chicken, pat dry and rub well with the salt, then with the garlic, pepper, oregano and olive oil. Place in a non-reactive container and dribble the vinegar over it. Let stand for at least 1/2 hour.

2. Heat a 1/2"-deep layer of oil in a large frying pan over medium-high heat. Brown the chicken and set aside.

3. In a clean *caldero* or deep chicken fryer heat 2 tablespoons of the browning oil over moderate heat.

4. Sauté the ham for 3 minutes. Add the uncooked condiment or diced vegetables and sauté for 5 more minutes.

5. Add the tomato sauce, olives and capers. Cook for 5 minutes.

6. Add the chicken and 1/4 cup of the water. Stir and cook for 5 minutes.

7. Add the rest of the water and the potatoes. Bring to a boil.

Reduce the heat to low, cover and simmer for 40 minutes or until the chicken and the potatoes are tender. Turn both over once.

8. Add the peas and cook uncovered until done —about 5 minutes.

NOTE: This recipe gains in flavor by reheating.

Serves: 6

BRAISED CHICKEN

(Pollo al caldero)

3 pounds chicken, dressed weight
2 1/2 teaspoons salt
3 large pressed garlic cloves
1/4 teaspoon ground pepper
1/4 teaspoon ground oregano
1 tablespoon olive oil
1 teaspoon vinegar
1/3 cup vegetable oil
3 or 4 peeled medium potatoes
3/4 cup water

1. Rinse and pat dry the chicken. Rub the salt into the cavity and over the skin.

2. Mix the garlic, pepper, oregano and oil and rub over the surface of the chicken. Truss.

3. Place in a non-reactive container and dribble the vinegar over it. Let stand for at least half hour, or refrigerate covered overnight. Take out of the refrigerator at least one hour before braising.

4. Scrape the marinade from the chicken, but save along with any rendered juices.

5. Heat the vegetable oil in a *caldero* or deep chicken fryer over medium-high heat. Brown the chicken all over, moving it to prevent sticking to the pot. Remove and set aside.

6. Discard all but two tablespoons of the browning oil. Add the water and saved marinade to the pot. Bring to a boil.

7. Put the chicken on its side in the pot and place the potatoes around it.

8. Lower the heat to a simmer, cover and cook for 30 minutes. Move it occasionally to prevent sticking.

9. Turn the chicken and potatoes over. Braise for an additional 20 minutes.

10. Uncover, raise the heat to moderate, keeping it at a steady simmer and braise for 10 more minutes.

11. Remove from the pot, along with the potatoes. Keep these warm while the chicken rests for some 15 minutes before carving. Degrease the sauce.

12. Untruss and section the chicken into serving pieces. Put it back in the sauce with the potatoes and serve warm.

Serves: 6

CHICKEN IN DARK SAUCE

(Pollo en salsa oscura)

3 pounds chicken dressed weight
2 1/2 teaspoons salt
6 pressed medium garlic cloves
1/4 teaspoon ground pepper
1/4 teaspoon ground oregano
2 tablespoons olive oil
2 teaspoons vinegar
1/3 cup vegetable oil
2 sliced medium onions
1 quartered medium tomato
1 green frying pepper, seeded and sliced
8 unpeeled medium garlic cloves
1/2 cup water
1 to 2 teaspoons commercial browning sauce

1. Rinse the chicken and pat dry. Rub the cavity and skin with salt.

2. Mix the pressed garlic, pepper, oregano, olive oil, and rub over the skin of the chicken. Truss, place in a non-reactive container, dribble the vinegar over it and let stand for at least one hour.

3. Heat the vegetable oil in a *caldero* or deep chicken fryer over medium-high heat. Scrape the marinade from the chicken, but save.

4. Brown the chicken all over, moving it frequently to prevent sticking to the pot. Remove and set aside.

5. Discard all but two tablespoons of the oil. Lower the heat to moderate and sauté the onion, pepper, tomato and unpeeled garlic without browning for 5 to 10 minutes.

6. Add the water, reserved marinade, and the browning sauce. Bring to a boil.

7. Return the chicken to the pot, laying on its side. Bring to a simmer, cover, and cook for 30 minutes.

8. Turn the chicken over and cook for 30 more minutes.

9. Remove from the pot and let rest for 15 minutes before carving.

10. In the meantime, degrease the sauce.

11. Untruss and carve the chicken. Pour the sauce over it.

NOTE: You may either serve the sauce with the cooking vegetables, you may puree or strain them, according to preference.

Serves: 6

BRAISED STUFFED CHICKEN

(Pollo relleno al caldero)

3 1/2 pounds chicken, dressed weight
1 quart water
1/4 cup lemon juice
1 tablespoon salt
3 pressed large garlic cloves
1/4 teaspoon ground oregano
1/4 teaspoon ground pepper
1 tablespon olive oil
1 1/2 teaspoons vinegar
3/4 cup ground meat stuffing, p. 236
1 chopped hard-boiled egg
1/2 cup diced boiled potato
1/3 cup apple sauce
1/3 cup vegetable oil
1 sliced medium onion
1 quartered medium tomato
1 medium size green frying pepper, seeded and sliced
4 unpeeled medium garlic cloves
1/2 cup water

1. Soak the chicken in the water and lemon juice for 10 minutes. Drain and pat dry.

2. Rub the salt into the cavity and over the skin of the chicken.

3. Rub the pressed garlic, oregano, pepper and olive oil on the skin of the chicken. Place in a non-reactive container and dribble the vinegar over it.

4. Let stand for at least one hour, or refrigerate covered overnight. In that case, remove from the refrigerator one hour before stuffing and braising. Do not stuff before refrigerating.

5. Prepare the stuffing by adding the egg, potato and apple sauce to the ground meat stuffing. It may be prepared the day before, and refrigerated separately.

6. Scrape the marinade from the chicken, but reserve along with any rendered juices.

7. Stuff the bird. Sew the neck vent shut with cotton thread. Stuff the chicken through the tail vent, allowing space for the stuffing to expand while cooking. Fill the bird about 2/3 to 4/5 full. Any left-over stuffing may be cooked on the range over low heat, covered, and basted occasionally with the cooking juices from the chicken.

8. Sew the tail vent shut with the cotton thread. Truss the bird.

9. Heat the vegetable oil in a *caldero* or deep chicken fryer over medium-high heat. Brown the chicken all over, moving it to prevent sticking to the pan. Remove carefully and set aside.

10. Discard all but 2 tablespoons of the browning oil. Lower the heat to moderate, add the tomato, onion, pepper and unpeeled garlic cloves and sauté for 5 to 10 minutes.

11. Add the water and reserved marinade. Bring to a boil.

12. Return the chicken to the pot laying it on its side. Cover, lower the heat to simmer and cook for 30 minutes.

13. Turn the chicken over and braise for an additional half hour.

14. Turn the chicken over on its back and cook for 10 more minutes.

15. Remove from the pot and let rest for 20 minutes before untrussing and carving.

16. In the meantime degrease the cooking juices. The vegetables may be strained out or pureed into the sauce.

Serves: 6

POACHED CHICKEN

(Pollo hervido)

3 pounds chicken, dressed weight, whole and trussed or quartered
2 quarts cool water
5 teaspoons salt
1 quartered medium onion
2 large peeled garlic cloves
2 large sweet chili peppers, seeded and quartered
4 large *culantro* leaves

1. Rinse the chicken, put in a kettle and cover with the cool water.

2. Bring to a slow boil and remove the scum as it comes to the surface.

3. When the scum stops rising, add the salt and vegetables. If you wish you may tie the vegetables up in cheesecloth for easy removal.

4. Bring the water to a slow simmer, cover and cook for about one hour, or until the chicken is tender and the juices run clear when you pierce the meat of the thigh.

5. Remove and let rest for 15 minutes before carving into serving pieces.

6. The broth may be served as a first course. While the chicken is resting, simmer pasta or rice in it until cooked. Or just garnish with freshly chopped herbs.

NOTES: If the chicken is poached for use in any other recipe, let cool in the broth, as then it will be juicier. Time the simmering according to the age of the chicken: a stewing hen is tougher and takes longer to cook, but it is tastier. A very young chicken will disintegrate if overcooked.

Serves: 6

CHICKEN SALAD

(Ensalada de pollo)

3 cups chicken breast —2 pounds breasts— cooled and diced after poaching for 30-40 minutes, p. 199
1/4 cup olive oil
1 teaspoon lemon juice or wine vinegar
1 tablespoon grated onion
1/2 teaspoon salt
1/8 teaspoon ground pepper
1/2 cup diced celery
3/4 cup apples, peeled, cored and diced
mayonnaise

1. In a non-reactive bowl, blend well the olive oil, lemon juice or vinegar, grated onion, salt and pepper.

2. Add the chicken meat, celery and apples and toss well.

3. Cover and chill.

4. Just before serving blend in enough mayonnaise to taste —about 1/2 to 3/4 cup.

Serves: 6

CHICKEN SALAD WITH POTATOES AND EGGS

(Ensalada de pollo con papas y huevos)

2 cups chicken breasts —1 1/2 pounds— cooled and diced after poaching for 30-40 minutes, p. 199
1/4 cup olive oil
2 teaspoons lemon juice or 1 teaspoon wine vinegar
1 tablespoon grated onion
1/2 teaspoon salt
1/8 teaspoon ground pepper
1/3 cup diced celery
1/2 cup apples, peeled, cored and diced
1 1/3 cup potatoes, boiled in salted water and diced —3/4 pound potatoes
2 chopped hard-boiled eggs
mayonnaise

1. In a non-reactive container mix well the olive oil, lemon juice or vinegar, grated onion, salt and pepper.

2. Add the chicken meat, celery, apple, potatoes and eggs. Toss well.

3. Cover and chill.

4. Just before serving, fold in enough mayonnaise to taste —1/2 to 3/4 cup.

Serves: 6

CHICKEN SALAD SANDWICHES

(Emparedados de pollo)

- 2 cups chicken breast —about 1 1/2 pounds breast— cooled and shredded after poaching for 30-40 minutes, p. 199
- 2/3 cup mayonnaise
- 1/4 teaspoon salt
- 2 teaspoons grated onion
- 1/8 teaspoon ground pepper
- 24 slices sandwich bread
- butter

1. Blend the mayonnaise, onion, salt and pepper.

2. Fold in the chicken meat.

3. Trim the crust from the bread slices and butter one side.

4. Fill the sandwiches with the chicken mixture. Cut in half on the diagonal, or in four triangles for party sandwiches.

5. Put on a platter and cover with plastic wrap to keep moist until serving. They may be refrigerated.

NOTE: These may be done with toast, but do not fill until serving.

Yield: 12 regular or 48 party sandwiches.

CHICKEN CROQUETTES

(Croquetas de pollo)

2 cups finely chopped or ground poached chicken meat, p. 199
6 tablespoons butter
1 tablespoon minced onion
1/2 cup all-purpose flour
1 1/4 cup hot milk
1/2 teaspoon salt
1/8 teaspoon ground pepper
3 large eggs beaten with a pinch of salt
1 1/3 cup soda-cracker or bread crumbs
vegetable oil

1. Melt the butter in a medium saucepan over low heat. Add the onion and cook it for 1 minute. Blend in the flour with a wooden spoon and cook, stirring, for some 2 minutes to prepare the roux.

2. Remove the pan from the heat, pour the hot milk, salt and pepper and whip rapidly with a wire whisk until smooth and blended.

3. Return the pan to moderate heat and boil slowly, stirring, until it thickens to a creamy consistency.

4. Add the shredded chicken and continue stirring until the mixture is thick enough to separate from the sides and bottom of the pan.

5. Pour onto a platter and let cool.

6. Flour your hands and form ovals of the chicken mixture, using tablespoonful measures.

7. Roll the croquettes in soda-cracker or bread crumbs, dip in the beaten eggs and roll again in crumbs.

8. Let stand for 15 minutes, or refrigerate covered overnight.

9. Fry in an uncrowded layer in oil to cover over medium-high

heat until golden crisp. Adjust the heat to prevent over-browning.

10. Drain on paper towels and serve warm.

NOTE: The croquettes can be frozen before frying, but remove from the freezer 20 minutes before cooking.

Yield: 18 croquettes

CHICKEN MEATBALLS

(Albóndigas de pollo)

1 1/2 cups shredded poached chicken meat, p.199
2 1/2 cups potatoes, mashed with 1/4 cup milk and 1 tablespoon butter —about 1 pound potatoes
3 large eggs beaten with a pinch of salt and 1/8 teaspoon ground pepper
1 1/3 cups fine bread or soda-cracker crumbs
vegetable oil

1. Mix the shredded chicken with the mashed potatoes. If the mixture is too soft, add 2 or 3 teaspoons crumbs.

2. Flour your hands and form balls using tablespoonful measures.

3. Roll the balls in the crumbs. Dip in the egg and roll over crumbs again.

4. Let stand for 15 minutes or refrigerate covered overnight.

5. Deep-fry in vegetable oil over medium-high heat until golden crisp on the outside.

6. Drain on paper towels and serve warm.

Yield: 22 meatballs

ROAST CHICKEN

(Pollo asado)

3 1/2 pounds roasting chicken, dressed weight
1 tablespoon salt
4 pressed medium garlic cloves
1/4 teaspoon ground oregano
1/8 teaspoon ground pepper
2 tablespoons softened butter
1 coarsely chopped onion
1 coarsely chopped carrot
2 tablespoons melted butter

1. Rinse the chicken inside and out and pat dry. Rub the cavity and skin with the salt, then with the garlic, oregano and pepper.

2. Put the two tablespoons of the softened butter inside the bird's cavity and truss. Let stand for at least 1/2 hour.

3. Preheat the oven to 325°F.

4. Place the chopped onion and carrot on the bottom of a roasting pan large enough to hold the chicken comfortably, but not too large, this will prevent the burning of the juices.

5. Brush the chicken with some of the two tablespoons of melted butter and lay on its side on top of the vegetables in the pan.

6. Roast for 1 hour and 40 minutes, alternating sides every 25 minutes. Baste with the melted butter, then with the rendered juices every 15 minutes.

7. Turn on its back and roast for 20 minutes or until golden brown. Baste twice.

8. Test for doneness by piercing the thigh meat. If the juices run clear and yellow, it is done —185°F on a meat thermometer.

9. Remove from the pan and let stand for some 20 minutes before untrussing and carving.

NOTES: If the breast browns too quickly, before the chicken is done, place a loose sheet of aluminum foil over it. You may roast it on a pan with a rack, but basting is then more important.

Quarters of onion may also be placed inside the bird's cavity.

Serves: 6

TIMETABLE FOR ROASTING UNSTUFFED CHICKENS

(Tabla de tiempo para asar pollos sin rellenar)

Oven temperature: 325°F

2 pounds	1:20 hours
2 1/2	1:35
3	1:50
3 1/2	2
4	2:10
4 1/2	2:20
5	2:30
5 1/2	2:40
6	2:45
6 1/2	2:50
7	2:55

NOTES: These timings are for cleaned chicken (dressed weight). For stuffed chickens add 20 minutes to the above stated roasting times.

CHICKEN IN THE ENGLISH MANNER

(Pollo a la inglesa)

3 1/2 pound roasting chicken, dressed weight
2 1/2 teaspoons salt
3 pressed large garlic cloves
1/4 teaspoon ground pepper
1 tablespoon grated onion
5 teaspoons Worcestershire Sauce
5 teaspoons lemon juice
5 tablespoons melted butter

1. Rub the cavity and the skin of the chicken with the salt after rinsing and pat-drying it. Truss.

2. Mix together the garlic, pepper, onion, 3 teaspoons of the Worcestershire Sauce and three teaspoons of the lemon juice.

3. Place the chicken in a non-reactive container and rub this mixture all over the skin. Let stand for at least one hour.

4. Preheat the oven to 325°F.

5. Drain the chicken, but save the marinade and rendered juices.

6. Rub the chicken all over with 2 tablespoons of the melted butter. Set on its side in a roasting pan large enough to hold it comfortably, but not too large —otherwise the juices burn.

7. Roast for 1 hour and 40 minutes, alternating sides every 25 minutes. Baste with the marinade, to which you have added the rest of the melted butter, every 15 minutes.

8. Turn the chicken breast-side up. Baste with the additional 2 teaspoons of Worcestershire Sauce and two teaspoons of lemon juice. Roast for 20 more minutes, basting twice.

9. Remove from the pan and let stand for some 20 minutes before untrussing and carving.

Serves: 6

CHICKEN PIE

(Pastelón de pollo)

2 pounds chicken breasts, skinned, boned and cut into 3/4" cubes
1 1/4 teaspoon salt
2 tablespoons butter or olive oil
1 diced medium onion
1 medium size green frying pepper, seeded and diced
1 medium tomato, peeled, seeded and chopped
1 pressed large garlic clove
1/2 cup tomato sauce
6 green pitted olives, minced
1 teaspoon minced capers
1/4 teaspoon ground oregano
1/8 teaspoon ground pepper
1 medium potato, peeled and diced (3/4 cup)
1/2 cup water
2 chopped hard-boiled eggs
1 chopped large pimiento
1 double pie crust, p.324

1. Salt the chicken and let it stand.

2. Heat the butter or olive oil in a large skillet over moderate heat. Sauté the onion and pepper for 5 minutes.

3. Add the tomato, garlic, tomato sauce, olives, capers, oregano and pepper. Cook for 5 minutes.

4. Add the chicken meat and stir-cook for 5 minutes.

5. Add the water. Bring to a simmer and cook covered for 25 minutes.

6. Add the potato, bring again to a simmer, and cook covered for 10 more minutes, or until the potato and chicken are tender.

7. Take off the heat and add the eggs and pimiento.

8. While the chicken is cooking, prepare the crust.

9. Roll out the bottom crust onto a pie dish 9-9 1/2" diameter by 1 1/2" deep.

10. Fill the pie crust with the cooked chicken and brush the edges of the crust in the pie dish with a little water. Roll out the upper crust over it.

11. Trim the edges of the crusts to 1/2" beyond the rim of the pie dish. Fold back together to the edge of the dish, top crust under bottom crust. Crimp together with the tines of the fork and brush the edges with water.

12. Make six slits in a ray pattern in the center of the top crust to allow steam to escape. Brush the crust with milk.

13. Bake in a preheated 400°F oven for 20 minutes. Lower the heat to 375°F and bake for 30 additional minutes.

14. Let rest for some 10 minutes before serving.

NOTE: You may use frozen pie crust following the instructions on the package.

Serves: 6-8

CHICKEN LIVERS IN SHERRY

(Hígados de pollo al jerez)

- 2 pounds trimmed chicken livers
- 1 quart water
- 2 tablespoons vinegar or lemon juice
- 2 teaspoons salt
- 2 pressed medium garlic cloves
- 1/4 teaspoon ground pepper
- 3 tablespoons butter or margarine
- 3 tablespoons vegetable oil
- 6 tablespoons uncooked condiment, p. 47
- 4 sliced roasted pimientos, p.119
- 1 tablespoon flour
- 1 cup chicken stock
- 1 1/2 cup dry sherry
- 2 medium potatoes, peeled and diced

1. Soak the livers in the water and vinegar or lemon juice for 5 minutes. Drain well, cut in half if large and season with the salt, pressed garlic and pepper. Set aside.

2. In a large skillet heat the butter and oil over medium-high heat.

3. Sauté the livers lightly for about 3 minutes and set aside.

4. Remove all but two tablespoons of the fat from the skillet and cook the condiment and one of the pimientos over moderate heat for 5 minutes.

5. Sprinkle in the flour and continue cooking, stirring, for one or two minutes.

6. Stir in the stock and sherry, making sure that the flour is integrated.

7. Return the livers to the pan, add the potatoes and bring to a boil. Lower the heat, cover and simmer for 20 minutes, stirring occasionally.

8. Uncover, raise the heat to moderate and cook for 10 more minutes or until the sauce thickens.

9. Place the rest of the pimientos over the livers before serving.

Serves: 6

BRAISED CHICKEN GIZZARDS

(Mollejas de pollo estofadas)

2 pounds chicken gizzards
2 quarts water
1/4 cup vinegar or lemon juice
2 teaspoons salt
1 quartered medium onion
4 peeled large garlic cloves
4 large *culantro* leaves
3 tablespoons butter or margarine
1 tablespoon vegetable oil
2/3 cup tomato sauce
1 tablespoon grated onion
2 pressed large garlic cloves
1/2 teaspoon hot sauce
1 cup chicken stock

1. With a small knife trim off the membrane that separates the sections of the gizzards. Cut in half, or quarter according to size.

2. Rinse the gizzards in 1 quart of the water and the vinegar or lemon juice. Drain.

3. Bring to a boil the additional quart of water, add the gizzards and remove the scum that comes to the surface.

4. Add the salt, quartered onion, whole garlic cloves and *culantro* leaves.

5. Lower the heat to simmer, cover, and cook for one hour. Drain, but save the liquid.

6. In a large skillet, heat the butter or margarine and oil over medium high heat. Sauté the gizzards for 5 minutes. Set aside.

7. Lower the heat to moderate, add the tomato sauce, grated onion, garlic and the hot sauce. Cook for 5 minutes.

8. Return the gizzards to the skillet and add the stock. Lower the heat and simmer covered for 30 minutes.

Serves: 6

CHICKEN GIZZARDS IN WINE

(Mollejas de pollo en vino)

2 pounds chicken gizzards
1 quart water
1/4 cup vinegar
1 1/2 teaspoons salt
1/4 teaspoon pepper
3 tablespoons butter or margarine
1 tablespoon olive oil
2 thinly sliced medium onions
2 minced medium garlic cloves
1/2 cup tomato sauce
1/2 pound potatoes, peeled and diced
1 1/2 cups red wine

1. With a small knife trim off the membrane that separates the sections of the gizzards. Cut in half, or quarter according to size.

2. Soak the gizzards in the water and vinegar for 5-10 minutes. Drain well.

3. Salt and pepper and let stand for 30 minutes.

4. Heat the butter and oil in a large skillet over moderate heat. Sauté the onions for some 5 minutes. Add the tomato sauce and the garlic. Cook for 3 to 5 additional minutes.

5. Add the gizzards, lower the heat to simmer and cook covered for 30 minutes.

6. Add the wine and potatoes. Simmer covered for one hour or until the gizzards are tender and the sauce has thickened.

Serves: 6

STUFFED ROAST TURKEY

(Pavo relleno asado)

12 pound turkey, fresh or frozen
2 quarts water
1/2 cup vinegar
1/4 cup lemon juice
4 tablespoons salt —one teaspoon per pound
12 pressed small garlic cloves —one per pound
1/2 teaspoon ground pepper —one pinch per pound
1 1/2 teaspoon ground oregano —1/8 teaspoon per pound
1/2 teaspoon poultry seasoning —1/16 teaspoon per pound
4 tablespoons olive oil —one teaspoon per pound
2 tablespoons vinegar —1/2 teaspoon per pound
6 1/2 cups ground pork stuffing for poultry, p. 259
vegetable oil or butter
1 chopped onion

1. If using a frozen turkey, defrost according to the package instructions. Remove the giblets and neck.

2. Pull back the neck skin until you locate the wishbone. With a small paring knife, slit the flesh around it. Once it is free, pull it out with your fingers. This eases the carving of the breast.

3. Rinse the bird and the giblets in one quart of the water mixed with the 1/2 cup of vinegar. The giblets may be used, except the liver, to prepare stock for the gravy. Follow the instructions for chicken broth on page 72

4. Drain well and soak in the other quart of water mixed with the lemon juice for 5-10 minutes.

5. Drain well and pat dry.

6. If there is a skin flap at the neck opening, trim it off, but do leave enough skin to sew the vent shut after stuffing the neck cavity. Save the cut-off flap for spanning the tail vent, if necessary.

7. Loosen the skin over the breast by putting your fingers under it, starting at the neck opening and moving towards the tail. Be careful not to tear it.

8. Rub the salt into the bird's cavity, over the skin, and between the skin and flesh. Put some softened butter under the skin covering the breast.

9. Mix the garlic, pepper, oregano, poultry seasoning and olive oil. Place the bird in a non-reactive container. Rub the skin all over with this marinade and dribble with the 2 tablespoons of vinegar. Cover and refrigerate overnight. Stuff only just before roasting, although you may prepare the stuffing the day before and refrigerate it. Remove both from the refrigerator one hour before roasting.

10. Stuff the bird partly through the neck opening. Sew shut with cotton thread. Stuff the bird through the tail vent only 3/4 full to allow for expansion. Sew the bird shut. If necessary, use the neck skin flap to span the vent.

11. Truss the bird.

12. Weigh the stuffed bird to determine roasting time according to the timetable at the end of the recipe. It should weight about 14 pounds.

13. Preheat the oven to 325°F.

14. Rub the turkey all over with vegetable oil or melted butter and place breast side down on a roasting pan provided with an adjustable rack.

15. Pour 2 cups of water, or stock made with the giblets, and the chopped onion over the bottom of the pan. This adds humidity and prevents burning of the drippings.

16. Put in the oven.

17. Roast for 3 3/4 hours, basting every 20 minutes, at first with more vegetable oil or butter, then with the pan drippings. If the turkey browns too quickly, before it is done, place a loose sheet of tin foil over it.

18. Turn the bird over and roast for 30 more minutes to brown the breast. Baste every 10 minutes.

19. Check for doneness by piercing the thigh meat. If the juices run clear, it is done —a reading of 180°F on a meat thermometer.

20. Remove from the oven and let stand for 30 minutes before carving.

21. In the meantime, degrease the pan juices and prepare a gravy with them and with stock, p. 60

22. Untruss, remove the threads and serve.

NOTE: If a roasting pan with adjustable rack is not available, roast breast side up on the bottom of a pan. Do not add water or stock to the pan, but strew the chopped onion around the turkey. Cover the breast with strips of blanched fatback or slab bacon, 1/4" thick. Remove these for the last 30 minutes of roasting to brown the breast.

Serves: 15-18

TIMETABLE FOR ROASTING STUFFED TURKEYS

(Tabla de tiempo para asar pavos rellenos)

Oven temperature: 325°F
These weights are for already-stuffed birds.

5-7 pounds	28 minutes per pound
8-10	23 minutes per pound
11-14	18 minutes per pound
15-19	16 minutes per pound
20-25	13 minutes per pound

Variation:

ROAST TURKEY STUFFED WITH MASHED POTATOES

(Pavo asado relleno con papas majadas)

Follow the recipe for Stuffed Roast Turkey but substitute the following stuffing:

1 cup bread crumbs
3/4 cup chicken stock, p. 72
10 bacon strips, fried and crumbled
1 tablespoon butter
2/3 cup minced onion
1/8 teaspoon salt
1/8 teaspoon ground pepper
1/4 teaspoon poultry seasoning (optional)
2 pounds potatoes, peeled and boiled until tender in 1 1/2 quart water and 1 tablespoon salt
2 ounces butter or margarine
1/2 cup warm milk

1. Mix the bread crumbs and chicken stock and set aside.

2. Heat the tablespoon of butter over medium heat in a frying pan. Add the onion and cook for 5 minutes or until tender, but not browned. Remove from the heat and add the salt, the pepper and the optional poultry seasoning.

3. Mash the potatoes and blend well with the 2 ounces of butter or margarine and the milk. You should have 4 cups of mashed potatoes.

4. Add the onion, the bread crumbs and stock, and the crumbled bacon. Mix well.

5. Use to stuff a 12 pound turkey.

NOTE: This stuffing must be prepared on the same day of roasting.

Serves: 15-18

GUINEA HEN FRICASSEE

(Fricasé de guinea)

3 pounds young guinea hen parts
2 cups water
2 tablespoons lemon juice
2 1/2 teaspoons salt
2 pressed medium garlic cloves
1/4 teaspoon ground oregano
1/8 teaspoon ground pepper
1 teaspoon olive oil
vegetable oil
2 ounces diced smoked ham
1/3 cup uncooked condiment, p.47, or 1 small tomato, onion, green frying pepper (seeded) and 2 sweet chili peppers (seeded), all finely minced
1/3 cup tomato sauce
1 teaspoon minced capers
6 pitted green olives
3 medium potatoes, peeled and quartered
1 1/2 cups water

1. Soak the guinea pieces in 2 cups of water and the lemon juice. Drain and pat dry.

2. Rub with the salt, then with the garlic, oregano, pepper and olive oil. Let stand for at least 30 minutes.

3. Heat a 1/2"-deep layer of vegetable oil over medium-high heat in a *caldero* or chicken fryer. Brown the guinea hen parts and set aside.

4. Discard all but 2-3 tablespoons of the browning oil and lower the heat to medium-low. Cook the ham for 5 minutes. Add the uncooked condiment or minced vegetables and cook for 5 additional minutes.

5. Add the tomato sauce, capers and olives and cook for 5 minutes.

6. Add the guinea hen, potatoes and 1 1/2 cup water. Bring to a boil. Lower the heat and simmer covered for 45 minutes or until the meat and potatoes are tender and the sauce has thickened.

Serves: 6

GUINEA HEN HUNTER'S STYLE

(Guinea a la cazadora)

3 - pound young guinea hen, dressed and split lengthwise keep the giblets
2 cups water
2 tablespoons lemon juice
2 1/2 teaspoons salt
2 pressed medium garlic cloves
1/4 teaspoon ground pepper
1 teaspoon olive oil
4 tablespoons butter
1 large frying green pepper, seeded and diced
1 diced medium onion
1 tomato, peeled, seeded and chopped, p.132
1 teaspoon flour
1/3 cup tomato sauce
1/2 cup red wine
1/2 cup dry sherry
vegetable oil

1. Soak the guinea hen and giblets in the water and lemon juice for 5-10 minutes. Drain and pat dry.

2. Rub with the salt, then with the garlic, pepper and olive oil. Let stand for at least 30 minutes.

3. Prepare the sauce in the meantime. In a skillet set over moderate heat, sauté the onion, pepper, chopped gizzard, heart and liver in the butter for 5 to 10 minutes.

4. Add the tomato and cook for 5 more minutes.

5. Blend in the flour and cook, stirring, for 2-3 minutes.

6. Add the tomato sauce, wine, and sherry. Blend well and cook for 5-10 minutes. Set aside.

7. Preheat the oven to 350°F.

8. In another skillet, heat a 1/4"-deep layer of vegetable oil over medium-high heat. Brown the guinea hen.

9. Place in the baking dish, skin side up, pour the sauce over it and bake for 45 minutes.

NOTE: You may remove the skin before serving.

Serves: 6

CHAPTER VIII
BEEF, PORK, VEAL AND KID

TENDERLOIN SMOTHERED IN ONIONS

(Filete encebollado)

2 pounds beef tenderloin
1 3/4 teaspoons salt
2 pressed medium garlic cloves
1/8 teaspoon ground pepper
2 sliced medium onions
2 tablespoons olive oil
vegetable oil

1. Trim off any membranes or connective tissues from the tenderloin. Cut slices against the grain about 3/4 inch thick.

2. Pound lightly each slice to make it thinner. Rub with the salt.

3. Blend the garlic, pepper and olive oil and rub the slices with them. Put the onions on top, cover and set aside for at least 30 minutes.

4. Heat a 1/4 inch-deep layer of vegetable oil in a skillet over medium-high heat. Sear the meat on both sides. Lower the heat to moderate and continue cooking until done to taste. Turn once or twice.

5. Remove the meat to a platter and keep warm.

6. Discard all but 2 tablespoons of the oil in the pan. Sauté the onion slices for about 5 minutes over moderate heat. Add the juices rendered by the meat on the platter, and stir.

7. Place the onions on top of the meat and pour the pan juices over all.

Serves: 6

BEEFSTEAK SMOTHERED IN ONIONS

(Biftec encebollado)

2 pounds boneless sirloin or round of beef in one piece
1 3/4 teaspoons salt
3 pressed medium garlic cloves
1/4 teaspoon ground oregano
1/4 teaspoon ground pepper
2 sliced medium onions
1 tablespoon olive oil
vegetable oil

1. Trim off any membranes or connective tissues from the meat. Cut against the grain into slices about 1/4 inch thick.

2. Thin each slice by pounding lightly and rub with the salt.

3. Mix the garlic, oregano and pepper. Rub the slices with this mixture. Put the onion slices on top and dribble the olive oil over all. Cover and set aside for at least 30 minutes.

4. Heat a 1/4-inch deep layer of vegetable oil in a skillet set over medium-high heat. Sauté the beef slices one or two minutes on each side according to taste in doneness.

5. Remove the meat to a platter and keep warm.

6. Discard all but 2 tablespoons of the oil in the pan. Sauté the onion slices for about 5 minutes over moderate heat. Remove the onions and put on top of the meat.

7. Add 2 tablespoons water and the juices rendered by the meat on the platter to the skillet. Boil lightly for 1-2 minutes and pour over the meat and onions.

Serves: 6

EGG-DIPPED BEEFSTEAK

(Biftec rebozado)

2 pounds boneless sirloin, tenderloin or round of beef
1 3/4 teaspoons salt
1/8 teaspoon ground pepper
1/3 cup flour
3 extra-large eggs beaten with a pinch of salt
vegetable oil

1. Trim off any membranes or connective tissues from the meat. Cut slices across the grain about 1/4 inch thick.

2. Thin each slice by pounding lightly.

3. Salt and pepper the slices. Cover and set aside for at least 15 minutes.

4. Heat a 1/4 inch deep layer of vegetable oil in a skillet over moderate heat.

5. Dredge each slice in flour and shake off excess. Dip into the beaten egg. Cook each slice for about two minutes on each side, or until the egg is golden yellow.

6. Drain on paper towels and keep warm until all the steaks are done.

NOTE: Dredge in flour and dip into the egg each slice just before frying, not all at a time.

Serves: 6

BREADED BEEFSTEAK

(Biftec empanado)

2 pounds boneless sirloin, tenderloin or round of beef
1 3/4 teaspoons salt
1/2 teaspoon garlic powder
1/4 teaspoon ground pepper
3 extra-large eggs beaten with a pinch of salt
2 1/2 cups soda-cracker or bread crumbs
vegetable oil

1. Trim off any membranes or connective tissues from the meat. Cut against the grain into 1/4 inch thick slices.

2. Thin each slice by pounding lightly.

3. Rub the slices with the salt, garlic powder and pepper. Cover and set aside for at least 30 minutes.

4. Heat a 1/4 inch deep layer of vegetable oil in a frying pan set over moderate heat.

5. Dip each slice in the egg and cover completely with cracker or bread crumbs, patting them lightly into the meat. Only dip and bread as many as you can cook in one single layer.

6. Fry in the skillet 2 minutes per side, or until golden brown. Remove off any burnt crumbs from the pan, or add more oil if necessary, during the frying.

7. Drain on paper towels.

Serves: 6

OLD RAGS

(Ropa vieja)

2 pounds brisket, simmered in seasoned stock until tender, or left-over beef from soup or stock, shredded
1/4 cup olive oil
1/2 teaspoon salt
2 thinly sliced medium onions
1 large frying pepper, seeded and sliced
2 medium tomatoes, peeled, seeded and chopped, p. 132
3 pressed medium garlic cloves
1 cup tomato sauce
1/2 teaspoon pimenton
1/4 teaspoon ground oregano

1. Heat the oil in a large frying pan over medium-high heat. Brown the shredded meat briefly. Salt and set apart.

2. Lower the heat to moderate. Add the onion and pepper slices. Sauté for 5 minutes.

3. Add the tomatoes, garlic, tomato sauce, pimenton and oregano. Cook, stirring, for 5 minutes.

4. Return the meat to the pan, mix well, and cook for an additional 5-10 minutes.

Serves: 6

LARDED POT ROAST

(Carne mechada)

3 - pound eye of round roast —after-trimming weight
2 teaspoons salt
2 ounces minced cooking ham
1 ounce minced fatback
2 tablespoons minced onion
2 teaspoons minced green olives
6 pressed medium garlic cloves
1/4 teaspoon ground oregano
1/4 teaspoon ground pepper
3 tablespoons olive oil
2 teaspoons vinegar
1/2 cup vegetable oil
1 sliced medium onion
1 medium tomato, peeled, seeded and chopped, p.132
1 medium frying pepper, seeded and sliced
6 medium unpeeled garlic cloves
1/3 cup tomato sauce
2 cups hot water
6 medium potatoes, peeled and halved

1. Trim off any membranes, connective tissues and fat from the meat.

2. Make an incision lengthwise through the center of the roast. Rub the incision and the surface with the salt.

3. Mix the ham, fatback, minced onion and olives. Stuff the incision with this mixture.

4. Place the meat in a non-reactive container. Mix the pressed garlic, oregano and ground pepper with a tablespoon of the olive oil. Rub the meat all over with this mixture.

5. Mix the additional olive oil with the vinegar. Dribble over the meat. Cover and let stand for no less than an hour, but preferably, refrigerate overnight.

6. Take the roast out of the refrigerator an hour before cooking.

7. Scrape off the marinade from the meat to prevent its burning when browning it. Reserve the liquid rendered in the marinade container.

8. Heat the vegetable oil in a *caldero* or deep chicken fryer over medium-high heat. Brown the roast all over, turning frequently.

9. Remove the roast from the caldero and discard all but 2 tablespoons of the oil. Lower the heat to moderate-low and sauté the onion, tomato, frying pepper, whole garlic cloves and tomato sauce for some 10 minutes, stirring occasionally.

10. Add the scraped marinade and rendered liquid. Cook for two more minutes.

11. Return the roast to the pot. Add the water and bring to a boil. Lower the heat, cover, and simmer for 2 to 3 hours, or until almost tender. Turn once or twice.

12. Add the potatoes and simmer for 30 more minutes, or until the meat and potatoes are tender.

13. Remove the roast and potatoes from the pot. Let the meat rest for 20 minutes before carving.

14. Degrease the sauce. Strain the cooking vegetables or puree them into the sauce.

15. You may carve the roast at the table, serving the sauce separately, but reheat the potatoes briefly in the sauce before placing them around the roast. Or you may slice the roast in the kitchen, surround it with the potatoes and pour the sauce over them.

NOTE: This roast gains flavor from reheating. It can also be frozen into serving portions once sliced. It is traditional to carve it into 1/2" slices.

Serves: 6

Variation:

LARDED POT ROAST IN DARK SAUCE

(Carne mechada en salsa oscura)

Follow the instructions and ingredients for Larded Pot Roast, but with the following variations:

Omit the tomato, the tomato sauce and the potatoes. Add 6 peeled medium garlic cloves, one additional sliced medium onion, and two teaspoons browning sauce along with the water. Simmer covered for 2 to 3 hours, or until the meat is tender.

Serves: 6

BOTTOM ROUND ROAST IN DARK SAUCE

(Masa larga de res en salsa oscura)

3 -pound bottom round roast —trimmed weight
1/4" - thick slice of slab bacon, diced
2 teaspoons salt
5 pressed medium garlic cloves
1/4 teaspoon ground oregano
1/4 teaspoon ground pepper
3 tablespoons olive oil
1 teaspoon vinegar
1/2 cup vegetable oil
2 sliced medium onions
1 frying pepper, seeded and sliced
2 cups water
8 large unpeeled garlic cloves
2 teaspoons browning sauce

1. Trim off any membranes, connective tissues and fat from the meat.

2. Make about 5 or 6 one inch deep incisions all over the meat and stuff with the bacon.

3. Rub with the salt and then with a mixture of the pressed garlic, oregano, pepper and one tablespoon of the olive oil.

4. Place in a non-reactive container. Mix the additional olive oil with the vinegar and dribble over the meat.

5. Set aside for no less than one hour, but preferably, refrigerate covered overnight.

6. Remove from the refrigerator one hour before cooking.

7. Scrape off the marinade from the meat to prevent its burning during the browning. Reserve with the liquid rendered in the marinade container.

8. Heat the vegetable oil in a *caldero* or deep chicken fryer over medium-high heat. Brown the meat all over turning frequently. Remove and discard all but two tablespoons of the browning oil.

9. Lower the heat to medium-low and sauté the onion and pepper slices for 10 minutes.

10. Add the scraped marinade and rendered liquid. Cook for 2 minutes.

11. Return the roast to the pot. Add the whole garlic cloves, the water and browning sauce and bring to a boil. Cover, lower the heat, and simmer for 2 to 3 hours or until tender. Turn once or twice.

12. Remove the roast from the pot. Let rest for 20 minutes before carving.

13. In the meantime, degrease the sauce. Strain the cooking vegetables or puree them into the sauce.

14. You may carve the roast at the table, serving the sauce separately, or you may slice it in the kitchen and serve with the sauce poured over it.

NOTE: This roast gains in flavor by reheating. It may be frozen in individual servings of beef slices and sauce.

Serves: 6

BEEF STEW

(Carne de res guisada)

2 pounds boneless beef rump, chuck, or round, cut into 2" cubes —trimmed weight
1 3/4 teaspoons salt
3 pressed medium garlic cloves
1/4 teaspoon ground oregano
1/8 teaspoon ground pepper
1 tablespoon olive oil
vegetable oil
1/3 cup uncooked condiment —p.47, or 1 small tomato, 1 small onion, 1 small frying pepper, seeded, and 2 large sweet chili peppers, seeded, all finely chopped
10 small green pitted olives
2 teaspoons small capers
1/3 cup tomato sauce
2 1/2 cup hot water or stock
4 medium potatoes, peeled and quartered

1. Trim off any membranes, connective tissues or fat from the meat.

2. Rub well with the salt, then with the garlic, oregano, pepper and olive oil. Marinade the meat for at least 30 minutes.

3. In a large *caldero* or stew pot heat 1/2" layer of vegetable oil over medium-high heat. Brown the meat cubes, without crowding, on all sides. Set apart as the pieces are browned.

4. Discard all but 2 tablespoons of the oil from the pan. Lower the heat to moderate-low and sauté the uncooked condiment or chopped vegetables for 5 minutes.

5. Add the olives, capers and tomato sauce. Cook for 5 minutes.

6. Return the meat to the pan, add the water or stock and bring to a boil. Lower the heat, cover, and simmer for 1 1/2 hours.

7. Add the potatoes and continue simmering for 30 minutes, or until the meat and potatoes are tender, and the sauce has thickened.

Serves: 6

COCKTAIL MEATBALLS

(Albondiguitas)

1 pound lean ground beef
3 slices crustless white bread
1/2 cup milk
1 teaspoon salt
1/4 teaspoon garlic powder
1/8 teaspoon ground oregano
1/4 teaspoon ground pepper
1 tablespoon grated onion
vegetable oil

1. Dice the bread, soak in the milk, and mash well.

2. Mix the meat with the salt, garlic powder, oregano, pepper and onion, stirring with a fork.

3. Drain off the excess milk from the mashed bread. Mix with the meat.

4. Make the meatballs about 3/4" in diameter, keeping your hands moist to prevent sticking.

5. Roll the balls in flour and gently shake off excess.

6. Heat a 1" deep layer of vegetable oil in a frying pan over moderate heat.

7. Deep fry for 6 minutes in the oil or until golden brown.

8. Drain on paper towels. Serve either warm or at room temperature with your favorite cocktail sauce.

NOTE: After formed, the meatballs may be frozen, unfloured, but take out of the freezer 30 minutes before frying. Fry them for 8 minutes. They may also be baked in a 350°F oven for 10 minutes, turning to brown evenly.

Yield: 75 meatballs

MEATBALL STEW

(Albóndigas guisadas)

1 1/2 pound lean ground beef
5 slices of crustless white bread or 6 tablespoons bread crumbs
1/2 cup milk
3 1/4 teaspoons salt
1/4 teaspoon garlic powder
1/4 teaspoon ground oregano
1/8 teaspoon pepper
2 tablespoons chopped parsley
2 beaten large eggs
vegetable oil
1/2 cup uncooked condiment, p.47, or 1 tomato, 1 onion, 1 seeded frying pepper, and 2 seeded sweet chili peppers, all finely chopped
2 large pressed garlic cloves
2 teaspoons minced capers
1/2 cup tomato sauce
1 3/4 cup hot water
4 medium potatoes, peeled and quartered

1. Dice the bread slices and soak in the milk. Mash well.

2. Mix the meat with 1 1/2 teaspoons of the salt, garlic powder, oregano, pepper and parsley, stirring with a fork.

3. Drain off excess milk from the bread, add to the meat and mix well.

4. Add the beaten eggs and blend well.

5. Make the meatballs about 1 1/2" diameter keeping your hands moistened to prevent sticking.

6. Roll the meatballs in flour and gently shake off excess.

7. Heat a 1/2" deep layer of vegetable oil in a large skillet over medium-high heat. Brown the meatballs all over and transfer to a stew pot or a *caldero*.

8. Discard all but 2 tablespoons of the oil from the skillet, lower the heat to medium-low and sauté the uncooked condiment or chopped vegetables, garlic, capers and tomato sauce for 10 minutes, stirring occasionally.

9. Add the water and additional 1 3/4 teaspoon of salt. Bring to a boil and transfer to the stewpot or *caldero*.

10. Add the potatoes and simmer covered for 30 minutes or until the potatoes are tender and the sauce has thickened.

Serves: 6

BEEF AND HAM ROLLS

(Rollos de res y jamón)

1 1/2 pound lean ground beef
1/2 pound ground smoked ham
1 3/4 teaspoon salt
3/4 teaspoon ground nutmeg
3/4 teaspoon ground pepper
3/4 cup fine soda-cracker or bread crumbs
3 large beaten eggs
2 tablespoons dry vermouth or white wine

Poaching Liquid
2 quarts water
1 tablespoon salt
1 quartered onion
2 sweet chili peppers, quartered and seeded
3 garlic cloves, peeled and halved
4 whole spice cloves

1. In a large bowl mix well the beef and ham. Add the 1 3/4 teaspoon salt, nutmeg, pepper and crumbs. Mix well stirring with a fork.

2. Blend the beaten egg with the vermouth or wine. Add to the meat mixture and blend well with your hands until it forms a ball that separates from the sides of the bowl. If it sticks, add more crumbs.

3. Divide the ball into three portions and make rolls 7" long by 1 1/2" in diameter.

4. Cut three 8" x 10" rectangles of double-thick cheesecloth. Rinse well, but keep damp. You may also use washed white cotton handkerchiefs.

5. Spread the cheesecloth on a flat surface and brush with vegetable oil.

6. Place a roll at the bottom of the long side of one of the pieces of cheesecloth. Roll up tightly and tie both ends securely with kitchen twine. Wrap the other two rolls.

7. In a pan where the rolls will fit comfortably, bring the water, 1 1/2 tablespoon salt, onion, sweet chili peppers, garlic and spice cloves to a boil.

8. Add the rolls, cover, lower the heat and poach gently for 1 1/2 hours, turning once.

9. Remove from the poaching liquid. Let cool and unroll from the cheesecloth.

10. Wrap in plastic wrapping and refrigerate before slicing and serving.

Yield: 3 rolls

SAUTEED GROUND BEEF WITH ROAST PEPPERS

(Picadillo de carne con pimientos asados)

- 2 pounds lean ground beef
- 2 ounces diced fatback
- 4 ounces ham, diced small
- 1 1/2 teaspoons salt
- 1 chopped medium onion
- 2 medium frying peppers, seeded and chopped
- 2 large tomatoes, peeled, seeded and coarsely chopped, p. 132
- 4 sweet chili peppers, seeded and minced
- 2 pressed large garlic cloves
- 2 tablespoons capers, minced after measuring
- 15 small pimiento-stuffed green olives
- 1/4 teaspoon ground oregano
- 3/4 cup tomato sauce
- 2 large red or green bell peppers, roasted, peeled, seeded and sliced into strips, p. 119
- 3 extra-large chopped hard-boiled eggs

1. Sauté the fatback in a *caldero* or chicken fryer over medium heat until lightly browned. Set aside.

2. In the fat rendered by the fatback brown the meat and ham lightly over medium-high heat. Remove from the pot, add to it the crispy pieces of fatback and salt.

3. Discard all but 2 tablespoons of fat from the pan. Lower the heat to moderate-low and sauté the onion and frying pepper for 5 minutes.

4. Add the tomato, sweet chili peppers, garlic, capers, olives, oregano and tomato sauce. Cook, stirring, for some 5 minutes.

5. Add the meat and ham mixture. Mix well and cook uncovered at moderate heat for 15 minutes. Stir occasionally.

6. Add the roast peppers and chopped eggs. Cook for 2 minutes or until these warm up.

Serves: 6

GROUND MEAT STUFFING

(Picadillo para rellenos)

1 pound lean ground beef or pork, or any combination of them
1 ounce fatback, diced small or 2 tablespoons of olive oil
2 ounces minced cooking ham
3/4 teaspoon salt
1/2 cup uncooked condiment or 1 small onion, 1 small tomato, 1 small seeded frying pepper and 2 seeded sweet chili peppers, all finely chopped
1 pressed medium garlic clove
9 small chopped pitted green olives
1 tablespoon minced capers
1/4 teaspoon ground oregano
1/2 cup tomato sauce
3 tablespoons seedless raisins (optional)

1. Render the fat from the fatback in a large skillet over medium heat, or heat the olive oil over medium-high heat.

2. Raise the heat to medium-high and sauté the meat and ham until lightly browned. Remove, salt and set aside.

3. Discard all but two tablespoons of fat from the skillet. Lower the heat to medium-low and sauté the uncooked condiment, or chopped vegetables, for 5 minutes.

4. Add the garlic, olives, capers, oregano, tomato sauce and optional raisins. Cook for 5 minutes.

5. Return the meat to the pan. Cook uncovered for 15 minutes, stirring occasionally.

6. Continue with your recipe, or refrigerate or freeze until ready to use.

Yield: 3 1/2 cups

GROUND MEAT TURNOVERS

(Pastelillos de carne)

1 cup ground meat stuffing, p. 236
2 cups all-purpose flour
1/2 teaspoon salt
1/2 cup cold vegetable shortening
1/2 cup cold water
vegetable oil or lard

1. Sift together the flour and salt in a bowl. Add the shortening and work it in with two forks or a pastry blender until the mixture forms pea-size pieces.

2. Start sprinkling with the water by tablespoons and work it in until the dough holds together. If necessary, you may knead it slightly.

3. Form into a ball and refrigerate wrapped in plastic for 30 minutes.

4. Divide the dough into 8 portions and keep covered until ready to roll out each portion.

5. On a cool floured surface, flatten each portion and start rolling with the pin from the center out, dusting flour over the top of the dough if it sticks to it. Roll into a 6-6 1/2" diameter circle.

6. Put an inverted 5 1/2" diameter saucer over the dough circle and cut out the edges.

7. Lift up the circle before filling to make sure that it has not stuck to the surface.

8. Fill each circle with a heaping tablespoon of filling and spread it out in the center.

9. Moisten lightly the edges and fold over itself to form a half circle. Crimp the edges together with the tines of a fork.

10. Place on a floured platter and refrigerate, covered, until ready to fry.

11. Deep fry in vegetable shortening or lard until golden brown.

12. Drain on paper towels and serve warm.

NOTE: The turnovers can be frozen. Remove from the freezer 30 minutes before frying.

Yield: 8 turnovers

STUFFED CHEESE

(Queso relleno)

3 cups ground meat stuffing, p. 236
3 - pound Edam cheese
2 large pieces of banana leaf, wilted, p.141, or aluminum foil

1. Cut a 2 1/2" diameter slice off the top of the cheese. Set apart.

2. Carefully scrape out the interior of the cheese until the sides are about 1/4" to 1/2" thick. Be careful not to pierce the sides or scrape out the edge of the opening.

3. Scrape out carefully the wax covering and peel off the rind. Do the same to the slice cut off the top.

4. Soak the cheese and top in cool water to cover for two hours.

5. Drain well and stuff with the ground meat or with a mixture of this and part of the scraped-out cheese. Cover with the top.

6. Line an oven-proof mould where the cheese fits snugly with banana leaves, if available.

7. Bake uncovered for 30 minutes in a preheated 300°F oven, or until lightly browned on top.

8. Remove from the oven and serve immediately directly from the mould.

Serves: 6-8

RECONSTITUTING JERKED BEEF (*TASAJO*)

(Tasajo —cómo reconstituir)

1. Trim off any connective tissues, membranes and fat from the jerked beef. Cut into 2" square pieces.

2. Soak in cold water to cover for 2 hours.

3. Boil in fresh water to cover the meat by 3" for 10 minutes.

4. Rinse, and simmer in fresh water to cover by 3" for 2 1/2 hours or until the beef is tender.

5. Let cool and shred.

6. Proceed with your recipe.

JERKED BEEF WITH SCRAMBLED EGGS

(Carne cecina con huevos revueltos)

- 1 pound jerked beef (tasajo), reconstituted, simmered and shredded, v. above
- 2 tablespoons olive oil
- 1 thinly sliced small onion
- 6 large eggs, beaten with 1/8 teaspoon salt

1. Sauté the onion slices in the olive oil in a large skillet set over moderate heat for 5 minutes.

2. Add the shredded beef. Sauté for 5 minutes.

3. Add the beaten eggs and scramble until done to taste.

Serves: 6

CATALONIAN JERKED BEEF

(Carne cecina a la catalana)

1 pound jerked beef (*tasajo*), reconstituted, simmered and shredded, p. 239
1/3 cup olive oil
3 large garlic cloves, halved
1 thinly sliced medium onion
2 medium size green frying peppers, roasted, seeded and cut into strips, p. 119
3/4 cup tomato sauce
1/4 cup water
1 tablespoon chopped parsley
4 ounces sliced pimientos

1. Heat the oil in a large skillet or a *caldero* over medium-low heat.

2. Sauté the garlic briefly until it starts to get golden. Remove and discard.

3. Cook the onions for 5 minutes. Add the green pepper strips, tomato sauce and water. Cook for 5 more minutes.

4. Preheat the oven to 300°F.

5. Mix the meat with the sauce and the parsley.

6. Put in an ovenproof casserole. Adorn with the pimiento slices in a basket-weave pattern, and bake uncovered for 10 minutes.

7. Serve with boiled green bananas, p. 91, or your favorite boiled tropical roots dribbled with sauce of the meat.

Serves: 6

SAUTEED CANNED CORNED BEEF

(Salteado de carne curada enlatada)

12-ounce can corned beef, shredded
2 tablespoons olive oil
1 thinly sliced small onion
2 tablespoons uncooked condiment, p. 47
1 pressed garlic clove
1/8 teaspoon ground oregano
3/4 cup tomato sauce
1/4 teaspoon sugar
3 tablespoons water

1. Heat the oil in a skillet over medium-low heat. Sauté the onion and condiment for 5 minutes.

2. Add the garlic, oregano, tomato sauce, sugar and water. Cook for 5 minutes.

3. Add the shredded corned beef, blend well with the sauce, and cook until warm for 2 or 3 minutes.

Serves: 6

BEEF LIVER SMOTHERED IN ONIONS

(Hígado de res encebollado)

1 1/2 pound beef liver
3/4 cup of milk
1 1/2 teaspoon salt
3 pressed medium garlic cloves
1/8 teaspoon ground oregano
1/8 teaspoon ground pepper
3 thinly sliced medium onions
2 tablespoons olive oil
vegetable oil

1. Trim off the liver any membranes or connective tissues. Cut into 1/4 inch thick slices.

2. Soak the slices in the milk for at least 5 minutes. Drain and pat dry.

3. Mix the salt, garlic, oregano and pepper. Rub this mixture on the liver slices. Cover with the onions and dribble the olive oil over all.

4. Cover and let stand for at least 30 minutes.

5. Heat a 1/8-inch layer of vegetable oil in a skillet set over medium-high heat. Sauté the liver slices for 2 minutes on each side —medium rare— and remove to a platter. Keep warm.

6. Discard all but one tablespoon of oil from the pan. Sauté the onion slices for about 5 minutes over moderate heat. Add the juices rendered by the liver on the platter.

7. Place the onions on top of the liver and pour the pan juices over all.

Serves: 6

BEEF LIVER STEW

(Hígado de res guisado)

1 1/2 pound beef liver
1/2 cup milk
2 teaspoons salt
2 tablespoons vegetable oil
1/2 cup uncooked condiment, p. 47
3 large *culantro* leaves or 3 strips of flat-leaf parsley, minced
2 pressed garlic cloves
1/8 teaspoon ground oregano
1/8 teaspoon pepper
1 1/2 tablespoons capers, minced after measuring
12 small pitted green olives
1/3 cup tomato sauce
2 cups hot water
3 medium potatoes, peeled and cut into 1" cubes

1. Trim off the liver any membranes or connective tissues.

2. Cut the liver into 1/2" cubes and soak in the milk for at least 5 minutes.

3. Drain, pat dry, and salt.

4. Heat the oil over medium-low heat in a *caldero* or large saucepan. Sauté the condiment, *culantro*, garlic, oregano, pepper, capers, olives and tomato sauce for 10 minutes, stirring often.

5. Raise the heat to medium-high. Add the liver, and stir-fry for one minute.

6. Add the hot water and potatoes. Cover, bring to a simmer and cook for 50 to 60 minutes, or until the liver is tender and the sauce has thickened.

Serves: 6

BEEF TONGUE IN DARK SAUCE

(Lengua de res en salsa oscura)

3-pound beef tongue
4 quarts water
6 1/2 teaspoons salt
1/4 teaspoon ground oregano
1/8 teaspoon ground pepper
1/2 cup vegetable oil
1 medium tomato, peeled, seeded and chopped, p. 132
1 medium frying pepper, seeded and sliced
2 sliced medium onions
10 large unpeeled garlic cloves
3/4 cup dry red wine
1 tablespoon browning sauce

1. Scrub the tongue under running water with a vegetable brush.

2. Place in a pot and cover with water and 6 teaspoons of the salt. Bring to a simmer —do not let boil— and remove the scum that rises to the surface of the water.

3. Cover and simmer gently for about 2 hours.

4. Let the tongue steep uncovered in the simmering water until cool enough to handle.

5. Remove from the pot, but reserve 2 1/2 cups of the simmering water.

6. With a sharp knife slit the skin of the tongue lengthwise at the top and the bottom. Peel off towards the sides.

7. Remove any bones or gristle.

8. On the underside of the tongue make a deep incision lengthwise. Salt the incision with most of the additional 1/2 teaspoon of salt, rubbing the surface with the rest.

9. Rub the tongue all over with the pepper and oregano. Place in a container and dribble with 2 tablespoons of the oil. Let stand for 30 minutes.

10. Heat the vegetable oil in a *caldero* or chicken fryer over medium-high heat. Brown the tongue all over, turning frequently. Remove.

11. Discard all but two tablespoons of the oil in the pot. Lower the heat to medium-low and sauté the tomato, pepper slices, onions and garlic cloves for 10 minutes, stirring occasionally.

12. Return the tongue to the pot, add the reserved simmering liquid and bring to a boil. Cover and simmer gently for 30 minutes.

13. Add the wine and browning sauce and simmer for an additional hour, or until tender.

14. Remove the tongue from the sauce and let rest for 20 minutes before slicing.

15. In the meantime, degrease the sauce.

16. Strain the vegetables out of the sauce, or pureé them in.

17. Lay the tongue on a cutting board, the base of the tongue on your left, underside facing you. Starting from the tip, slice with a sharp carving knife into 3/8" diagonal slices.

18. Return the slices to the sauce and reheat briefly before serving.

Serves: 6-8

PORK TENDERLOIN SMOTHERED IN ONIONS

(Filete de cerdo encebollado)

2 - pound pork tenderloin, sliced 1/2" thick
1 1/2 teaspoon salt
2 pressed medium garlic cloves
1/8 teaspoon ground oregano
1/8 teaspoon ground pepper
2 large onions, sliced 1/4" thick
2 tablespoons olive oil
vegetable oil

1. Trim off any membranes, connective tissues or fat from the tenderloin.

2. Rub the tenderloin slices with the salt, then with the garlic, oregano and pepper. Put in a container.

3. Place the onion slices over the meat, pour the olive oil over all and marinade covered for at least 30 minutes.

4. Heat a 1/4" deep layer of vegetable oil in a frying pan set over medium-high. Sauté the slices in one layer for about 2 minutes on each side. Remove to a platter and keep warm until all the slices are done.

5. Discard all but two tablespoons of the oil from the pan, lower the heat to moderate and sauté the onions until tender, stirring to deglaze the pan.

6. Add the juices rendered by the meat on the platter. Put the onions over the meat and pour the juices over all before serving.

Serves: 6

FRIED PORK MORSELS

(Carne de cerdo frita)

2 pounds boneless pork, preferably fresh ham, butt end, cut into 2" cubes
1 1/2 teaspoons salt
2 pressed medium garlic cloves
1/8 teaspoon ground oregano
1/4 teaspoon ground pepper
3/4 cup lard, vegetable shortening or oil

1. Trim off any connective tissues, membranes or excess fat from the meat. Do leave attached any pieces of rind.

2. Rub the meat with the salt, then with the garlic, oregano and pepper. Let stand for at least 30 minutes.

3. Heat the lard, shortening or oil in a *caldero* or frying pan large enough to hold the pork cubes in one layer.

4. Add the cubes one at a time, stirring to prevent them from sticking to the pan.

5. Lower the heat to moderate and cook covered for 15 minutes. Turn the meat over, cover and cook for 15 additional minutes.

6. Uncover, raise the heat to medium-high and cook for 15 to 20 minutes until the meat is golden brown. Turn once or twice to brown all over.

7. The pieces with rind attached may need a few extra minutes to allow the rind to become crackling.

8. Drain on paper towels and serve warm.

Serves: 6-8

FRIED PORK CHOPS

(Chuletas de cerdo fritas)

6 pork chops, 1/2" thick
1/2 teaspoon salt per pound of chops
2 pressed medium garlic cloves
1/4 teaspoon ground oregano
1/8 teaspoon ground pepper
1 teaspoon olive oil
vegetable oil

1. Trim off excess fat from the chops and score the edges to prevent curling.

2. Rub the chops with the salt then with the garlic, oregano, pepper and olive oil. Let stand for at least 30 minutes.

3. Heat a 1/4" deep layer of vegetable oil in a skillet over medium high heat.

4. Brown each chop on each side for some 2 minutes.

5. Lower the heat to moderate-low and cook for 3 more minutes on each side.

6. Drain on paper towels and serve warm.

Serves: 6

CAN-CAN PORK CHOPS

(Chuletas de cerdo can-can)

6 pork chops, 1" thick, cut from a loin that has the pork rind attached, 3/4 pound each
1/2 teaspoon salt per pound of chop
3 pressed medium garlic cloves
1/4 teaspoon ground oregano
1/4 teaspoon ground pepper
vegetable shortening or lard

1. Make cuts around the edges of the chops at 1 1/2" intervals from the rind, through the fat, up to the meat. These will give the chops the ruffled look that accounts for their name.

2. Rub well with the salt, then with the garlic, oregano and pepper. Let stand for at least 30 minutes, but preferably refrigerate covered overnight. Remove from the refrigerator one hour before frying.

3. Simmer the chops in water to cover for 25 minutes.

4. Drain and pat dry.

5. Deep fry in vegetable shortening or lard for some 10 minutes, or until the rind becomes crackling.

6. Drain on paper towels and serve warm.

Serves: 6

EGG-DIPPED PORK CHOPS

(Chuletas de cerdo rebozadas)

6 pork chops, 1/2" thick
1/2 teaspoon salt per pound of chops
1/2 teaspoon garlic powder
1/8 teaspoon ground pepper
1/2 cup flour
4 large eggs beaten with a pinch of salt
vegetable oil

1. Trim off excess fat from the chops and score the edges to prevent curling.

2. Rub with the salt, then with the garlic and pepper. Let stand for at least 30 minutes.

3. Heat a 1/4" deep layer of oil in a frying pan set over moderate heat. Sauté the chops 5 minutes on each side. Drain on paper towels.

4. Dredge the chops in flour and shake off excess. Dip into the beaten egg. Follow this process only for as many chops as you can fry in a single layer.

5. Heat a fresh layer of oil, 1/8" deep in a clean skillet over medium heat and fry the chops for about a minute on each side, or until the eggs sets a golden yellow. Add more oil as needed.

6. Drain on paper towels and keep warm until all the chops are done.

Serves: 6

BREADED PORK CHOPS

(Chuletas de cerdo empanadas)

6 pork chops, 1/2" thick
1/2 teaspoon salt per pound of chops
1/2 teaspoon garlic clove
1/4 teaspoon ground oregano
1/8 teaspoon ground pepper
2 teaspoons olive oil
2 extra-large eggs beaten with a pinch of salt
1 1/2 cup soda-cracker or bread crumbs
vegetable oil

1. Trim off excess fat from the chops and score the edges to prevent curling.

2. Rub with the salt, then with the garlic, oregano, pepper and olive oil. Let stand for at least 30 minutes.

3. Heat a 1/4" layer of oil in a frying pan over moderate heat.

Sauté the chops 5 minutes on each side. Drain on paper towels.

4. Heat a fresh layer of oil, 1/4" deep in a clean skillet set over medium-high heat.

5. Dip the chops in the beaten egg and cover with the crumbs, patting them into the meat. Follow this process only for as many chops as you can fry in a single layer.

6. Fry the chops in the oil about one minute on each side or until golden brown.

7. Drain on paper towels and keep warm until all the chops are done.

Serves: 6

BRAISED FRESH HAM

(Pernil de cerdo al caldero)

6-pound fresh ham, skinless
4 1/2 teaspoons salt
5 pressed medium garlic cloves
1/4 teaspoon ground pepper
1/2 teaspoon ground oregano
2 tablespoons olive oil
1 tablespoon vinegar
1/3 cup vegetable oil
1 1/4 cup hot water
8 peeled medium potatoes

1. Trim off all excess fat from the ham.

2. Make several 1" deep incisions all over the ham. Rub some salt into the incisions, and the rest on the surface.

3. Mix the garlic, pepper and oregano and rub the ham with it. Place in a non-reactive container.

4. Blend the olive oil and vinegar and dribble over the meat. Cover and let stand for no less than an hour, but preferably,

refrigerate overnight. Remove from the refrigerator at least one hour before cooking.

5. Just before cooking scrape off the marinade from the ham, but reserve along with any rendered juices.

6. Heat the vegetable oil over medium-high heat in a *caldero* or chicken fryer large enough to hold the ham and the potatoes. Pat dry and brown the ham all over.

7. Discard the browning oil, add the water and scraped marinade and rendered liquids. Bring to a boil and return the ham to the pot.

8. Lower the heat to simmer, cover, and cook for about 3 hours. Turn every hour.

9. An hour before it is done add the potatoes.

10. Once done, remove and let rest for 15-20 minutes before carving.

11. In the meantime, degrease the juices in the pot and prepare a gravy if so wished.

Serves: 12

ROAST FRESH HAM

(Pernil de cerdo asado)

6-pound fresh ham
4 1/2 teaspoons salt
5 pressed medium garlic cloves
1/2 teaspoon ground oregano
1/4 teaspoon ground pepper
3 tablespoons olive oil
1 tablespoon vinegar

1. With a boning knife separate the skin and fat from the meat at the butt end of the ham. Leave the skin attached to the shank end.

2. Pull back the skin towards the shank end and trim off all but 1/4" fat from it. Trim off any excess fat from the meat proper.

3. Make several 1" deep incisions in the meat, rub some salt into them, and rub the rest of the salt on the surface of the meat itself. Pull the skin back over the ham.

4. Mix the garlic, oregano, pepper and one tablespoon of the oil. Rub this all over the ham.

5. Put in a non-reactive container. Mix the rest of the oil with the vinegar and dribble all over the ham.

6. Cover and marinade for no less than one hour, but preferably refrigerate overnight. Take out of the refrigerator 2 hours before roasting.

7. Preheat the oven to 400°F.

8. Put the ham on a roasting pan. Fasten the skin to the meat at the butt end 1" from the edge with trussing needles. Pour the marinade liquids over it.

9. Put a pan with water on the lower rack of the oven, but remove it for the last minutes of roasting to crisp the skin.

10. Put the ham in the oven. After 10 minutes reduce the heat to 325°F.

11. Roast 30 minutes per pound or until a meat thermometer reads an internal temperature of 170°F. Baste with the pan fat every 20 minutes.

12. Remove from the oven and let rest 20 minutes before carving.

13. Remove the crackling in one piece. Break it into serving pieces, and serve along with carved slices of meat.

14. If you wish, degrease and deglaze the roasting pan to use the juices for a gravy.

NOTE: You may omit steps one and two and instead simply score the skin and fat up to the surface of the meat in a diamond pattern. When carving, do not remove the crackling, but carve along with the meat.

Serves: 10

FRESH HAM SANDWICHES

(Emparedados de pernil)

Braised or roast fresh ham, pp.250, 251, thinly sliced
- 12 slices white sandwich bread
- mayonnaise
- 6 leaves leaf lettuce
- 6 slices tomato
- salt

1. Remove the crust of the bread and spread one side of each slice with mayonnaise to taste.

2. Sandwich between two bread slices, slices of ham, a lettuce leaf and a tomato slice. Salt to taste.

3. Cut the sandwich diagonally.

NOTE: This is the simplest version of a standard ham sandwich to which one can add pickles and cheese, or which can be made with *pan de agua* (French bread).

Yield: 6 sandwiches

FRESH HAM, WALNUTS AND PINEAPPLE SALAD

(Ensalada de pernil de cerdo, nueces y piña)

- 3 cups lean braised or roast fresh ham, pp.250, 251, cut into 1/2" cubes
- 3/4 cup mayonnaise
- 2 teaspoons grated onion
- 1 teaspoon lemon juice or vinegar
- 1/4 teaspoon salt
- 1/8 teaspoon pepper
- 3/4 cup chopped walnuts
- 1 1/2 cups pineapple cut into 1/2" cubes or canned pineapple chunks, drained

1. In a large bowl blend well the mayonnaise, onion, lemon juice or vinegar, salt and pepper.

2. Add the meat and walnuts and mix well.

3. Fold in the pineapple.

4. Cover and chill before serving.

Serves: 6

BRAISED PORK LOIN

(Lomo de cerdo al caldero)

6-chop center cut pork loin, chine bone either removed or cut through in between the chops, fat trimmed off
3/4 teaspoon salt per pound
1 pressed medium garlic clove per pound
1/16 teaspoon ground pepper per pound
1/8 teaspoon ground oregano per pound
1 teaspoon olive oil per pound
1/4 teaspoon vinegar per pound
1/3 cup vegetable oil
1 cup hot water
6 peeled medium potatoes

1. Make 1" deep incisions all over the meat.

2. Rub salt over the loin, introducing some into the incisions.

3. Mix the garlic, pepper, oregano, olive oil and vinegar. Put the loin in a non-reactive container and rub well with this blend.

4. Let stand covered for no less than an hour, but preferably, refrigerate overnight. Remove from the refrigerator one hour before braising.

5. Scrape off the marinade to prevent its burning when browning the loin, but save along with any rendered juices.

6. Heat the vegetable oil in a *caldero* or chicken fryer large

enough to hold the loin and the potatoes over medium-high heat.

7. Pat dry the loin and brown all over. Discard the browning oil.

8. Add the water and saved marinade. Bring to a boil. Lower the heat, cover, and simmer for one hour.

9. Add the potatoes and simmer for an additional 1 1/4 hour, or until the meat and potatoes are tender.

10. Remove and put in a warm platter. Let rest for 15 minutes before carving at the table.

11. In the meantime, degrease and strain the pot juices. Rewarm the potatoes in the sauce before serving.

Serves: 6

BRAISED PORK TENDERLOIN

(Filete de cerdo al caldero)

2-pound pork tenderloin
1 1/2 teaspoon salt
4 pressed medium garlic cloves
1/8 teaspoon ground oregano
1/4 teaspoon ground pepper
2 tablespoons olive oil
1 teaspoon vinegar
1/4 cup vegetable oil
1 large onion, sliced 1/4" thick
4 unpeeled medium garlic cloves
1 cup water
1 teaspoon browning sauce
6 peeled medium potatoes

1. Trim off all membranes or fat from the tenderloin.

2. Make a deep incision in the center of the tenderloin's thicker end. Salt inside the incision and all over the surface of the meat.

3. Mix the pressed garlic, oregano and pepper with one tablespoon of the olive oil and rub the tenderloin all over with this blend.

4. Put in a non-reactive container. Blend the rest of the olive oil with the vinegar and dribble over the meat.

5. Let stand for at least 30 minutes, but preferably refrigerate covered overnight. Remove from the refrigerator one hour before braising.

6. Scrape the marinade off to prevent burning it while browning the tenderloin, but save along with the rendered juices.

7. Heat the oil in a *caldero* or chicken fryer over medium-high and brown the tenderloin all over. Remove and set aside.

8. Discard all but 2 tablespoons of oil from the pot. Lower the heat to moderate and sauté the onion and garlic cloves for 5 minutes.

9. Return the meat to the pot. Add the water, browning sauce, marinade and rendered juices and potatoes. Bring to a boil, cover and lower the heat. Simmer for 1 1/4 hour. Turn the potatoes and meat once.

10. Remove from the pot. Let rest for 15 minutes before carving.

11. In the meantime, degrease the sauce.

12. Slice the tenderloin and return to the pot along with the potatoes just long enough to reheat them in the sauce; or, carve at the table surrounded by the potatoes reheated in the sauce.

Serves: 6

PORK STEW

(Carne de cerdo guisada)

2 pounds lean boneless pork, preferably fresh ham, butt end, cut into 2" cubes
1 3/4 teaspoon salt
3 pressed medium garlic cloves
1/4 teaspoon ground oregano
1/8 teaspoon ground pepper
1 teaspoon olive oil
1/4 cup vegetable oil
1/3 cup uncooked condiment, p.47, or 1 small tomato, 1 small onion, 1 small seeded frying pepper, and 2 seeded sweet chili peppers, all minced
1/3 cup tomato sauce
10 pitted green olives
2 teaspoons minced capers
2 cups hot water
3 medium potatoes, peeled and halved

1. Trim off any excess fat or membranes from the meat.

2. Rub the meat with the salt, then with the garlic, pepper, olive oil and let stand for at least 30 minutes.

3. Heat the vegetable oil in a stew pot or *caldero* over medium-high heat. Brown the meat on all sides. Remove.

4. Discard all but 2 tablespoons of the browning oil. Reduce the heat to medium-low and sauté the uncooked condiment or minced vegetables for 5 minutes.

5. Add the tomato sauce, olive and capers and cook for 5 more minutes.

6. Return the meat to the pot along with any rendered juices. Add the water and bring to a boil. Cover, lower the heat, and simmer for one hour.

7. Add the potatoes and simmer covered for an additional hour or until the meat and potatoes are tender.

Serves: 6

PORK CHOPS IN DARK SAUCE

(Chuletas de cerdo en salsa oscura)

6 pork chops, 3/4" thick
3/4 teaspoon salt per pound of chops
3 pressed medium garlic cloves
1/8 teaspoon ground pepper
vegetable oil
2 sliced medium onions
1 chopped medium tomato
1 medium frying pepper, seeded and sliced
6 unpeeled medium garlic cloves
1 cup hot water
2 teaspoons browning sauce

1. Trim off excess fat from the chops and score the edges to prevent curling.

2. Rub the chops with the salt, then with the pressed garlic and pepper. Let stand for at least 30 minutes.

3. Heat a 1/4" deep layer of vegetable oil over medium-high heat in a skillet large enough tc hold the chops in one layer or slightly overlapping.

4. Brown the chops on both sides and set aside.

5. Discard all but 2 tablespoons of oil from the pan. Lower the heat to medium-low and sauté the onions, tomato, garlic cloves and pepper slices for 10 minutes.

6. Return the chops to the pan laying them under the vegetables.

7. Add the water and browning sauce and bring to a boil. Cover, lower the heat, and simmer gently for an hour, turning the chops once.

8. Remove the chops and keep warm while degreasing the sauce.

9. Drain off the vegetables or puree into the sauce.

NOTE: You may use boneless loin chops.

Serves: 6

GROUND PORK STUFFING FOR POULTRY

(Picadillo de cerdo para relleno de aves)

1 1/2 pound lean ground pork
4 tablespoons vegetable oil
1 tablespoon salt
1 cup finely chopped onion
2 ounces *alcaparrado* or 1 ounce pimiento-stuffed green olives and 1 ounce capers, minced
4-ounce jar chopped pimientos, plus their liquid
1/2 cup seedless raisins
1 pound applesauce
3 chopped hard-boiled eggs

1. Heat the oil in a large skillet over medium-high heat. Brown the meat lightly. Remove, salt, and set aside.

2. Discard all but 1 tablespoon of the browning oil. Reduce the heat to medium-low, add the onions and sauté for 5 minutes.

3. Add the *alcaparrado*, pimientos and their liquid. Cook for 5 minutes.

4. Add the raisins, return the meat to the pan and cook uncovered for 15 minutes, stirring occasionally.

5. Remove from the heat. Add the applesauce and chopped eggs. Mix well.

6. Refrigerate or freeze if not using immediately.

Yield: 6 1/2 cups

PORK AND BEEF ROLLS

(Rollos de carne de cerdo y res)

1/2 pound lean ground pork
1/2 pound lean ground beef
1/4 pound ground smoked ham
1/2 teaspoon salt
1/4 teaspoon thyme or 1/8 teaspoon oregano
1/4 teaspoon ground nutmeg
1/4 teaspoon ground pepper
1 tablespoon grated onion
1/2 cup fine soda-cracker or bread crumbs
1 teaspoon Worcestershire Sauce
1 teaspoon vinegar
2 large beaten eggs

Poaching Liquid

2 quarts water
1 tablespoon salt
1 quartered onion
2 sweet chili peppers, quartered and seeded
3 garlic cloves, peeled and halved
2 whole spice cloves

1. Mix well the pork, beef, ham, 1/2 teaspoon salt, thyme, nutmeg, pepper, grated onion and crumbs in a large bowl.

2. Mix the Worcestershire Sauce, vinegar and eggs. Add to the meat mixture and blend well with your hands until it forms a ball that separates from the sides of the bowl. If it does not, add more crumbs.

3. Divide into two portions and form 2 rolls 7" long by 1 1/2" in diameter.

4. Cut two 8" x 10" rectangles of double-thick cheesecloth, rinse and keep damp. You may also use rinsed white handkerchiefs.

5. Spread the cheesecloths on a flat surface and brush with melted lard or vegetable oil.

6. Place the rolls at the bottom of the long side of the cheese-

cloth pieces. Roll up tightly and tie both ends securely with kitchen twine.

7. In a pan large enough to hold the rolls comfortably, bring to a boil the water, tablespoon salt, onion, chili peppers, garlic and spice cloves.

8. Add the rolls, cover, lower the heat and poach gently for 1 1/2 hour, turning once.

9. Remove from the poaching liquid. Let cool and unroll from the cheesecloth.

10. Wrap in plastic and chill before slicing and serving.

NOTE: Instead of the beef and pork, you may use 1 pound of pork.

Yield: 2 rolls

GLAZED HAM BAKED IN RED WINE

(Jamón planchado)

12-pound processed boneless ham
1 2/3 cup red dry wine
whole spice cloves
4 cups dark brown sugar
1 cup pineapple juice, or 1/2 cup juice and 1/2 cup syrup from the canned pineapple slices
12 pineapple slices, freshly poached or canned
12 maraschino cherries

1. Trim off any excess gelatin or fat from the ham.

2. Place fat side up on a baking pan where it fits snugly and pour 2/3 cup of the wine over it.

3. Bake in a preheated 325°F oven for 40 minutes, basting frequently. Remove from the oven and discard the wine which has become salty.

4. Raise the oven temperature to 350°F.

5. Cut crisscrossing diagonal lines 1 1/2" apart on the top of the ham to create a diamond pattern.

6. Stud the intersections of the lines with the spice cloves.

7. Mix 3 cups of the sugar with the rest of the wine and the pineapple juice —and syrup if using any.

8. Pour this mixture over the ham. Return to the oven and bake for one hour, basting regularly.

9. Remove from the oven and raise the temperature to 400°F.

10. Put the pineapple slices on top and sides of the ham securing them with wooden toothpicks. Place a cherry on the center of each slice.

11. Spread the additional cup of sugar over all and bake for 30 more minutes. Baste once or twice.

12. Remove the ham to a serving platter and let cool to room temperature.

13. Strain and degrease the sauce and let cool. Do not add any juices rendered by the ham on the platter to prevent its clouding.

14. Carve thinly at the table, serving pieces of pineapple and cherries along with the meat. Serve the sauce separately.

NOTE: This ham may be served at room temperature or chilled.

Serves: 25-40

Variation:

GLAZED HAM IN DRY VERMOUTH

(Jamón planchado con vermouth seco)

Follow the instructions for Glazed Ham Baked in Red Wine as above, but substitute dry vermouth for the red wine.

POACHED BRINED SPARERIBS

(Costillas de cerdo en salmuera hervidas)

4 pounds brined or salted pork spareribs
1 medium size breadfruit, peeled, quartered and boiled, p. 109
12 green bananas, peeled and boiled, p. 91
1 avocado, peeled and sliced
Ajilimójili, p.65, or vinaigrette, p.64

1. Cut the spareribs into 2 or 3-rib segments.

2. Rinse and soak in cold water to cover for 1 hour.

3. Rinse again. Bring 5 quarts of water to a boil, add the ribs, lower the heat and simmer covered 1 1/2-2 hours, or until tender.

4. Taste the water after 30 minutes into the simmering. If too salty, remove one quart of the pot water and add a quart of fresh hot water. Bring again to boil and lower the heat to simmer.

5. Serve with the warm quarters of breadfruit, bananas and with the slices of avocado.

6. Serve the *ajilimójili* or vinaigrette separately to add to taste over the vegetables.

Serves: 6

VIENNA SAUSAGE, POTATOES AND EGGS STEW

(Guisado de salchichas vienesas, papas y huevos)

2 five-ounce cans of Vienna sausages
2 tablespoons vegetable oil
1/3 cup uncooked condiment, p.47, or 1 small tomato, 1 small seeded frying pepper, 1 small onion, and 2 seeded sweet chili peppers, all minced
1 pressed large garlic clove
6 tablespoons tomato sauce
3/4 cup water or 1/2 cup water and 1/4 cup liquid from the cooked peas
1/8 teaspoon salt
5 medium potatoes, boiled in 1 1/2 quart water and 1 1/2 teaspoon salt, peeled and diced into 1" cubes —about 1 1/4 pound potatoes
4 hard boiled eggs, sliced lengthwise
1 cup cooked peas —fresh, frozen or canned

1. Cut the sausages in half.

2. Sauté the condiment or minced vegetables in the vegetable oil for 5 minutes over medium-low heat in a *caldero* or chicken fryer.

3. Add the garlic and tomato sauce and cook for 5 more minutes.

4. Add the water, and pea liquid, if using it, the salt, sausages and potatoes. Stir well, bring to a boil and cover. Lower the heat and simmer for 15 minutes or until the sauce thickens.

5. Remove from the heat and fold in gently the eggs and the peas.

Serves: 6

PORK CRACKLINGS

(Chicharrones de cerdo)

3 pounds pork skin with no less than 1/4" layer of fat attached
1 1/2 cups lard
salt

1. Cut the pork skin into 1 1/2"-2" squares. Leave a fat layer no thicker than 1/4".

2. Melt the lard in a very large *caldero* or chicken fryer over medium-high heat.

3. Add the skin pieces, fat side down, cover and cook at low heat for 15-20 minutes, or until tender.

4. Raise the heat to moderate and put the cover ajar to allow vapor to escape and crisp the cracklings.

5. Fry for 15-20 minutes or until crisp.

6. Drain on paper towels and salt to taste.

NOTE: They may be refrigerated loosely covered.

Serves: 6

PIGS FEET WITH CHICK PEAS

(Patitas de cerdo con garbanzos)

2 pounds salted pigs feet, split lengthwise
7 cups water
2 tablespoons olive oil
1/3 cup uncooked condiment, p. 47
2 pressed medium garlic cloves
1/3 cup tomato sauce
1/3 pound pumpkin, peeled, seeded and cut into 1 1/2" cubes
2/3 pound dried chick peas, boiled, plus their boiling liquid, p.305

1. Rinse the pigs feet and soak overnight in water to cover.

2. Blanch the feet for 5 minutes in fresh water to cover. Drain and discard the water.

3. Simmer in 7 cups of fresh water for 2 1/2 hours or until tender.

4. Remove from the pot. Degrease the simmering water and save 2 1/2 cups.

5. In a pot large enough to hold all the ingredients, cook the uncooked condiment and garlic in the olive oil for 5 minutes over medium low heat.

6. Add the tomato sauce and cook for 5 more minutes.

7. Add the 2 1/2 cups of the water saved from boiling the pigs feet and 1 1/2 cups of the water from the boiled chick peas.

8. Add the pigs feet, the chick peas and pumpkin. Taste for salt and bring to a boil.

9. Reduce the heat and simmer with the pot lid slightly ajar for 40 minutes or until the sauce thickens to taste.

Serves: 6

PORK OFFAL RAGOUT

(Gandinga de cerdo)

3 pounds pork offal —liver, heart and kidneys
1 tablespoon salt
1 tablespoon annatto lard or oil, p. 47
1/2 cup uncooked condiment, p.47, or 1 small onion, 1 small seeded frying pepper, 4 seeded sweet chili peppers, all minced
2 pressed medium garlic cloves
4 minced cilantro sprigs
4 *culantro* leaves or four additional cilantro sprigs, minced
12 pimiento-stuffed green olives
2 teaspoons minced capers
1/4 teaspoon ground pepper
1/4 teaspoon ground oregano
1/2 bay leaf
3/4 cup tomato sauce
3 cups hot water
3 large potatoes, peeled and diced

1. Rinse well the offal. .

2. Trim off all membranes and veins from the liver and cut into 1/2" cubes.

3. Trim off all membranes, veins and fat, and remove any blood clots from the heart. Cut into 1/2" cubes.

4. Trim off any membranes and fat from the kidneys. Split lengthwise and trim off any veins or white tissue on them. Boil them in water to cover for 3 minutes. Drain well and cut into 1/2" cubes.

5. Salt the meats and set aside.

6. Heat the oil in a *caldero* or chicken fryer over medium-low heat. Sauté the uncooked condiment, or minced vegetables, for 5 minutes.

7. Add the garlic, cilantro, culantro, olives, capers, pepper,

oregano, bay leaf and tomato sauce. Cook for 5 more minutes.

8. Raise the heat to moderate, add the meats and stir-cook for 5 additional minutes.

9. Add the water, bring to a boil, lower the heat and simmer covered for 45 minutes.

10. Add the potatoes and simmer for an additional 30-40 minutes or until the meat and potatoes are tender and the sauce has thickened.

Serves: 6

SIMMERED PORK STOMACH

(Cuajo hervido)

pork stomach
per pound of meat:
- 1 quart water
- 3 tablespoons vinegar
- 6 additional cups of water
- 4 teaspoons salt
- 3 large *culantro* leaves or 3 sprigs cilantro
- 1 quartered small onion
- 3 peeled garlic cloves

1. Trim off any fat from the pork stomach and rinse well under running water, scrubbing with a vegetable brush.

2. Cut into 2" square pieces and soak in the quart of water and vinegar for 15 minutes. Rinse.

3. Bring the 6 cups of water and salt to a boil in a pot, add the meat and remove the scum as it comes to the surface of the water.

4. Add the *culantro* or cilantro, onion and garlic. Cover. Reduce the heat to low and simmer for 1 1/2 hour or until tender.

5. Drain and proceed with your recipe.

NOTE: May be frozen at this point, but defrost for one hour before additional cooking.

FRIED PORK STOMACH

(Cuajo frito)

1 1/2 pound pork stomach, simmered and cut into 1" squares, p. 268
vegetable oil

1. Heat a 1/2" deep layer of vegetable oil in a large skillet set over moderate heat.

2. Fry the meat without crowding until golden brown and slightly crisp.

3. Drain on paper towels.

4. Let cool to room temperature and serve with your favorite hot sauce or Russian dressing.

Serves: 6

BREADED PORK STOMACH

(Cuajo empanado)

1 1/2 pound pork stomach, simmered and cut into 1" x 2" pieces, p. 268
1/2 cup flour
3 large eggs beaten with a pinch of salt
2 cups soda cracker or bread crumbs
vegetable oil

1. Dredge the pieces of meat in flour and shake off excess. When ready to fry, dip into the beaten egg and then cover completely with crumbs patting them in. Follow this procedure only for as many pieces of meat as you can fry in a single layer.

2. Heat a 1" deep layer of vegetable oil in a large skillet over medium-high heat.

3. Fry the breaded pieces until golden brown. Skim off any burnt crumbs as you fry.

4. Drain on paper towels and keep warm until all the meat is fried.

5. Serve with your favorite hot sauce.

Serves: 6

PORK STOMACH IN PIQUANT SAUCE

(Cuajo en salsa picante)

1 1/2 pound pork stomach, simmered and cut into 1" pieces, p. 268
3 tablespoons butter
1 teaspoon grated onion
1/4 cup tomato sauce
4 teaspoons flour
1 1/4 cups warm chicken stock
1 teaspoon *pique*, p.62, or 1/4 teaspoon bottled hot sauce —more to taste
1/4 teaspoon salt

1. Melt the butter over medium-low heat in a large skillet.

2. Add the onion and tomato sauce. Cook stirring for 5 minutes.

3. Blend well the flour with 1/4 cup of the chicken stock and add to the pan. Mix well and cook for 3 or 4 minutes.

4. Add the chicken stock gradually, stirring all the time to blend well.

5. Add the *pique* and the salt. Simmer for 10 minutes stirring occasionally.

6. Add the meat and cook until reheated.

Serves: 6

ROAST LEG OF VEAL

(Pernil de ternera asado)

4 1/2-pound leg of veal
1/4 cup vinegar
1 quart water
3 1/2 teaspoons salt
2 pressed large garlic cloves
1/4 teaspoon ground oregano
1/4 teaspoon ground pepper
2 tablespoons olive oil
1 teaspoon vinegar
fresh pork fat, sliced in strips 1/2" wide by 1/4" thick —you may use blanched slab bacon or fatback

1. Trim off any membranes and connective tissues from the veal.

2. Mix the 1/4 cup vinegar with the water and soak the veal in this for about 10 minutes. Rinse and pat dry.

3. Make a few incisions all over the leg and rub salt into them and on the surface of the meat. Place in a non-reactive container.

4. Mix the garlic, pepper and oregano. Rub the meat all over with them.

5. Blend the oil and teaspoon of vinegar and dribble over the meat. Cover and let stand for at least an hour, but preferably, refrigerate overnight. Remove from the refrigerator at least one hour before roasting.

6. Preheat the oven to 325°F.

7. Place the leg on a roasting pan, cover with the fat strips in a basket-weave pattern. Pour the marinade liquid over it.

8. Roast for about 2 hours, or 25 minutes per pound, until it reaches an internal temperature of 165°F on a meat thermometer.

Serves: 6

KID FRICASSEE

(Cabrito en fricasé)

3 pounds kid meat, cut into 2" cubes
1/2 cup sour orange juice, or 1/3 cup vinegar
1 tablespoon salt
3 pressed large garlic cloves
1/4 teaspoon ground oregano
1/4 teaspoon ground pepper
6 tablespoons olive oil
1 tablespoon olive oil
1 1/2 ounce diced smoked ham
1 large sliced onion
1 large frying pepper, sliced and seeded
1 large tomato, peeled, seeded and chopped, p.132
6 tablespoons tomato sauce
8 pimiento-stuffed green olives
2 teaspoons minced capers
1 bay leaf
3 medium potatoes, peeled and halved

1. Trim off any membranes, connective tissues and fat from the meat.

2. Soak in the sour orange juice or vinegar for some 20 minutes. Drain and pat dry after rinsing.

3. Rub the salt and then the garlic, oregano, pepper and the tablespoon olive oil on the meat. Place in a non-reactive container and marinate, covered, for at least one hour.

4. Heat the olive oil in a *caldero* or chicken fryer over medium-low heat. Sauté the ham briefly without browning.

5. Add the onion and pepper slices and cook for 5 minutes.

6. Add the tomato, tomato sauce, olives, capers and bay leaf. Cook for 5 additional minutes.

7. Raise the heat to moderate, add the meat and stir-fry for 5 minutes.

8. Reduce the heat to low, cover, and simmer gently for an hour.

9. Add the potatoes and simmer for one more hour or until the meat and potatoes are tender.

Serves: 6

BRAISED KID

(Cabrito estofado)

3 pounds kid meat, cut into 2" cubes
1/2 cup sour orange juice or 1/3 cup vinegar
1 tablespoon salt
1/4 cup olive oil
1 1/2 ounce diced smoked ham
1 sliced large onion
1 medium frying pepper, sliced and seeded
1 large tomato, peeled, seeded and chopped, p. 132
3/4 cup tomato sauce
4 large unpeeled garlic cloves
8 minced pitted green olives
2 teaspoons minced capers
1 bay leaf
1/4 teaspoon ground oregano
1/4 teaspoon peppercorns
1/2 cup dry red wine
3 potatoes, peeled and quartered

1. Trim off any membranes, connective tissues and fat from the meat.

2. Soak in the sour orange juice or vinegar for some 20 minutes. Drain and pat dry after rinsing. Salt.

3. Heat the oil in a *caldero* or stew pot over medium-high heat. Brown the meat a few pieces at a time. Remove and set aside as you brown.

4. Discard all but one tablespoon of the oil. Lower the heat to

medium-low and sauté the smoked ham, onion and pepper slices for 5 minutes.

5. Add the tomato, tomato sauce, garlic cloves, olives, capers, bay leaf, oregano and peppercorns. Cook for 5 minutes.

6. Return the meat to the pot, reduce the heat to low, cover and simmer gently for 1 hour.

7. Add the red wine and potatoes. Bring again to a simmer and cook for an additional hour or until the meat and potatoes are tender, and the sauce has thickened.

Serves: 6

CHAPTER IX: RICE AND BEANS . . . AND OTHER GRAINS

SIMMERED SHORT-GRAIN WHITE RICE

(Arroz blanco)

3 cups short-grain white rice
3 cups water
3 tablespoons lard or vegetable oil
1 tablespoon salt

1. Rinse the rice in cold running water until the water runs clear. Drain.

2. Bring the water to a boil in a *caldero* or appropriate heavy-bottommed pan. Add the salt and lard or vegetable oil.

3. Add the rice, stir, and lower the heat to moderate.

4. Cook uncovered until the water level reaches the surface of the rice.

5. Stir the rice from the bottom up. Reduce the heat lo low, cover and cook for 20 minutes.

6. Stir the rice again from the bottom up, mounding it.

7. Cover and cook for an additional 20 minutes or until the grains are tender. Fluff with a fork.

NOTE: For softer rice use 3 1/2 cups water.

Serves: 6

SIMMERED LONG-GRAIN WHITE RICE

(Arroz blanco de grano largo)

3 cups parboiled long-grain rice
3 1/2 cups water
3 tablespoons lard or vegetable oil
1 tablespoon salt

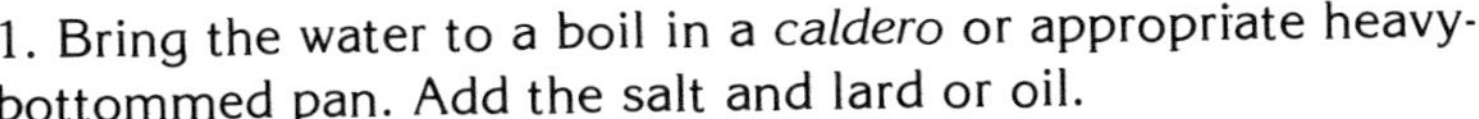

1. Bring the water to a boil in a *caldero* or appropriate heavy-bottommed pan. Add the salt and lard or oil.

2. Stir in the rice and bring back to a boil.

3. Reduce the heat to moderate and cook uncovered until the water level reaches the surface of the rice.

4. Reduce the heat to low, cover, and cook for 15 minutes.

5. Stir the rice from the bottom up, mounding it, cover and cook for 15 more minutes. Fluff with a fork.

Serves: 6

RICE WITH ONIONS AND DRY VERMOUTH

(Arroz con cebollas y vermouth seco)

3 cups long-grain parboiled rice
4 tablespoons butter
3/4 cup finely chopped onion
3 1/2 cups water
1 tablespoon salt
1/3 cup extra-dry vermouth

1. Sauté the onion in 3 tablespoons of the butter in a *caldero* or heavy pot over medium-low heat until tender but not browned —about 5 minutes.

2. Add the water and salt, raise the heat, and bring to a boil.

3. Stir in the rice and bring again to a boil.

4. Lower the heat to moderate and cook uncovered until the water level reaches the surface of the rice.

5. Reduce the heat to low, cover and cook for 10 minutes.

6. Add the vermouth and additional tablespoon of butter. Stir the rice from the bottom up.

7. Cover and cook for an additional 20 minutes. Fluff with a fork.

Serves: 6

RICE WITH OKRA

(Arroz con guingambós)

3 cups short-grain white rice
3 tablespoons annatto oil or lard, p. 47
1 ounce diced fatback
2 ounces diced cooking ham
1/2 cup uncooked condiment, p. 47
2 pressed medium garlic cloves
1 tablespoon capers minced after measuring
1/3 cup tomato sauce
3 1/2 cups water
1 tablespoon salt
1 pound fresh okra, tips and stems trimmed off, and sliced into 3/4" rings or frozen okra, defrosted

1. Sauté the fatback and cooking ham in the lard or oil in a *caldero* or heavy-bottommed pan set over medium-low heat for 5 minutes.

2. Add the uncooked condiment, garlic, capers and tomato sauce. Cook for 5 minutes.

3. Rinse the rice under running cool water until this runs clear. Drain.

4. Add the water and salt. Raise the heat and bring to a boil. Stir in the rice and bring back to a boil. Stir in the okra.

5. Reduce the heat to moderate and cook until the liquid level reaches the surface of the rice.

6. Stir the rice from the bottom up. Reduce the heat to low, cover and cook for 15 minutes.

7. Stir the rice once more, mounding it up, and cook for 15 additional minutes. Fluff with a fork.

Serves: 6-8

DORA ROMANO'S SEAFOOD RICE

(Arroz con mariscos a la Dora Romano)

2 cups short-grain white rice
1/4 cup olive oil
1 large minced onion
1 large green frying pepper, seeded and minced
3 medium-size sweet chili peppers, seeded and minced
1/2 teaspoon ground oregano
2/3 cup tomato sauce
1 pound raw lobster meat cut into medallions
1 pound raw shrimp, shelled and deveined
1 pound white-flesh fish fillets, cut into 2 1/2" square pieces
5 cups fish stock, p. 73
5 teaspoons salt
8 ounces cooked petit-pois
10 ounces cooked asparagus tips
4-ounce jar sliced roasted pimientos

1. Rinse the rice under running cold water until the water runs clear. Drain.

2. Sauté for 5 minutes the onion, pepper, sweet chili peppers and garlic in the olive oil in a *caldero* or heavy pot over medium-low heat.

3. Add the oregano and tomato sauce. Cook for 5 more minutes.

4. Raise the heat to moderate. Add the lobster, shrimp and fish. Stir fry for 2-3 minutes.

5. Add the fish stock and salt. Raise the heat and bring to a boil.

6. Stir in the rice, return the heat to moderate and cook uncovered for 10 minutes.

7. Reduce the heat to low, cover, and cook for 20 minutes, or until the rice is tender. Fluff with a fork.

8. Place in a platter and garnish with the peas, asparagus tips and pimiento slices.

Serves: 6-8

RICE WITH SALT CODFISH

(Arroz con bacalao)

3 cups short-grain white rice
1/2 pound salt-codfish fillet
3 tablespoons lard or annatto oil, p. 47
1 ounce diced fatback
2 ounces diced ham
1/2 cup uncooked condiment, p. 47
1 pressed large garlic clove
1/4 cup tomato sauce
8 pitted green olives
1 tablespoon capers minced after measuring
1 teaspoon pimenton
salt, if needed
7-ounce jar roasted pimientos, sliced
3 1/2 cups water

1. Cut the codfish fillet into 2" pieces and soak in plenty of cold water for one hour. Drain.

2. Trim off any skin and remove any bones. Shred and set aside.

3. Sauté the fatback and ham in the lard or annatto oil for 5 minutes in a *caldero* or heavy pot set over medium-low heat.

4. Add the uncooked condiment and garlic. Cook for 5 minutes.

5. Add the tomato sauce, olives, capers, pimenton, one of the sliced roasted pimientos and the codfish. Cook for 5 minutes.

6. Add the water, raise the heat, and bring to a boil. Reduce the heat and simmer covered for 10 minutes.

7. In the meantime, rinse the rice under running cool water until the water runs clear. Drain.

8. Taste the liquid for salt, adjusting to the saltiness of the codfish. Add salt by half-teaspoons if needed at all, remembering that the rice will absorb salt.

9. Add the rice, stir, and lower the heat to moderate. Cook uncovered until the liquid level reaches the surface of the rice.

10. Reduce the heat to low and cook covered for 15 minutes.

11. Stir the rice from the bottom up, mounding it, and cook covered for 15 more minutes. Fluff with a fork.

12. Place on a platter and garnish with the additional sliced roasted pimientos.

NOTE: If the salt codfish is too salty, adjust or omit the salt asked for in the recipe.

Serves: 6-8

RICE WITH SQUID

(Arroz con calamares)

3 cups short-grain white rice
1/4 cup olive oil
1/2 cup uncooked condiment, p. 47
3 pressed large garlic cloves
3 tablespoons tomato sauce
3 teaspoons salt
1/4 teaspoon ground pepper
6 tins of squid, 4 3/8 ounces each
1 diced large roasted pimiento
3 1/2 cups water

1. Sauté the uncooked condiment and garlic in the olive oil in a *caldero* or heavy pot over medium-low heat for 5 minutes.

2. Add the tomato sauce, salt and pepper and cook for 3 more minutes.

3. Add the squid and its liquid, and the pimiento. Cook, stirring, for 3 minutes.

4. Rinse the rice under running cool water until the water runs clear. Drain.

5. Add the water to the pot, raise the heat to bring to a boil.

6. Stir in the rice, reduce the heat to moderate and cook until the liquid level reaches the surface of the rice.

7. Stir the rice from the bottom up. Reduce the heat to low and cook covered for 15 minutes.

8. Stir the rice again, mounding it, and cook for 15 more minutes. Fluff with a fork.

NOTE: You may use fresh squid, cut into pieces, along with its ink. The color of the rice will be lighter, though, than that made with tinned squid. The taste will also be milder.

Serves: 6-8

RICE WITH GREAT LAND CRAB

(Arroz con jueyes)

3 cups short-grain white rice
3 tablespoons annatto oil or lard, p. 47
3/4 cup uncooked condiment, p. 47
2 pressed medium garlic cloves
1/4 cup tomato sauce
1/4 teaspoon ground oregano
3 teaspoons salt
2 cups boiled land crab meat, p. 179
3/4 cup corals and crab fat from the boiled crabs
2 3/4 cup water
2 ounces sliced roasted pimientos

1. Rinse the rice under running cool water until the water runs clear. Drain.

2. Sauté the uncooked condiment and garlic cloves in the annatto oil or lard in a *caldero* or heavy pot set over medium-low heat for 5 minutes.

3. Add the tomato sauce, oregano and salt. Cook for 5 minutes.

4. Stir in the crabmeat, corals and crab fat. Cook, stirring, for 3 minutes.

5. Add the water and raise the heat to bring to a boil.

6. Stir in the rice. Lower the heat to moderate and cook until the liquid level reaches the surface of the rice.

7. Stir the rice from the bottom up. Reduce the heat to low and cook covered for 15 minutes.

8. Stir the rice again, mounding it, and cook for 15 additional minutes.

9. Uncover and cook for 5 more minutes. Fluff with a fork.

10. Serve garnished with the slices of roasted pimientos.

Serves: 6-8

RICE WITH CHICKEN

(Arroz con pollo)

2 1/2 cups short-grain white rice
3 pounds chicken pieces
5 teaspoons salt
3 tablespoons annatto lard or oil, p.47, or olive oil
1 ounce diced fatback
2 ounces diced cooking ham
1/2 cup uncooked condiment, p. 47
1 tablespoon capers, minced after measuring
8 pitted green olives
3 pressed medium garlic cloves
1/2 cup tomato sauce
1/4 teaspoon ground oregano
3 cups water
4 - ounce jar of sliced roasted pimientos

1. Salt the chicken pieces with 2 1/2 teaspoons of the salt. Set aside.

2. Sauté the fatback and ham in the annatto lard or oil, or olive oil, in a *caldero* or heavy pot set over medium-low heat for 5 minutes.

3. Add the uncooked condiment, capers, olives and garlic. Sauté for 5 minutes.

4. Add the tomato sauce, oregano, and the remaining 2 1/2 teaspoons of salt. Cook for 5 minutes.

5. Stir in the chicken pieces, cover and cook for 10 minutes over low heat. Turn once.

6. In the meantime, rinse the rice under running cool water until this runs clear. Drain.

7. Add the water to the pot and raise the heat to bring to a boil. Stir in the rice.

8. Lower the heat to medium and cook uncovered until the liquid level reaches the surface of the rice.

9. Stir the rice from the bottom up. Cover, reduce the heat to low and cook for 15 minutes.

10. Stir again, mounding it, and cook for 15 minutes. Fluff with a fork.

11. Serve garnished with the slices of roasted pimientos.

Serves: 6

DORA ROMANO'S RICE WITH CHICKEN

(Arroz con pollo a la Dora Romano)

3 cups parboiled long-grain rice
1 1/2 pounds chicken pieces
4 1/2 teaspoons salt
1/2 pound lean pork, cut into 1/2" cubes
1/4 cup olive oil
1/2 cup uncooked condiment, p. 47
1/3 cup tomato sauce
1 pressed large garlic clove
1 large bay leaf
20 strands of saffron
1 teaspoon pimenton
4 1/2 cups chicken stock
1/3 cup extra-dry vermouth
7-ounce jar sliced roasted pimientos

1. Salt the chicken pieces with 1 1/2 teaspoons of the salt and set aside.

2. Brown the pork cubes in the olive oil in a *caldero* or heavy pot ser over medium-high heat. Do not let the oil burn. Remove the pork cubes and save.

3. Reduce the heat to medium-low and sauté the uncooked condiment for 5 minutes.

4. Add the tomato sauce, garlic, bay leaf, saffron, pimenton and the rest of the salt. Cook for 5 minutes.

5. Add the chicken pieces and pork. Cover, reduce the heat to low and cook for 10 minutes. Turn over once.

6. Add the stock and raise the heat to bring to a boil. Add the rice and stir.

7. Reduce the heat to moderate and cook uncovered until the liquid level reaches the surface of the rice.

8. Reduce the heat to low. Cover and cook for 15 minutes.

9. Add the vermouth. Stir the rice from the bottom up, mound-

ing it. Cover and cook for 20 more minutes. Fluff with a fork.

10. Serve garnished with the pimiento slices.

Serves: 6-8

MOLDED RICE STUFFED WITH CHICKEN FRICASSEE

(Arroz relleno con fricasé de pollo)

Chicken Fricasee
2 1/2 pounds boneless chicken meat, cut into 1 1/2" pieces
1 1/2 teaspoon salt
3 pressed medium garlic cloves
1/4 teaspoon ground oregano
1/8 teaspoon ground pepper
1 teaspoon olive oil
1/4 cup vegetable oil
1/2 cup uncooked condiment, p. 47
1 1/2 cup tomato sauce
6 chopped pitted green olives
1 teaspoon minced capers
1 small bay leaf
2 cups water

Rice
4 cups parboiled long-grain rice
3 tablespoons vegetable oil
1 cup chopped onion
1/2 cup tomato sauce
1 tablespoon salt
5 1/2 cups chicken stock, p. 72
1/2 cup extra-dry vermouth
3/4 cup parmesan cheese

1. Blend the 1 1/2 teaspoons salt with the garlic, oregano, pepper and teaspoon of olive oil. Rub the chicken pieces with this and let stand for at least 30 minutes.

2. Brown the chicken in the 1/4 cup vegetable oil in a *caldero*

or heavy pot over medium-high heat. Do not burn the oil. Remove the chicken and save.

3. Reduce the heat to medium-low. Add the uncooked condiment and cook for 5 minutes.

4. Add the tomato sauce, olives, capers and bay leaf. Cook for 5 more minutes.

5. Add the 1 1/2 cup water. Raise the heat to bring to a boil, then add the chicken pieces. Lower the heat, cover, and simmer for 30 minutes, or until the chicken is tender and the sauce thickens. Uncover the pot if necessary to thicken the sauce.

6. In the meantime, prepare the rice. Sauté the cup of onion in the 3 tablespoons of vegetable oil in a *caldero* or heavy pot over medium-low heat until tender but not browned —about 5 minutes.

7. Add the tomato sauce and tablespoon of salt. Cook for 5 minutes.

8. Add the chicken stock and vermouth. Raise the heat to bring to a boil.

9. Add the rice, stirring it in. Reduce the heat to moderate and cook until the liquid level reaches the surface of the rice.

10. Stir the rice from the bottom up.

11. Reduce the heat to low, cover, and cook for 15 minutes. It should not be too dry or completely cooked as it will finish cooking in the oven.

12. Preheat the oven to 350°F.

13. Grease a 13" x 9 1/2" x 2" oven-tempered glass mold.

14. Spread half of the rice on the bottom of the mold and place the chicken on top, saving half of the chicken sauce.

15. Sprinkle with half of the parmesan cheese and cover with the rest of the rice.

16. Dribble the rest of the chicken fricasee sauce over the rice and sprinkle with the rest of the cheese.

17. Bake uncovered for 20 minutes.

NOTE: You may do 3 layers of rice and 2 of chicken if you so prefer, following the above-stated sequence. You may also use any other shape of mold large enough to hold all the ingredients.

Serves: 8

PAELLA

2 cups parboiled long-grain rice
2 1/2 pounds chicken pieces
1/2 pound lean pork or veal, cut into 1" cubes
5 teaspoons salt
vegetable oil
2/3 cup olive oil
3/4 cup diced onion
1/2 cup green frying pepper, seeded and diced
1 large pressed garlic clove
2 medium tomatoes, peeled, seeded and chopped, p. 132
25 saffron threads
1 teaspoon pimenton
1/2 cup tomato sauce
4 1/2 cups warm chicken or fish stock, pp.72, 73, or a combination of them. You use the clam juice if using canned clams
1/2 pound raw shrimp, shelled and deveined
1/2 pound raw lobster medallions
12 live clams in the shell or 8 ounces canned shucked clams
1 cup fresh or defrosted green peas
6 or 8 artichoke hearts, fresh or defrosted
2 large sliced roasted pimientos
cooked asparagus tips, fresh or frozen
parsley
halved lemon slices

1. Salt the chicken with 2 1/2 teaspoons of the salt, and the pork or veal with 1/2 teaspoon. Set aside.

2. In a large skillet or *caldero* brown the chicken pieces in the vegetable oil. Remove and set aside.

3. In the same oil, brown the pork or veal. Remove and set aside.

4. Preheat the oven to 350°F.

5. Discard the vegetable oil.

6. In the same skillet or *caldero* sauté the onion, pepper and garlic in the olive oil for 5 minutes over moderate heat.

7. Add the tomato, saffron, pimenton, tomato sauce and additional salt. Cook for 5 minutes.

8. Raise the heat to medium-high. Add the rice and 1/2 cup of the stock. Cook stirring for 5 minutes.

9. Transfer this to the *paellera* or to a heavy skillet or ovenproof casserole large enough to hold all the ingredients.

10. Stir in the rest of the warm stock.

11. Add the chicken, pork or veal, and arrange the shrimp, lobster, clams and artichoke hearts and peas. Make sure the artichokes and peas are covered by the stock.

12. Cook in the oven for 40-45 minutes or until all of the liquid is absorbed.

13. Garnish with the asparagus tips, pimiento slices, parsley and lemon slices.

NOTE: If using fresh clams, you may wish to scrub them and steam in a separate container before adding to the *paellera*. Discard any that do not open and add the juice to the stock. If using frozen shrimp and lobster, defrost before cooking. You may also add slices of chorizo when you sauté the onion, pepper and garlic. Reduce the olive oil accordingly, for chorizos render fat.

Serves: 8

RICE WITH PIT-ROASTED PORK

(Arroz con lechón asado)

3 cups short-grain white rice
2 tablespoons annato oil or lard, p.47, or vegetable oil
1/3 cup uncooked condiment, p. 47
3 pressed medium garlic cloves
1/3 cup tomato sauce
1/4 teaspoon ground oregano
1 pound pit-roasted pork, cut into 1 1/2-2" cubes
3 1/2 cups water
1 tablespoon salt

1. In an appropriate *caldero* or heavy pot, sauté the uncooked condiment and garlic in the oil or lard for 5 minutes over medium-low heat.

2. Add the tomato sauce and oregano. Cook for 5 minutes.

3. Add the roast pork and stir-fry for 2-3 minutes.

4. Add the water and half of the salt. Bring to a boil, reduce the heat to low and simmer covered for 5 minutes.

5. Add more salt, if necessary, adjusting it to the saltiness of the roast pork used.

6. Rinse the rice under running cool water until this runs clear. Drain and stir into the pot.

7. Bring to a boil, reduce the heat to moderate and cook uncovered until the liquid level reaches the surface of the rice.

8. Stir the rice from the bottom up. Reduce the heat to low and cook covered for 15 minutes.

9. Stir the rice again, mounding it, and cook for 15 more minutes. Fluff with a fork.

Serves: 6-8

RICE WITH SPARERIBS

(Arroz con costillas)

3 cups short-grain white rice
2 pounds country-style or regular spareribs, divided into 2-rib sections
3 tablespoons annato oil or lard, p.47, or vegetable oil
2 ounces diced cooking ham
1/2 cup uncooked condiment, p.47
4 pressed medium garlic cloves
1/4 teaspoon ground oregano
1 tablespoon capers, minced after measuring
1/2 cup tomato sauce
4 1/4 teaspoons salt
4 cups water

1. Rinse the spareribs, pat dry and salt with 2 teaspoons salt. Let stand for 30 minutes.

2. Sauté the ham for 3 minutes in the oil or lard in a *caldero* or heavy pot set over medium-low heat.

3. Add the uncooked condiment, garlic, oregano and capers. Cook, stirring, for 5 minutes.

4. Add the tomato sauce and cook for 5 minutes.

5. Bring the heat to medium-high. Add the spareribs and stir-fry for 2-3 minutes.

6. Add the water and bring to a boil. Cover, reduce the heat to low and simmer for 40-50 minutes or until the ribs are tender.

7. Rinse the rice under running cool water until this runs clear. Drain.

8. Raise the heat to bring the liquid in the pot to a boil. Stir in the rice and the rest of the salt.

9. Reduce the heat to moderate and cook uncovered until the liquid level reaches the surface of the rice.

10. Stir the rice from the bottom up, cover, reduce the heat to low, and cook for 15 minutes.

11. Stir the rice again, mounding it, and cook for 15 additional minutes. Fluff with a fork.

Serves: 6-8

RICE WITH FATBACK

(Arroz con tocino)

3 cups short or medium-grain white rice
4 ounces fatback, diced after trimming off the rind
3 1/2 cups water
2 1/2 teaspoons salt

1. In a *caldero* or heavy pot render the fatback over moderate to medium-low heat until the pieces are crisp and golden.

2. Add the water and salt and raise the heat to bring to a boil.

3. Rinse the rice under running cool water until the water runs clear. Drain.

4. Stir the rice into the pot and bring to a boil.

5. Reduce the heat to moderate and cook uncovered until the liquid level reaches the surface of the rice.

6. Reduce the heat to low. Stir the rice from the bottom up and cook covered for 15 minutes.

7. Stir the rice again, mounding it, and cook for 15 more minutes. Fluff with a fork.

Serves: 6-8

RICE WITH VIENNA SAUSAGE

(Arroz con salchichas vienesas)

2 1/2 cups short-grain white rice
3 tablespoons annatto oil or lard, p.47, or vegetable oil
1/2 cup uncooked condiment, p. 47
2 pressed large garlic cloves
6 chopped medium pitted green olives
2 teaspoons capers, minced after measuring
1/4 cup tomato sauce
1/4 teaspoon ground oregano
2 1/2 teaspoons salt
3 cups water
3 large chopped *culantro* leaves
2 five-ounce cans of Vienna Sausage and their stock

1. Cut the sausages into three pieces each.

2. Sauté the uncooked condiment, garlic, olives and capers in the oil or lard for 5 minutes in a *caldero* or heavy pot set over medium-low heat.

3. Add the tomato sauce, oregano and salt. Cook for 5 minutes.

4. Add the water, *culantro*, sausages and their stock. Raise the heat to bring to a boil.

5. Rinse the rice under running cool water until this runs clear. Drain, add to the pot and stir.

6. Reduce the heat to moderate and cook uncovered until the liquid level reaches the surface of the rice.

7. Stir the rice from the bottom up. Reduce the heat to low and cook covered for 15 minutes.

8. Stir again, mounding it, and cook for 15 more minutes. Fluff with a fork.

Serves: 6-8

RICE WITH *LONGANIZA* SAUSAGE

(Arroz con longaniza)

2 1/2 cups short-grain white rice
2 tablespoons vegetable oil or lard
1/3 cup uncooked condiment, p.47
1 pressed large garlic clove
1/4 teaspoon ground oregano
2 1/2 teaspoons salt
1/2 pound *longaniza* sausage, removed from its casing and coarsely chopped
3 cups water

1. In a *caldero* or heavy pot, sauté the uncooked condiment and garlic in the oil or lard over medium-low heat for 5 minutes.

2. Add the oregano and salt. Cook for 5 minutes.

3. Raise the heat to medium-high, add the sausage meat, and stir-fry for 3-4 minutes.

4. Add the water and raise the heat to bring to a boil.

5. Rinse the rice under running cool water until this runs clear. Drain and add to the pot, stirring it.

6. Reduce the heat to moderate and cook uncovered until the liquid level reaches the surface of the rice.

7. Reduce the heat to low, stir the rice from the bottom up and cook covered for 15 minutes.

8. Stir the rice again, mounding it, and cook for 15 more minutes. Fluff with a fork.

Serves: 6-8

Variation:

RICE WITH *LONGANIZA* SAUSAGE AND PIGEON PEAS

(Arroz con longaniza y gandules)

Follow the recipe for Rice with *Longaniza* Sausage, but add along with the rice:

> 1 pound fresh pigeon peas, boiled in salted water until tender, p.307; frozen peas cooked following the package instructions; or one 16-ounce can of cooked pigeon peas.
>
> Use 4 cups of water instead of 3 1/2.

RICE WITH SPARERIBS AND PIGEON PEAS

(Arroz con costillas y gandules)

- 2 1/4 cups short-grain rice
- 2 tablespoons annatto oil or lard, p.47, or vegetable oil
- 2 ounces diced cooking ham
- 1/2 cup uncooked condiment, p. 47
- 2 pressed medium garlic cloves
- 1/4 cup tomato sauce
- 1/4 teaspoon ground oregano
- 1 tablespoon salt
- 1 pound country-style or regular pork spareribs, cut into 2-rib segments
- 3 cups water
- 3 large chopped *culantro* leaves
- 1 pound fresh pigeon peas, boiled in water until tender, p. 307

1. Sauté the ham in the oil or lard in a *caldero* or heavy pot for 3 minutes over medium-low heat.

2. Add the uncooked condiment and garlic. Cook for 5 minutes.

3. Add the tomato sauce, oregano and salt. Cook for 5 more minutes.

4. Raise the heat to medium-high. Add the spareribs and stir-fry for 3 minutes.

5. Add the water and *culantro*. Cover and simmer at low heat for 30-45 minutes, or until the ribs are tender.

6. Rinse the rice under running cool water until this runs clear. Drain.

7. Stir in the rice and the drained pigeon peas into the pot. Bring to a boil.

8. Reduce the heat to moderate and cook uncovered until the liquid level reaches the surface of the rice.

9. Reduce the heat to low, stir the rice from the bottom up and cook covered for 15 minutes.

10. Stir the rice again, mounding it, and cook for 15 more minutes. Fluff with a fork.

NOTE: You may use frozen pigeon peas, cooked according to the package instructions, or canned cooked peas.

Serves: 6-8

RICE WITH *PASTELES* FLAVOR

(Arroz apastelado)

3 cups short-grain white rice
3 tablespoons annatto oil or lard, p. 47
1 1/2 pound pork meat—fresh ham, butt end, or Boston shoulder —cut into 2" cubes
1/3 cup uncooked condiment, p. 47
2 pressed medium garlic cloves
2 large sweet chili peppers, seeded and minced
1 tablespoon capers, minced after measuring
12 small pimiento-stuffed olives
1/2 cup tomato sauce
1/4 teaspoon ground oregano
1 tablespoon chopped *culantro* leaves
4 teaspoons salt

3 1/2 cups water
1/2 cup grated green plantain, p.91, mixed with 1 cup of water or with one cup of the liquid from the boiled chick peas
2 cups chick peas, boiled in salted water until tender, p.305, or one 20-ounce can of cooked chick peas, drained
1 piece banana leaf, p.141, about the diameter of the cooking pot

1. In a *caldero* or heavy pot brown lightly the pork in the oil or lard over medium-high heat. Remove, season with 1 1/2 teaspoons of the salt and set aside.

2. Reduce the heat to medium-low and cook the uncooked condiment, garlic, sweet chili peppers, capers and olives for 5 minutes.

3. Add the tomato sauce, oregano, *culantro*, and cook for 5 minutes.

4. Return the meat to the pot. Add the 3 1/2 cups water, and raise the heat to bring to a boil. Cover, reduce the heat to low and simmer 30-45 minutes, or until the meat is tender.

5. Rinse the rice under running cool water until the water runs clear. Drain.

6. Bring the liquid back to a boil. Stir in the chick peas, the grated plantain with its liquid, and the rest of the salt. Bring to a boil.

7. Stir in the rice. Reduce the heat to moderate and cook until the liquid level reaches the surface of the rice.

8. Stir the rice from the bottom up. Lay the banana leaf over it. Cover and cook at medium-low heat for 15 minutes.

9. Stir the rice once more. Lay the leaf on top of it again. Cook covered for 10 more minutes.

10. Remove the leaf and cook uncovered for 5 more minutes. Fluff with a fork.

NOTES: This rice is less fluffy than usual due to the grated plantain. After peeling the green plantain, cut it into 4 pieces and place it in salted water for 10 minutes. Drain and grate. If you cooked dried chick peas, you may use their boiling liquid instead of the 3 1/2 cups of water to cook the meat.

Serves: 6-8

CONGRI

(Congrí)

- 2 cups white rice
- 3 bacon slices cut into 8 pieces each
- 1/4 pound pork meat —fresh ham or Boston shoulder— cut into 3/4" cubes
- 2 ounces diced cooking ham
- 1/2 cup uncooked condiment, p. 47
- 2 pressed large garlic cloves
- 1/4 cup tomato sauce
- 1 tablespoon minced *culantro* leaves
- 1 small bay leaf
- 1/4 teaspoon ground oregano
- 3/4 teaspoon ground cumin
- 2 1/2 teaspoons salt
- 1/2 pound boiled dried black beans, p.305, or one 16-ounce can of boiled beans
- 3 cups liquid from the boiled beans, sediment drained out, or water

1. In a *caldero* or heavy pot fry the bacon pieces until crisp. Remove and save.

2. Brown the pork cubes in the bacon fat. Adjust the heat so that the fat does not burn. Remove the pork and set aside.

3. Reduce the heat to medium-low. Cook the ham, uncooked condiment and garlic for 5 minutes.

4. Add the tomato sauce, *culantro*, bay leaf, oregano, cumin and salt. Cook for 5 minutes.

5. Raise the heat to moderate. Add the beans and stir-cook for 3 minutes.

6. Add the liquid and pork cubes. Raise the heat to bring to a boil.

7. Rinse the rice under running cool water if using short-grain rice until the water runs clear. Drain.

8. Stir the rice into the pot. Lower the heat to moderate and cook uncovered until the liquid level reaches the surface of the rice.

9. Stir the rice from the bottom up. Reduce the heat to low and cook covered for 15 minutes.

10. Stir the rice again, mounding it, and cook for 15 more minutes.

11. Crumble the bacon and stir into the rice before serving. Fluff with a fork.

Serves: 6-8

RICE WITH TASAJO

(Arroz con tasajo)

- 3 cups white-short grain rice
- 3 tablespoons annatto oil or lard, p. 47
- 1 ounce diced fatback
- 2 ounces diced cooking ham
- 1/2 cup uncooked condiment, p. 47
- 1 pressed large garlic clove
- 1 tablespoon capers, minced after measuring
- 1/4 cup tomato sauce
- 2 teaspoons salt
- 1 pound jerked beef —tasajo— reconstituted and shredded, p. 239
- 3 1/2 cups water or the liquid from the reconstitution of the beef, if not too salty

1. In a *caldero* or heavy pot, sauté the fatback and ham for 3-4 minutes in the oil or lard over medium-low heat.

2. Add the uncooked condiment, garlic, and capers. Cook for 5 minutes.

3. Add the tomato sauce and beef. Cook for 5 minutes.

4. Add the liquid and raise the heat to bring to a boil. Taste. Add just enough salt to make the liquid taste slightly briny —approximately 1-2 teaspoons, depending on the saltiness of the beef.

5. Rinse the rice under running cool water until this runs clear. Drain.

6. Stir the rice into the liquid, reduce the heat to moderate and cook uncovered until the liquid level reaches the surface of the rice.

7. Stir the rice from the bottom up and cook covered over low heat for 15 minutes.

8. Stir the rice again, mounding it, and cook for 15 more minutes. Fluff with a fork.

Serves: 6-8

SHRIMP *ASOPAO*

(Asopao de camarones)

1 1/2 cup short-grain white rice
3 tablespoons olive oil
1/2 cup uncooked condiment, p. 47
2 pressed medium garlic cloves
1/2 cup tomato sauce
1/4 teaspoon ground oregano
1/8 teaspoon ground pepper
4 teaspoons salt
2 pounds medium or large raw shrimp, shelled and deveined, or defrosted frozen shrimp
8 cups fish stock, p. 73
7-ounce jar roasted pimientos, sliced
10 ounces asparagus tips, freshly cooked, frozen or canned

1. Sauté the uncooked condiment and garlic for 5 minutes in the olive oil in a *caldero* or heavy pot over medium-low heat.

2. Add the tomato sauce, oregano, pepper, salt and the slices from two of the roasted pimientos. Cook for 5 minutes.

3. In the meantime, rinse the rice under running cool water until this runs clear. Drain.

4. Add the shrimp to the pot and stir-fry for 1 minute.

5. Add the fish stock and raise the heat to bring to a boil.

6. Stir in the rice.

7. Reduce the heat to moderate and cook uncovered for 25-30 minutes, stirring occasionally, until the rice is tender and the *asopao* is as liquid or as thick as you like it.

8. Garnish with the rest of the pimientos and the asparagus tips.

NOTE: *Asopao*, as it name implies should not be as liquid as a soup, nor as dry as cooked rice, it is actually a "soupy" rice.

Serves: 6

Variation:

LOBSTER *ASOPAO*

(Asopao de langosta)

Follow the instructions for the Shrimp *Asopao*, but substitute for the shrimp:

2 pounds raw fresh or defrosted lobster meat cut into medallions or cubes.

Serves: 6

CHICKEN *ASOPAO*

(Asopao de pollo)

1 1/2 cup short-grain white rice
4 1/2 teaspoons salt
3 pressed medium garlic cloves
1/4 teaspoon oregano
1/8 teaspoon ground pepper
2 teaspoons olive oil
2 1/2 pounds chicken pieces
2 tablespoons annatto oil or lard, p.47, or vegetable oil
1 ounce diced fatback
2 ounces diced cooking ham
1/2 cup uncooked condiment, p. 47
2 large sweet chili peppers, seeded and minced
1/2 cup tomato sauce
6 large *culantro* leaves
8 cups water or chicken stock, p. 72
8 ounces defrosted frozen sweet peas
4-ounce jar sliced roasted pimientos
10 ounces asparagus tips, freshly cooked, frozen or canned

1. Rub the chicken pieces with 2 1/2 teaspoons of the salt and then with the garlic, oregano, pepper and olive oil. Let stand for at least 30 minutes.

2. In a *caldero* or heavy pot, sauté the fatback and ham in the annatto oil or lard for 3 minutes over medium-low heat.

3. Add the uncooked condiment and sweet chili peppers. Cook for 5 minutes.

4. Add the tomato sauce, *culantro* and the rest of the salt. Cook for 5 more minutes.

5. Add the chicken pieces, and cook turning once, for 3-4 minutes over moderate heat.

6. Add the chicken stock or water to the pot and raise the heat to bring to a boil. Cover, reduce the heat and simmer for 10-15 minutes.

7. Rinse the rice under running cool water until this runs clear. Drain.

8. Stir the rice into the pot. Raise the heat to bring again to a boil, then reduce to moderate. Cook uncovered for 20 minutes, stirring occasionally.

9. Add the peas and cook for 5-10 minutes until the rice is tender and the *asopao* as liquid or as dry as you prefer.

10. Garnish with the sliced pimientos and asparagus tips.

NOTE: *Asopao*, as the name implies is a "soupy rice", neither as runny as a soup, nor as dry as cooked rice.

Serves: 6

PORK AND PIGEON PEAS *ASOPAO*

(Asopao de cerdo y gandules)

3/4 cup short-grain white rice
2 tablespoons annatto oil or lard, p. 47, or vegetable oil
1/2 cup uncooked condiment, p. 47
2 pressed large garlic cloves
2 large sweet chili peppers, seeded and minced
1/2 cup tomato sauce
6 large *culantro* leaves
1/4 teaspoon ground oregano
1/8 teaspoon ground pepper
3 teaspoons salt
1 1/2 pound pork meat —fresh ham or Boston shoulder— cut into 1 1/2" cubes
5 cups of water or a mixture of water and the boiling liquid from the pigeon peas
3/4 pound boiled fresh pigeon peas, p. 307, frozen and boiled according to the package instructions, or canned and drained

1. In a *caldero* or heavy pot set over medium-low heat, sauté for 5 minutes the uncooked condiment, garlic, and sweet chili peppers in the oil or lard.

2. Add the tomato sauce, *culantro*, oregano, pepper and salt. Cook for 5 minutes.

3. Raise the heat to moderate. Add the pork and stir-fry for 3-4 minutes.

4. Add the liquid and raise the heat to bring to a boil. Cover, reduce the heat to low, and simmer for 45-50 minutes or until the meat is tender. (If you are using frozen pigeon peas, you may add them at some point during this time, instead of cooking them separately. For the timing consult the package instructions.)

5. Rinse the rice under running cool water until this runs clear.

6. Drain the rice and stir into the pot with the pigeon peas. Raise the heat to bring again to a boil.

7. Reduce the heat to moderate and cook uncovered for 25-30 minutes or until the rice is tender and the *asopao* as liquid or as dry as you prefer it.

NOTE: *Asopao* means literally "soupy rice". It should be neither as dry as cooked rice, nor as runny as soup.

Serves: 6

BOILED DRIED BEANS AND PEAS

(Habichuelas y guisantes secos hervidos)

1/2 pound dried beans or peas
2 quarts water for soaking
2 quarts water for boiling

1. Spread the beans or peas on a flat surface and pick out any foreign matter or damaged specimens.

2. To rehydrate the beans or peas, soak overnight in 2 quarts of water —but no less than 8 hours— or bring the beans or peas to a boil in 2 quarts of water, boil for 2 minutes, remove from the heat and soak covered for one hour.

3. Discard the soaking water and any floating specimens or skins.

4. Bring the beans or peas to a boil in 2 quarts of fresh water. Boil for 10 minutes, skimming off the scum that rises to the surface.

5. Cover the pot, reduce the heat to low and simmer until tender. Start testing for tenderness after the first half hour as they vary. Test by squeezing a bean or pea between two fingers.

NOTE: You may add aromatics to the boiling liquid, such as a quartered onion, two quartered and seeded sweet chili peppers and 4 *culantro* leaves. This is particularly good if you plan to eat the beans or peas either plainly boiled or dressed as salad.

Serves: 6

TIMING TABLE FOR BOILING DRIED BEANS AND PEAS
(Tabla de tiempo de cocción de habichuelas y guisantes secos)

Black beans	1	-	1 1/2 hours
Black-eyed peas	1/2	-	1
Chick peas	1	-	2
Lima beans	1/2	-	1
Navy beans	1	-	1 1/2
Pigeon peas	1 1/2	-	2
Pink beans	1 1/2	-	2
Pinto beans	1 1/2	-	2
Red kidney beans	1	-	2

BOILED FRESH BEANS AND PEAS

(Habichuelas y guisantes frescos hervidos)

1/2 pound fresh beans or peas
2 quarts water

1. Spread the beans or peas on a flat surface and pick out any foreign matter or damaged specimens.

2. In the case of pigeon peas *only*, soak for 20 minutes in 3 cups of water and 1 1/2 teaspoon salt to eliminate any bitter taste. Drain. Other beans and peas do not need this treatment.

3. Bring the beans or peas to a boil in the 2 quarts of water and skim off the scum or any specimens that rise to the surface.

4. Boil for 10 minutes, then lower the heat and simmer covered until tender. Start testing for tenderness after the first 15 minutes, as these take less time to cook than dried beans or peas. Test by squeezing a specimen between two fingers. Do not overcook.

NOTE: You may add aromatics, such as quartered onions, sweet chili peppers, seeded and quartered, or *culantro* leaves. This is especially good if you plan to eat the beans or peas either in salad, or plainly boiled.

Serves: 6

STEWED BEANS OR PEAS

(Habichuelas o guisantes guisados)

1/2 pound dried or fresh beans or peas in their boiling liquid, pp.306, 307 —see note
1 1/2 tablespoons annatto oil or lard, p.47, or vegetable oil
2 ounces diced cooking ham
4 tablespoons uncooked condiment, p. 47
1 pressed medium garlic clove
1 large sweet chili pepper, seeded and minced
4 tablespoons tomato sauce
1/8 teaspoon ground oregano
4 chopped *culantro* leaves
1 teaspoon salt
1/4 pound pumpkin, peeled, seeded and cut into 1 1/2" cubes or half a ripe medium plantain, peeled and cut into 1" rings

1. In a small skillet set over medium-low heat, sauté the ham in the annatto lard or oil for 2-3 minutes.

2. Add the uncooked condiment, garlic and sweet chili pepper. Cook for 5 minutes.

3. Add the tomato sauce, oregano, *culantro* and salt. Cook for 5 minutes. This sauce is called the *sofrito.*

4. Add to the beans or peas in their boiling pot, but leave only enough of their boiling liquid to cover them by at least one inch —about 1 3/4 cup.

5. Bring to a boil.

6. Stir in the pumpkin or plantain.

7. Lower the heat and simmer with the pot lid slightly ajar until the sauce thickens to taste, about 15-20 minutes. The sauce should neither be too runny or too thick.

8. Serve to accompany simmered white rice, pp. 277-278. The persons at table serve themselves of the rice and either top it with the beans or put them next to it in about equal proportions —though this varies with personal taste.

NOTES: This recipe is appropriate for black-eyed peas, lima beans, navy beans, pink and pinto beans and red kidney beans. Recipes for black beans, chick peas and pigeon peas are found in following pages.

You may use frozen or canned beans or peas. In the case of frozen, boil according to the package instructions; in the case of canned, just rinse and add enough water to cover them by at least 1 inch.

Serves: 6

STEWED BLACK BEANS

(Habichuelas negras guisadas)

1/2 pound dried black beans in their boiling water, p. 305
1/4 cup olive oil
1/2 cup finely chopped onion
1 large frying green pepper, seeded and quartered lengthwise
1 pressed garlic clove
2 large sweet chili peppers, seeded and minced
1/8 teaspoon ground oregano
1 small bay leaf
1 1/4 teaspoon salt
1/4 teaspon cumin
1/4 teaspoon sugar
1 teaspoon vinegar

1. In a small skillet set over low heat, cook the onion, green pepper, garlic, sweet chili peppers, oregano, bay leaf, salt, cumin and sugar in the olive oil for 5-10 minutes.

2. Add to the beans, but first leave only enough liquid to cover by at least one inch —about 1 3/4 cup of the boiling liquid. Bring to a boil and add the vinegar.

3. Reduce the heat and simmer with the pot lid slightly ajar for 15-20 minutes, or until the sauce thickens to taste, yet, neither too runny, nor too thick. If it is too runny, mash 1/2 cup of the beans and stir into it.

4. Serve with simmered white rice, pp.

Serves: 6

STEWED CHICK PEAS

(Garbanzos guisados)

1/2 pound chick peas in their boiling water, p. 305
1 1/2 tablespoons annatto oil or lard, p.47, or vegetable oil
2 ounces diced cooking ham
4 tablespoons uncooked condiment, p. 47
1 pressed medium garlic clove
4 tablespoons tomato sauce
1 1/4 teaspoon salt
1/4 pound pumpkin, peeled and seeded, and cut into 1 1/2" cubes
2 ounces green cabbage, cut into 2" pieces

1. In a small skillet set over medium-low heat, cook the ham, uncooked condiment and garlic in the oil or lard for 5 minutes.

2. Add the tomato sauce and salt. Cook for 5 more minutes.

3. Add to the chick peas, but leave enough of their boiling liquid to cover by at least 1"—1 3/4 cup. Bring to a boil.

4. Stir in the pumpkin and cabbage.

5. Reduce the heat and simmer with the pot lid slightly ajar until the sauce thickens to taste. This recipe has a thicker sauce than that of stewed beans.

6. Serve with simmered white rice, pp. 277-278

NOTE: You may use 2 one-pound cans of boiled chick peas, rinsed and drained. On step 3, instead of the 1 3/4 cup of water just add enough to cover them by one inch.

Serves: 6

STEWED FRESH PIGEON PEAS

(Gandules verdes guisados)

1/2 pound fresh pigeon peas in their boiling water, p. 307
1 small green plantain or 2 green bananas, peeled and cut into 4 segments, and boiled until tender, p.91
1 tablespoons annatto oil or lard, p.47, or vegetable oil
2 ounces diced cooking ham
4 tablespoons uncooked condiment, p. 47
1 pressed medium garlic clove
3 tablespoons tomato sauce
1/8 teaspoon ground oregano
1 teaspoon salt

1. Puree the boiled green plantain or bananas in a food processor or pound in a mortar. Make balls 1 - 1 1/2" diameter and set apart.

2. In a small skillet set over medium-low heat, cook the ham in the lard or oil for 3-4 minutes.

3. Add the uncooked condiment and garlic. Cook for 5 minutes.

4. Add the tomato sauce, oregano and salt. Cook for 5 more minutes.

5. Add to the pigeon peas, but first leave about 1" of their boiling liquid to cover —1 3/4 cup. Bring to a boil.

6. Add the plantain or banana balls.

7. Reduce the heat and simmer with the pot lid slightly ajar until the sauce thickens to taste, neither too runny, nor too thick.

NOTE: You may use 2 one-pound cans boiled pigeon peas, rinsed and drained. On step 5, instead of the 1 3/4 cup of water just add enough to cover the peas by one inch.

Serves: 6

Variation:

STEWED DRIED PIGEON PEAS

(Gandules secos guisados)

Follow the recipe for Stewed Pigeon Peas, but boil following the Boiled Dried Beans and Peas recipe, p. 305

Serves: 6

CHICK PEAS WITH CHORIZOS

(Garbanzos con chorizos)

1/2 pound boiled dried chick peas, p. 305
2 tablespoons olive oil
2 medium chorizos, sliced 1/4" thick
1/4 cup uncooked condiment, p. 47
1 pressed medium garlic clove
3 tablespoons tomato sauce
4-ounce jar roasted pimientos, sliced into strips
3/4 teaspoon salt
1 1/2 cup water from the boiling of the chick peas
liquid from the roasted pimientos

1. In a *caldero* or heavy pot set over low heat, cook the chorizos in the olive oil for 5 minutes. Remove and save.

2. Add the uncooked condiment and cook for 5 minutes.

3. Add the garlic, tomato sauce, one of the sliced roasted pimientos and the salt. Cook for 5 minutes.

4. Add the water and the liquid from the pimientos. Bring to a boil.

5. Stir in the chick peas and sausage.

6. Reduce the heat and simmer with the pot lid slightly ajar for 20 minutes or until the sauce thickens to taste. Stir once or twice.

7. Garnish with the additional slices of the roasted pimientos.

NOTES: You may use 2 one-pound cans of boiled chick peas, rinsed and drained. If using canned chorizos remove their covering fat.

Serves: 6

FRIED CHICK PEAS WITH BACON

(Garbanzos fritos con tocineta)

1/2 pound boiled dried peas, p.305, or 2 one-pound cans boiled chick peas, rinsed, drained and dried
12 slices of bacon, cut into 6-8 pieces each

1. Fry the bacon over moderate heat until crisp. Remove and save.

2. Strain the bacon fat into a *caldero* or chicken fryer and add enough lard or vegetable oil to have a 1" deep layer.

3. Heat over moderate heat until a haze starts to form on its surface.

4. Add the chick peas and fry, stirring occasionally, until golden brown.

5. Remove with a slotted spoon or skimmer and drain on paper towels.

6. Toss with the bacon pieces and serve warm. Salt to taste.

NOTE: These may be used in salad instead of croutons.

Serves: 6

Variation:

FRIED PIGEON PEAS WITH BACON

(Gandules fritos con tocineta)

Follow the recipe for Fried Chick Peas With Bacon, but substitute for the chick peas:

1/2 pound boiled fresh pigeon peas, p.307, drained and dried on paper towels, or 2 one-pound cans of boiled pigeon peas, rinsed, drained and dried.

PICKLED NAVY BEANS

(Habichuelas blancas en escabeche)

1/2 pound dried or fresh boiled navy beans, pp. 305, 307 drained
1/3 cup olive oil
1 thinly sliced medium onion
2 medium garlic cloves, halved lengthwise
1 small bay leaf
4 peppercorns
1 teaspoon salt
3 tablespoons vinegar

1. Cook the onion and garlic in the olive oil over very low heat, until the onion is transparent. Do not brown.

2. Add the bay leaf, peppercorns, salt and vinegar. Cook for 10 minutes.

3. Let cool and mix well with the beans.

Serves: 6

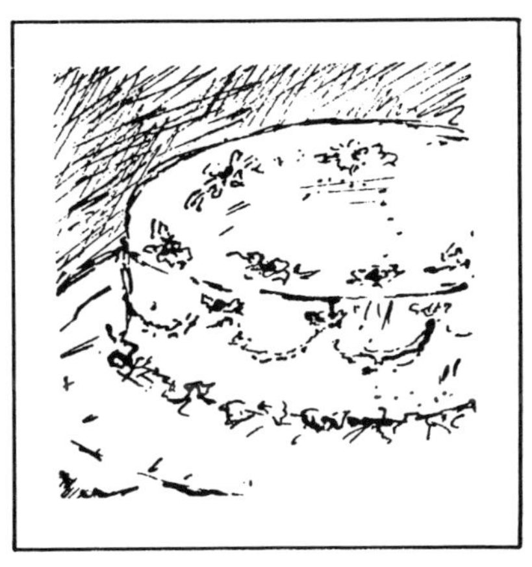

CHAPTER X: CAKES, PIES, BEIGNETS AND TURNOVERS

POUND CAKE

(Ponqué)

1/2 pound butter
1 1/3 cup sugar
1 teaspoon vanilla extract
1/8 teaspoon ground mace (optional)
6 large eggs —separate two, save the whites for the frosting
2 cups sifted cake flour
2 teaspoons baking powder
1/4 teaspoon salt
1/2 cup milk
cake mold —either a 10" x 3" tube, or a 10 1/2" x 2" tubeless round mold
butter
flour

1. Bring all the ingredients to room temperature.

2. Butter the inside of the mold with about 1 1/2 teaspoons butter and dust well with flour. Shake off any excess.

3. Beat together the sugar and 1/2 pound butter until smooth and pale in color —about 20 minutes by hand, much less by machine.

4. Add the vanilla and optional mace.

5. Add the 2 yolks from the separated eggs. Mix well.

6. Beat in the additional 4 whole eggs one by one.

7. Preheat the oven to 325°F.

8. Sift together the flour, baking powder and salt.

9. Add to the butter mixture, alternating with the milk, mixing well each time. Start and end with flour.

10. Pour into the mold and bake 50-60 minutes or until done —that is, when the surface is springy to the touch, the cake sides shrink from the pan or a cake tester inserted slightly off the center of the cake comes out clean.

11. Let cool in the mold for 5 minutes.

12. Turn over onto a wire rack and let cool before icing with Meringue Icing, V. below or your favorite one.

NOTE: For a lighter cake you may separate all the eggs, beat the whites until they form soft peaks and fold them in after step 9.

Yield: 20 slices

MERINGUE ICING

(Azucarado de merengue)

3/4 cup water
1 1/2 cup sugar
2 egg whites from large eggs —2 ounces of whites
1/4 teaspoon cream of tartar
1/2 teaspoon vanilla extract or 1 teaspoon almond extract
5 drops food color for a light pastel shade (optional)

1. Dissolve the sugar in the water and bring to a boil in a saucepan set with a candy thermometer.

2. Lower the heat to medium and boil without stirring. Clean

the sides of the pan occasionally with a moist pastry brush to prevent the formation of sugar crystals.

3. When the thermometer reaches 230°F, after some 15 minutes, add the vanilla or almond extract.

4. Continue boiling until the temperature reaches 240°F —softball stage.

5. In the meantime, beat the whites with the cream of tartar and the optional food color until they form stiff peaks.

6. When the syrup is ready, dribble into the egg whites beating continuously until you reach the desired consistency —about 5-10 minutes.

7. Ice the cake immediately as this icing hardens very fast.

NOTE: To make a different quantity, use the following proportions: 3/4 cup of sugar and 6 tablespoons of water per ounce of egg white.

Yield: sufficient for a 10" x 3" round cake.

SPONGE ROLL

(Brazo gitano)

4 large eggs
1 cup sugar
1/2 teaspoon grated acid lime rind
3 tablespoons cold water
1/2 teaspoon lemon juice
1/2 cup sifted all-purpose flour
1/2 cup sifted cornstarch
1 teaspoon double-action baking powder
1/4 teaspoon salt
jelly-roll pan —10 1/2" x 15 1/2" x 1/2"
butter
wax paper
1/4 cup confectioner's sugar
kitchen towel (non-terry cloth)
Pastry cream, p. 321, or jelly

1. Bring all the ingredients to room temperature, except the pastry cream or jelly.

2. Butter the mold and line with wax paper leaving a 1/2" overhang at each end. Butter lightly the paper.

3. Preheat the oven to 350°F.

4. Separate the egg whites from the yolks.

5. Beat the yolks, 1/2 cup of the sugar and the lime rind until the mixture is thick and pale in color.

6. Add the water and lemon juice. Blend well and set apart.

7. Beat the egg whites only until they form soft peaks. Gradually add the additional 1/2 cup sugar and beat until stiff and glossy. Fold into the yolks.

8. Sift together the sifted flour and cornstarch, baking powder and salt. Fold gradually into the eggs until well blended.

9. Spread the mixture in the pan and bake 12-15 minutes or until just done. Do not overbake, otherwise the cake will crack when rolling.

10. Dust the kitchen towel or wax paper with part of the confectioner's sugar.

11. Separate the edges of the cake from the pan with a knife and turn over onto the towel. Remove the pan and strip off carefully the lining wax paper. Cut off with a bread knife any hard edges of the cake.

12. Roll up the cake lengthwise in the towel and let cool on a wire rack for 25 minutes.

13. Unroll carefully and spread with the pastry cream or jelly almost to the edges.

14. Roll again without the towel, pressing lightly as you go.

15. Wrap in wax paper for 20 minutes or until it seals.

16. Unwrap and place in a serving platter. Dust with the additional confectioner's sugar.

17. Slice with a bread or cake knife.

NOTE: If you are using pastry cream and are not serving immediately, refrigerate covered with plastic wrap.

Yield: 14-16 slices

PASTRY CREAM

(Crema repostera)

2 cups milk
2 egg yolks
4 tablespoons cornstarch
6 tablespoons sugar
1/4 teaspoon salt
1/2 teaspoon acid lime rind or 1 teaspoon vanilla extract

1. Dissolve the cornstarch in 1/2 cup of the milk, add the egg yolks and mix well.

2. Add to the rest of the milk, sugar, salt and rind (if using this), in a heavy-bottomed saucepan.

3. Set over medium to medium-high heat and cook, stirring constantly, until it thickens —from 10 to 15 minutes.

4. Remove from the heat, add the vanilla extract (if using this), and beat for 5 minutes to cool slightly.

5. Cover with a thin film of cold milk to prevent crusting. Refrigerate once cool until ready to use. Pour out the film of milk before using.

Yield: 2 1/4 cups

SPONGE CAKE

(Bizcocho esponjoso)

6 large eggs —separate yolks from whites
1 cup sugar
1/2 teaspoon grated acid lime rind
1 tablespoon lemon juice
3 tablespoons cold water
1 cup sifted all-purpose flour
1 teaspoon double-action baking powder
1/4 teaspoon salt
cake mold, 9" x 9" x 2"
wax paper, 12" x 12" sheet
butter

1. Bring all the ingredients to room temperature.

2. Butter the pan.

3. Cut 2" squares off the corners of the wax paper sheet. Use the resultant cross-shaped paper to line the mold. Butter lightly.

4. Preheat the oven to 325°F.

5. Beat the egg yolks, 1/2 cup of the sugar, and the lime rind until smooth and pale in color.

6. Blend in the lemon juice and water. Set apart.

7. Beat the egg whites until they form soft peaks. Add the rest of the sugar gradually while beating, until the whites form stiff, glossy peaks. Set apart.

8. Sift together the flour, baking powder and salt. Fold into the egg yolk mixture.

9. Fold in the egg whites mixing well.

10. Pour the batter into the mold and bake for 45 minutes or until done —that is, when the surface is springy to the touch and a cake tester inserted slightly off the center comes out clean.

11. Let cool in the mold for 5 minutes.

12. Turn over onto a wire rack, remove the paper carefully and let cool.

Yield: one 9" x 9" x 2" cake.

DRUNKEN SOUP

(Sopa borracha)

1 sponge cake, 9" x 9" x 2", p. 322
2 1/2 cups sugar
2 cups water
1 cup Muscat wine or cream sherry
2 large egg whites
4 tablespoons additional sugar
1/2 teaspoon lemon juice
multi-colored décors (non-pareils)

1. Dissolve the 2 1/2 cups sugar in the water and bring to a boil in a saucepan set with a candy thermometer.

2. Lower the heat to medium and cook until the temperature reaches 228°F —thread stage, about 30-40 minutes.

3. Remove from the heat and let cool. Add the wine and mix well.

4. Cut the cake into 16 two-inch cubes. Place in a serving platter and soak with the syrup-wine mixture.

5. Beat the whites with the lemon juice until they form soft peaks, add the 4 tablespoons additional sugar and beat until it reaches a stiff meringue consistency.

6. Cover the tops of the cake pieces with the meringue and sprinkle with the décors.

7. Refrigerate before serving.

Yield: 16 servings

COCONUT SAUCE FOR CAKES

(Bienmesabe)

2 cups coconut milk, pp. 26, 416
2 cups sugar
1 cup water
4 large egg yolks
1/16 teaspoon salt

1. Bring the water and sugar to a boil, stirring until you dissolve the sugar.

2. Reduce the heat to medium low and cook for 8-10 minutes or until you get a light syrup —222°F on a candy thermometer.

3. Put the syrup in a larger saucepan and let cool completely.

4. Beat the egg yolks lightly with the salt and beat in the coconut milk. Strain into the cool syrup and mix well.

5. Bring slowly to a boil, stirring all the time.

6. Remove from the heat as soon as it comes to a boil. Let cool before refrigerating in a covered container.

7. Serve over sponge cake, p. 322, lady fingers, or any mild tasting cake.

Yield: about a quart, 12-16 servings

PIE CRUST

(Corteza para pasteles)

3 cups all-purpose flour
1 teaspoon salt
1 cup cold vegetable shortening
1/2 cup cold water

1. Sift the flour and salt into a bowl.

2. Using two knives in a criss-cross motion, or a pastry blender,

chop the shortening into the flour until you get pea size particles.

3. Start sprinkling with the water by tablespoons while working it up with a fork until it all sticks together.

4. Form a ball and chill for an hour before rolling it out.

5. Divide the dough in half and roll into a 12" x 1/8" circle on a flour-dusted wax paper sheet.

6. Roll onto the rolling pin and unroll onto the bottom of a 9" pie pan. Fit well and cut off any excess.

7. Roll out the other half of the dough into the same dimensions as the first one and set aside.

8. Put the filling in the crust on the pie pan and cover with the top crust by rolling it on the pin and rolling it out over the filling.

9. Moisten the edge of the lower crust and crimp both edges with the tines of a fork. Cut any excess of the top crust.

10. Cut 6 slits on the top crust in a ray pattern to allow vapor to escape.

11. Moisten the edges of the crust with water and brush the top with milk with a pastry brush.

12. Bake according to your recipe.

Yield: 1 double pie crust

PRUNE PIE

(Pastel de ciruelas secas)

1 pound pitted prunes
1 1/4 cup water
1 cup sugar
2 medium cinnamon sticks
2 teaspoons lemon juice
3 tablespoons rum
1 double pie crust, p. 324

1. Bring the prunes, water, sugar and cinnamon to a boil.

2. Lower the heat to medium and cook uncovered for 20 minutes or until the temperature reaches 220°F on a candy thermometer —slightly below thread stage.

3. Remove from the heat and add the lemon juice. Let cool.

4. Drain the prunes and chop coarsely. Add 5 tablespoons of the syrup and the rum. Mix well.

5. Fill and cover the pie following steps 6 thru 11 on p. 325

6. Bake in a preheated 425°F oven for 35 minutes or until golden brown.

NOTE: You may use commercial frozen pie crusts. Follow the package instructions.

Yield: one 9" pie

PINEAPPLE PIE

(Pastel de piña)

2 one-pound cans pineapple tidbits or crushed pineapple
1 1/4 cup sugar
2 tablespoons butter
3 tablespoons rum
1 double pie crust, p. 324

1. Cook the pineapple and sugar uncovered over moderate heat for some 45 minutes, or until the temperature reaches 220°F on a candy thermometer —slightly below thread stage.

2. Remove from the heat, blend in the butter and rum and let cool.

3. Fill and cover the pie following steps 6 thru 11 on p.325, and bake in a preheat 425°F oven for 35 minutes or until golden brown.

NOTE: You may use commercial frozen pie crusts. Follow the package instructions.

Yield: one 9" pie

APPLE PIE

(Pastel de manzanas)

6 medium tart apples
2/3 cup sugar
1 tablespoon flour
1/2 teaspoon ground cinnamon
2 tablespoons butter
3 tablespoons rum
1 double pie crust, p. 324

1. Peel, quarter and core the apples. Slice lengthwise 1/4" thick.

2. Mix the sugar, flour and cinnamon.

3. Lay half of the apple slices in the bottom crust and sprinkle with half of the sugar, flour, cinnamon and rum. Dot with butter pieces.

4. Lay the rest of the slices on top and sprinkle with the rest of the sugar, flour, cinnamon, rum and butter.

5. Cover with the top crust.

6. Cut 6 slits on the crust in a ray pattern to allow vapor to escape.

7. Bake in a preheated 450°F oven for 15 minutes.

8. Lower the heat to 350°F and bake for 35 additional minutes.

9. Serve warm or cold.

NOTE: You may use commercial frozen pie crusts. Follow package instructions for temperature and timing.

Yield: one 9" pie

BEIGNETS

(Buñuelos de viento)

1 cup water
1 teaspoon sugar
2 tablespoons butter
1/4 teaspoon salt
1 cup all-purpose flour
2 large eggs
vegetable shortening

1. Bring to a boil the water, sugar, butter and salt in a saucepan large enough to hold all the ingredients.

2. Remove from the heat and beat in the flour until well blended —about 5 minutes.

3. Add the whole eggs one at a time, beating them in well.

4. Continue beating until the batter holds together.

5. Deep fry by teaspoonfuls in the vegetable shortening over medium-high heat until golden. Do not crowd in the pan as they swell up when frying.

6. Drain on paper towels and serve with cinnamon syrup, p. 329

Yield: 36 beignets

Variation:

ORANGE FLAVORED BEIGNETS

(Buñuelos con licor de naranjas)

Follow the recipe for Beignets, but add after beating in the eggs:

2 tablespoons orange liqueur
1 teaspoon grated orange rind

Yield: 36 beignets

CHEESE BEIGNETS

(Buñuelos de queso)

1 cup all-purpose flour
1 teaspoon sugar
1 teaspoon double-action baking powder
1/4 teaspoon salt
1/4 cup grated parmesan cheese
1 large egg, lightly beaten
1/2 cup milk
vegetable shortening

1. Sift together the flour, sugar, baking powder and salt.

2. Add the cheese and whole egg, mix well.

3. Add the milk. If the mixture is too runny add more flour by teaspoons.

4. Deep fry by teaspoonfuls until golden in the vegetable shortening over medium-high heat.

5. Drain on paper towels and serve with cinnamon syrup, V. below.

Yield: 24 beignets

CINNAMON SYRUP

(Almíbar de canela)

1 1/4 cup sugar
1 cup water
1 thick 2" long cinnamon stick

1. Bring the ingredients to a boil while stirring to dissolve the sugar.

2. Reduce the heat to moderate and cook uncovered for 10 minutes for a light syrup —222°F on a candy thermometer.

3. Let cool and serve with beignets.

NOTE: You may create other flavors by using lemon, orange, mandarin orange rinds or liqueurs.

Yield: 1 cup

FRUIT TURNOVERS

(Pastelillos de frutas)

2 cups all-purpose flour
1/4 teaspoon salt
1/2 cup cold vegetable shortening
1/2 cup cold water
1/2 teaspoon sugar dissolved in the water
vegetable oil or lard
chewey coconut compote, p.378, pineapple preserve, or chopped guava paste

1. Sift together the flour and salt in a bowl. Add the shortening and work it with two knives in a criss-cross motion or a pastry blender until the mixture forms pea-size pieces.

2. Start sprinkling with the water and sugar by tablespoons and work it in until the dough holds together. If necessary, you may knead it lightly.

3. Form into a ball and refrigerate wrapped with plastic for 30 minutes.

4. Divide the dough into 8 portions and keep covered until ready to roll out each one.

5. On a cool floured surface, flatten each portion and start rolling with the pin from the center out, dusting flour over the top of the dough if it sticks to it. Roll into a 6-6 1/2" diameter circle.

6. Put an inverted 5 1/2" diameter saucer over the dough circle and cut out the edges.

7. Lift up the circle before filling to make sure that it has not stuck to the surface.

8. Fill each circle with a heaping tablespoon of filling and spread it out in the center.

9. Moisten lightly the edges and fold over itself to form a half circle. Crimp the edges together with the tines of a fork.

10. Place on a floured platter and refrigerate covered until ready to fry.

11. Deep fry in vegetable shortening or lard until golden brown.

12. Drain on paper towels.

NOTE: The turnovers can be frozen. Remove from the freezer 30 minutes before frying.

Yield: 8 turnovers

CHAPTER XI: FLANS AND CUSTARDS

GLAZING CARAMEL

(Caramelo para glacear moldes)

1 cup sugar
non-porous heavy metal saucepan or skillet

1. Put the sugar in the pan over low to moderate heat.

2. Stir continuously with a wooden spoon until the sugar is completely melted. Continue cooking until you reach the desired color, from light to dark. Do not make too dark, though, as it will taste bitter.

3. Keep over very low heat while glazing the mold.

4. Pour the caramel in a metal, or heat-resistant mold. Tilt the mold around with your hands, working rapidly until the bottom and sides are caramelized. Set aside to cool.

FLAN

3 cups milk
3/4 cup plus 2 tablespoons sugar
1/4 teaspoon salt
6 whole large eggs plus 2 additional yolks
1 1/2 teaspoon vanilla or 3/4 teaspoon grated acid lime rind
caramel made with 1 cup sugar, v. above
flan mold-round, 8" x 2 1/2"
larger mold for the bain-marie

1. Caramelize the flan mold and set aside.

2. Preheat the oven to 325°F.

3. Add water to the bain-marie mold to come up to 2/3 the height of the flan mold and set in the oven.

4. Mix well the milk, sugar, and salt without foaming, then scald in a saucepan. Do not let come to a boil.

5. Beat the eggs and additional yolks lightly, just enough to blend them. Do not foam up, as this will produce a grainy flan.

6. Add the scalded milk and strain.

7. Add the vanilla or acid lime rind.

8. Pour into the caramelized mold and set in the pan already in the oven.

9. Bake for 1 1/2 hours or until a cake tester inserted slightly off the center comes out clean.

10. Remove from the oven and let cool for 2 hours before refrigerating.

11. Refrigerate covered. To serve, turn over in a platter with a rim which will hold the liquified caramel.

NOTE: You may use a blender or processor to mix the ingredients. Let the foam subside before straining into the mold.

Serves: 8-10

PIÑA COLADA FLAN

(Flan a la piña colada)

1 cup unsweetened pineapple juice
1 1/2 cups fresh coconut milk, p. 416
1 cup sugar
1/4 teaspoon salt
1/3 cup rum
8 large eggs, lightly beaten
caramel made with one cup sugar, p. 335
flan mold-round, 7" x 3"
larger mold for the bain-marie

1. Caramelize the flan mold and set aside.

2. Preheat the oven to 325°F.

3. Add water to the bain-marie mold to come up to 2/3 the height of the flan mold and set inside the oven.

4. Mix the pineapple juice, coconut milk and sugar. Stir until the sugar is dissolved.

5. Add the rum and eggs. Blend well without foaming.

6. Strain into the flan mold and wait until any foam has subsided.

7. Set into the large pan already in the oven and bake for 1 1/2 hours or until a cake tester inserted slightly off the center comes out clean.

8. Let cool for 2 hours before refrigerating covered.

9. Before serving, turn over on a platter with a rim that will hold the liquified caramel.

Serves: 8

ALMOND FLAN

(Flan de almendras)

2 1/2 ounces shelled, blanched, almonds
2/3 cup sugar
2 cups milk
4 eggs
3/4 teaspoon acid lime rind
1/4 teaspoon salt
6 to 7 four-ounce oven-proof custard cups
caramel made with one cup sugar, p. 335
larger mold to hold the custard cups in bain-marie

1. Caramelize the custard cups and set aside.

2. Preheat the oven to 325°F.

3. Add water to the bain-marie mold to come up to 2/3 the height of the custard cups and set in the oven.

4. Grind the almonds finely in a blender or food processor.

5. Add the rest of the ingredients and blend at high speed.

6. Let the froth subside before pouring into the custard cups.

7. Pour into the cups and set into the container already in the oven.

8. Bake for 1 1/4 hour or until a cake tester inserted off the center comes out clean.

9. Let cool before refrigerating.

10. Serve in the custard cups or turn over on individual dessert plates.

Yield: 6-7 flans

PINEAPPLE FLAN I

(Flan de piña I)

2 cups unsweetened pineapple juice
1 cup sugar
8 large eggs
1/4 teaspoon salt
caramel made with one cup sugar, p. 335
8 four-ounce custard cups
larger mold to hold the custard cups in bain-marie

1. Caramelize the custard cups and set aside.

2. Bring the sugar and juice to a boil, stirring to dissolve the sugar.

3. Lower the heat to moderate and cook for 15 minutes or until it reaches the light syrup stage —220°F on a candy thermometer.

4. Remove from the heat, skim out the froth and let cool completely.

5. Preheat the oven to 325°F.

6. Add water to the bain-marie mold to come up to 2/3 the height of the flan mold and set in the oven.

7. Beat the eggs with the salt lightly, without frothing.

8. Combine with the pineapple syrup and strain.

9. Pour into the custard cups and bake for 50-60 minutes or until a cake tester inserted near the center comes out clean.

10. Let cool, then refrigerate covered, before serving either in the cups or turned over on individual dessert plates.

NOTE: You may also bake this flan in a caramelized 7" x 3" round mold.

Serves: 8

PINEAPPLE FLAN II

(Flan de piña II)

1 twelve-ounce can evaporated milk
1 cup unsweetened pineapple juice
1/2 cup sugar
1/4 teaspoon salt
5 large eggs
caramel made with one cup sugar, p. 335
8 four-ounce custard cups
larger mold to hold the custard cups in bain-marie

1. Caramelize the custard cups and set aside.

2. Preheat the oven to 325°F.

3. Add water to the bain-marie mold to come up to 2/3 the height of the custard cups and set inside the oven.

4. Put all the ingredients, except the eggs, in a food processor and process until the sugar is dissolved.

5. Add the eggs and process only until well mixed.

6. Let the foam subside before straining into the custard cups.

7. Pour into the cups and set in the larger mold already in the oven.

8. Bake for 50-60 minutes or until a cake tester inserted near the center comes out clean.

9. Let cool before refrigerating covered.

10. Serve in the custard cups or turned over individual dessert plates.

NOTE: This flan may also be baked in a 7" x 3" round pan.

Yield: 8 flans

COCONUT FLAN I

(Flan de coco I)

2 1/2 cups freshly grated coconut, p. 415
2 cups sugar
1 1/4 cup water
1 teaspoon acid lime rind
1/4 teaspoon salt
8 lightly beaten eggs
caramel made with 1 cup sugar, p.335
round mold, 7" x 3"
larger mold for the bain-marie

1. Caramelize the flan mold and set aside.

2. Mix the water and sugar and boil over moderate heat to a

thread-stage syrup —230°F on a candy thermometer— about 30 minutes.

3. Preheat the oven to 325°F.

4. Add water to the bain-marie mold to come up to 2/3 the height of the caramelized mold and set it inside the oven.

5. Add the syrup, salt and acid lime rind to the grated coconut. Stir well until it cools to prevent the eggs from curdling when added.

6. Pour the beaten eggs through a colander and stir well into the mixture.

7. Pour the mixture into the flan mold and set in the mold already in the oven.

8. Bake for 1 1/4 hour or until a cake tester inserted slightly off the center comes out clean.

9. Let cool in the mold for 5 minutes. Separate the sides from the mold with a thin knife.

10. Turn over on a platter with a short rim. Wait 5 minutes and remove the mold.

11. Let cool completely before refrigerating.

NOTES: You may use up to one more cup of grated coconut for a taller flan. In this flan, the grated coconut and the custad separate into two distinct layers.

Serves: 10-12

COCONUT FLAN II

(Flan de coco II)

2 cups freshly grated coconut, p. 415
1 twelve-ounce can evaporated milk
1 1/3 cup sugar
1/4 teaspoon salt
3/4 teaspoon grated acid lime rind
4 lightly beaten large eggs
caramel made with one cup sugar, p. 335
flan mold, round, 7" x 3"
larger mold to hold the flan mold in bain-marie

1. Caramelize the flan mold and set aside.

2. Preheat the oven to 325°F.

3. Add water to the bain-marie mold to come up to 2/3 the height of the flan mold and set inside the oven.

4. Dissolve the sugar and salt in the milk.

5. Add the acid lime rind and eggs and mix well.

6. Add the grated coconut and mix well.

7. Pour into the mold and set inside the larger mold already in the oven.

8. Bake for 1 1/4 hour or until a cake tester inserted off the center comes out clean.

9. Let cool in the mold for 5 minutes. Separate the sides from the mold with a thin knife and turn over on a platter with a short rim. Wait 5 minutes before removing the mold.

10. Let cool before refrigerating.

NOTES: You may use up to one additional cup of grated coconut for a taller flan. In this flan the coconut and custard separate into two distinct layers.

Serves: 10-12

PUMPKIN FLAN

(Flan de calabaza)

2 pounds pumpkin
1 quart water
1/4 teaspoon salt
1 1/2 cups milk
2 tablespons cornstarch
3/4 cup sugar
4 slightly beaten large eggs
1 1/2 teaspoon vanilla
2 tablespoons brandy
caramel made with 1 cup sugar, p. 335
flan mold, round, 7" x 3"
larger mold for the bain-marie

1. Caramelize the flan mold and set aside.

2. Cut the pumpkin into 6 pieces, peel and boil in one quart of water and one teaspoon salt for 10-15 minutes or until tender.

3. Preheat the oven to 350°F.

4. Add water to the bain-marie mold to come up to 2/3 the height of the flan mold and set it in the oven.

5. Puree the pumpkin pieces and press out any excess liquid.

6. Measure 2 tightly packed cups of the pumpkin puree. Set into a bowl.

7. Dissolve the cornstarch in the milk and stir in slowly into the pumpkin. Mix well.

8. Add the sugar, salt and beaten eggs. Mix well.

9. Add the vanilla and brandy and blend well.

10. Pour into the flan mold and set it into the mold already in the oven.

11. Bake for 60-70 minutes or until a cake tester inserted slightly off the center comes out clean.

12. Let cool for 2 hours before refrigerating covered.

13. Turn onto a platter before serving.

NOTES: You may use canned pumpkin puree. You may steam, instead of boiling, the pumpkin.

Serves: 8

SWEET POTATO FLAN

(Flan de batata)

1 pound white sweet potato
3 cups water
1/2 teaspoon salt
2 tablespoons butter
1/2 cup densely packed dark sugar
3/4 cup sugar
1/2 teaspoon ground cinnamon
1/8 teaspoon ground cloves
1/4 teaspoon ground nutmeg
1 teaspoon vanilla
6 large eggs
1 2/3 cup milk
round mold, 7" x 3"
larger mold for the bain-marie

1. Peel the sweet potatoes, quarter and boil in the water and salt until tender.

2. Preheat the oven to 350°F.

3. Add water to the bain-marie mold to come up to 2/3 the height of the flan mold and set it inside the oven.

4. Melt the butter in the flan mold over low heat. Sprinkle the dark sugar uniformly over the bottom. Let stand in the heat for three minutes. Remove and set apart.

5. In a food processor or blender large enough to hold all the ingredients, puree the sweet potatoes.

6. Add the sugar, cinammon, cloves, nutmeg and vanilla. Process.

7. Add the eggs and milk. Process or blend well.

8. Pour into the mold and set inside the larger one already in the oven.

9. Bake for 1 1/4 hour or until a cake tester inserted off the center comes out clean.

10. Cool for 1 1/2 hours, then refrigerate covered for three or four hours.

11. Before turning over on a platter, separate the sides from the mold with a fine knife.

Serves: 10

CHEESE FLAN

(Flan de queso)

4 ounces cream cheese, at room temperature
1 cup sugar
1/4 teaspoon salt
1 twelve-ounce can evaporated milk
1/2 cup water
5 slightly beaten large eggs
1 teaspoon vanilla
caramel made with one cup sugar, p. 335
round mold, 7" x 3"
larger mold for the bain-marie

1. Caramelize the flan mold and set aside.

2. Preheat the oven to 350°F.

3. Add water to the bain-marie mold to come up to 2/3 the height of the flan mold and set it in the oven.

4. Beat the cheese with the sugar and salt until smooth.

5. Mix the milk, water, eggs and vanilla, and strain over the cheese. Blend well.

6. Let the foam subside before pouring into the mold.

7. Set inside the larger mold in the oven and bake for 45 minutes.

8. Cover loosely with a sheet of aluminum foil. Bake for 45 additional minutes or until a cake tester inserted near the center comes out clean.

9. Let cool for 2 hours before refrigerating.

10. Turn over on a platter before serving.

NOTE: Instead of evaporated milk and water you may use an equal amount of half-and-half.

Serves: 8

HEAVENLY BACON

(Tocino del cielo)

3/4 cup water
1 1/2 cups sugar
1/4 teaspoon lemon juice
1/2 cup egg yolks —about 10-12 yolks
1/2 cup whole eggs —about 3 medium eggs
1 teaspoon grated acid lime rind or vanilla extract
1/4 teaspoon salt
caramel made with 1/2 cup sugar, p. 335
round mold, 6" x 2"
larger mold for the bain-marie

1. Bring the water, sugar and lemon juice to a boil. Reduce the heat to moderate and cook without stirring until you get a heavy syrup —226°F on a candy thermometer.

2. Remove from the heat and let cool completely.

3. In the meantime, caramelize the mold and set aside.

4. Preheat the oven to 350°F.

5. Add enough water to the bain-marie mold to come up to 2/3 the height of the caramelized mold. Set inside the oven.

6. Beat the whole eggs and yolks with the salt, but without foaming. Strain.

7. Add the acid lime rind or vanilla and a cup of the cooled syrup. Mix well without frothing.

8. Pour into the mold, cover with a loose sheet of aluminum foil and set into the larger pan already in the oven.

9. Bake for 2 hours or until a cake tester inserted near the center comes out clean.

10. Let cool before refrigerating. Invert on a platter before serving.

NOTE: The measurements for the eggs and egg yolks in this recipe must be exact.

Serves: 6-8

STIRRED ACID LIME CUSTARD

(Natilla de lima)

4 cups milk
4 tablespoons cornstarch, dissolved into some of the milk
1/2 cup sugar
1/4 teaspoon salt
4 egg yolks
8-10 strips acid lime peel

1. Blend well all the ingredients.

2. Cook in a heavy saucepan over moderate heat, stirring constantly until it coagulates.

3. Reduce the heat to low and cook for 5 additional minutes.

4. Remove the acid lime rind and pour into custard cups. Serve either warm or refrigerated.

NOTE: You may mix all the ingredients in a blender of food processor, except the lime peel. Add this just before cooking.

Serves: 6

STIRRED CHOCOLATE CUSTARD

(Natilla de chocolate)

- 2 ounces grated unsweetened chocolate
- 4 cups milk
- 2/3 cup sugar
- 1/4 teaspoon salt
- 4 tablespoons cornstarch, dissolved into some of the milk
- 4 lightly beaten egg yolks
- 1 teaspoon vanilla

1. Mix well the milk, sugar, salt and cornstarch.

2. Stir in the egg yolks and chocolate.

3. Cook in a heavy saucepan over moderate heat, stirring constantly, until the mixture coagulates.

4. Reduce the heat to low and cook for 5 more minutes.

5. Remove from the heat, stir in the vanilla, and pour into custard cups. Serve either warm or refrigerated.

NOTE: You may mix all the ingredients in a blender or food processor before cooking.

Serves: 6

IRONED CUSTARD

(Crema planchada)

3 cups milk
5 tablespoons cornstarch, dissolved into part of the milk
1/2 cup sugar
1/4 teaspoon salt
3 large egg yolks
1 teaspoon vanilla extract or grated acid lime rind
caramel made with 2/3 cup sugar, p. 335
additional caramel made with 3 tablespoons sugar
9-inch pie mold or 8 four-ounce custard cups

1. Caramelize the mold or custard cups with the 2/3 cup of sugar. Set aside.

2. Mix well all the ingredients, except the vanilla or lime rind and strain into a heavy saucepan. You may do this in a food processor or blender which is large enough.

3. Add the vanilla or acid lime rind.

4. Cook over medium to medium-high heat, stirring constantly until it coagulates.

5. Reduce the heat immediately to low and cook for 5 additional minutes, stirring all the time.

6. Remove from the heat and continue stirring for about 5 minutes to cool it slightly.

7. Pour into the mold or custard cups.

8. Prepare the additional caramel with the three tablespoons sugar and dribble over the custard.

9. Refrigerate covered before serving.

NOTE: This custard gets its name from the custom of caramelizing sugar sprinkled on its top with a hot cast-iron pressing iron. A similar effect can be achieved with a salamander.

Serves: 8

STIRRED COCONUT CUSTARD

(Tembleque)

4 cups coconut milk, p.416
1/2 cup cornstarch, dissolved into part of the coconut milk
3/8 teaspoon salt
2/3 cup sugar
ground cinnamon
1 quart round mold

1. Mix well the coconut milk, cornstarch, salt and sugar and strain into a heavy saucepan.

2. Cook at medium to medium-high heat, stirring constantly until it coagulates.

3. Reduce the heat immediately to low and cook for 5 more minutes, stirring occasionally.

4. Pour into the rinsed, drained, but moist mold.

5. Let cool before refrigerating covered.

6. Separate the sides of the custard from the mold with a fine knife and invert it on a platter.

7. Sprinkle the top with ground cinnamon.

Serves: 12

CHAPTER XII:
PUDDINGS, POLENTA AND PAP

BREAD PUDDING

(Budín de pan)

1 pound white bread
3 1/2 cups milk
4 tablespons melted butter
1 1/4 cup sugar
1/4 teaspoon salt
2 teaspoons vanilla
1 teaspoon ground cinnamon
1/2 cup seedless raisins
3 lightly beaten eggs
buttered mold, 9" x 9" x 2"

1. Preheat the oven to 350°F.

2. Trim off the bread crust.

3. Soak the bread in the milk until soft, then mash or puree. Add the butter and blend well.

4. Add the sugar, salt, vanilla, cinnamon and raisins. Mix well.

5. Add the eggs, mix well, and pour into the mold.

6. Bake for 1 1/4 hours or until a cake tester inserted near the center comes out clean. If by the first hour it is browning too fast, reduce the heat to 325°F.

7. Let cool in the mold.

Yield: 16 servings

BREAD PUDDING WITH SPIRITS

(Budín con licor)

1 pound French bread
2 1/2 quarts water
1 cup milk
1 1/2 cups sugar
1/2 teaspoon salt
4 tablespoons melted butter
2 teaspoons vanilla
1 teaspoon ground cinnamon
1/2 cup chopped seedless raisins
3 lightly beaten large eggs
1/3 cup brandy, vermouth, rum or sherry
caramel made with 1 cup sugar, p. 335
mold, 8" x 8" x 2"
larger mold for the bain-marie

1. Caramelize the pudding mold and set aside.

2. Cut the bread into 8 or 10 pieces and trim off the crust.

3. Soak the bread in the water for 15 minutes, remove and squeeze out the water.

4. Mash or puree the bread —you should have about 3 cups.

5. Preheat the oven to 375°F.

6. Add enough water to the bain-marie mold to come up to 2/3 the height of the pudding mold. Place in the oven.

7. Mix the bread with the milk, sugar, salt, butter, vanilla, cinnamon and raisins. Blend well.

8. Add the eggs and mix well.

9. Blend in the spirits.

10. Pour into the mold and set in the larger one already in the oven.

11. Bake for 1 hour, then raise the temperature to 400°F.

12. Bake for 10 more minutes or until a cake tester inserted near the center comes out clean.

13. Let cool for 5 minutes, then turn over on a platter. Let cool before serving.

Yield: 16 servings

SPANISH TOAST

(Torrejas)

12 slices French bread, cut 1/2" thick
1 1/4 cup milk
1/8 teaspoon salt
1/2 teaspoon ground cinnamon
1 1/2 cup sugar
3/4 cup water
1 cinnamon stick
4 large eggs beaten with a pinch of salt
vegetable shortening or butter

1. Trim the bread crust off the slices.

2. Mix the milk and salt. Soak the bread slices in it and dust them with cinnamon. Let stand 15-20 minutes.

3. In the meantime, boil the sugar, water and cinnamon stick over moderate heat to make a light syrup —222°F on a candy thermometer— about 10 minutes.

4. Dip the bread slices in the egg one at a time and fry until golden brown, turning once. Dip in egg only as many slices as you can fry at a time.

5. Drain on paper towels and set in one overlapping layer in an appropriate platter.

6. Pour the syrup over them and refrigerate before serving.

NOTE: You may add 1/3 cup cream sherry or Muscat wine to the milk.

Serves: 6

SIMPLE RICE PUDDING

(Arroz con leche)

3/4 cup short-grain white rice
3 cups water
1 medium cinnamon stick
2 1/4 cups milk
1/4 teaspoon salt
2/3 cup sugar
ground cinnamon

1. Bring the water and cinnamon stick to a boil in a heavy saucepan.

2. Rinse the rice under running cool water until this runs clear. Drain and stir into the saucepan. Reduce the heat to low and cook covered for 15 minutes or until the rice has absorbed the water.

3. Mix the milk with the sugar and salt. Add to the rice and stir. Bring to a boil.

4. Reduce the heat to moderate and cook uncovered for 15 minutes or until it thickens. Stir occasionally.

5. Serve sprinkled with ground cinnamon.

NOTE: This pudding may also be cooked without sugar.

Serves: 6

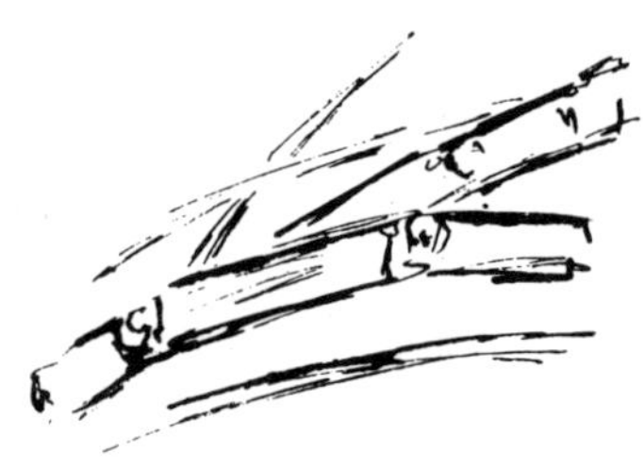

COCONUT RICE PUDDING

(Arroz con coco)

1 1/2 cups short grain white rice
1/2 cup grated coconut, p. 415
5 1/2 cups coconut milk, p. 416
1 1/2 cups sugar
2 additional tablespoons sugar
1 ounce fresh ginger, cut into 4 pieces and crushed
30 spice cloves
1 1/2 cup water
3/4 teaspoon salt
1/2 cup seedless raisins
2 tablespoons butter
ground cinnamon

1. Soak the rice in water to cover for 30 minutes.

2. Sweeten one cup of the coconut milk with the 2 additional tablespoons of sugar. Reserve.

3. Simmer the crushed ginger and cloves in the 1 1/2 cups water for 15 minutes and strain into a heavy saucepan where you will cook the rice. Add the ginger pieces.

4. Add the 4 1/2 cups of unsweetened coconut milk and the salt. Raise the heat to bring to a boil.

5. Rinse and drain the rice. Add to the saucepan. After it comes to a boil, lower the heat to moderate and cook uncovered for 15 minutes.

6. Add the sugar, raisins, and 1/2 cup of the sweetened coconut milk. Stir and reduce the heat to low.

7. Cook for 15 minutes, stirring twice to prevent it from sticking to the pan.

8. Add the rest of the coconut milk, the grated coconut and butter. Stir well and pour into a low glass mold.

9. Sprinkle with cinnamon before serving at room temperature.

NOTE: This pudding can be refrigerated but should be taken out of the icebox about one hour before serving.

Yield: 16 servings

PUMPKIN PUDDING

(Budín de calabaza)

3 pounds pumpkin
1 quart water
1/4 cup milk
1 cup sugar
1/4 teaspoon salt
2 tablespoons melted butter
6 tablespoons flour
1 1/2 teaspoon vanilla
1 teaspoon ground cinnamon
3 lightly beaten large eggs
buttered mold, 8" x 8" x 2"

1. Cut the pumpkin into 8-9 pieces and peel. Boil in the quart of water until tender —about 15 minutes.

2. Strain, puree, set in a colander or sieve and press out any excess water. Measure 3 tightly packed cups.

3. Preheat the oven to 400°F.

4. Mix the pumpkin with the rest of the ingredients, blending well.

5. Pour into the mold and set in the oven.

6. Bake for 25 minutes. Reduce the temperature to 350°F, and bake for 25 additional minutes or until a cake tester inserted near the center comes out clean.

7. Let cool in the mold before refrigerating.

NOTE: You may use canned pumpkin puree. You may also steam the pumpkin instead of boiling it.

Yield: 12-16 servings

SWEET POTATO AND COCONUT PUDDING

(Budín de batata y coco)

1 1/4 pounds white sweet potato
1 quart water
2 cups coconut milk, p. 416
1 cup sugar
1/4 teaspoon salt
1/4 cup flour, sifted after measuring
1/4 teaspoon ground ginger
4 tablespoons melted butter
4 lightly beaten large eggs
buttered mold, 8" x 8" x 2"

1. Cut the sweet potatoes and boil in the water for 20 minutes or until tender.

2. Remove from the water, peel and puree. Measure 2 tightly packed cups.

3. Preheat the oven to 375°F.

4. Add the coconut milk to the sweet potato gradually, stirring all the time.

5. Add the sugar, salt, flour, ginger and butter. Mix well.

6. Add the eggs and mix well.

7. Strain into the mold and bake for 25 minutes.

8. Reduce the heat to 350°F and bake for 25 additional minutes or until a cake tester inserted near the center comes out clean.

9. Let cool in the mold before refrigerating. Bring out of the icebox 30 minutes before serving.

Yield: 16 servings

SWEET POTATO AND PUMPKIN PUDDING

(Cazuela)

1 1/2 pound white sweet potato
1 1/2 pound pumpkin
2 quarts water salted with 1 1/2 teaspoons salt
1 cup coconut milk, p. 416
1 1/2 cup sugar
1/4 teaspoon salt
1/2 teaspoon ground cloves
1/2 teaspoon ground cinnamon
1/2 teaspoon ground ginger
1/4 cup wheat or rice flour
3 large beaten eggs
buttered mold, 8" x 8" x 2"

1. Peel the sweet potatoes and pumpkin and cut into pieces. Boil in the quarts of water until tender —about 15 minutes for the pumpkin, 20 for the sweet potato.

2. Preheat the oven to 350°F.

3. Drain and mash or puree the sweet potato and pumpkin.

4. Measure 3 tightly packed cups of sweet potato and 2 tightly packed cups of pumpkin.

5. Add the rest of the ingredients and blend well until smooth.

6. Pour into the mold and bake for 50-60 minutes or until a cake tester inserted near the center comes out clean.

7. Set under the broiler for 2-3 minutes or until golden brown on top.

8. Let cool in the mold. Then refrigerate to serve cold.

NOTE: You may caramelize the mold, p.335. Let the pudding rest for 5 minutes after baking, then turn over on a platter.

Yield: 16 servings

POLENTA WITH MILK

(Funche con leche)

1/2 cup cornmeal
1 1/2 cup milk
1 1/2 cup water
3/4 teaspoon salt
2 tablespoons butter

1. Put all the ingredients except the cornmeal in a saucepan and bring to a boil.

2. Remove from the heat and add the cornmeal gradually, stirring all the time with a wire beater or wood spoon.

3. Return the saucepan to the heat.

4. Lower the heat to medium-low and cook stirring until it thickens to taste.

5. Serve warm with sugar and more milk, if so desired.

Serves: 6

SWEET POLENTA

(Funche dulce)

1/2 cup plus one tablespoon fine cornmeal, sifted
2 1/4 cups water
3/4 cup milk
1/2 cup sugar plus one tablespoon sugar
2 tablespoons butter
1/2 teaspoon salt
1/4 cup seedless raisins

1. Bring all the ingredients to a boil in a saucepan, except the cornmeal.

2. Remove from the heat and add the cornmeal gradually while stirring all the time with a wire whisk or wood spoon.

3. Return the saucepan to the heat.

4. Lower the heat to medium-low and continue stirring until it thickens to taste.

5. Remove from the heat and stir to cool off lightly before pouring it onto a serving platter.

6. Let cool and refrigerate covered before serving.

Serves: 6

COCONUT POLENTA

(Funche con leche de coco)

1/2 cup plus one tablespoon cornmeal
3 cups coconut milk, p. 416
1/2 cup plus one tablespoon sugar
1/4 teaspoon salt
1 cinnamon stick or 1/4 cup seedless raisins
2 tablespoons grated coconut, p. 415
ground cinnamon

1. Bring the coconut milk, sugar, salt and cinnamon stick or raisins to a boil in a saucepan.

2. Remove from the heat and add the cornmeal gradually, stirring all the time with a wire whisk or wood spoon.

3. Reduce the heat to medium low. Add the grated coconut to the saucepan. Return to the heat and continue cooking until it thickens to taste. Stir constantly.

4. Pour on a plate, dust with cinnamon and either serve at room temperature or refrigerated.

Serves: 6

RICE FLOUR AND COCONUT MILK PAP

(Majarete con leche de coco)

1/2 cup sifted rice flour
3 cups coconut milk, p. 416
1/2 cup sugar
1/4 teaspoon salt
3 strips acid lime peel or 2 small tender sour orange leaves
2 teaspoons butter
ground cinnamon
6 four-ounce custard cups

1. Bring all the ingredients, except the rice flour, to a slow boil in a saucepan.

2. Remove from the heat and add the rice flour gradually, stirring all the time with a wire whisk or a wood spoon.

3. Return the saucepan to the heat.

4. Reduce the heat to medium-low and cook stirring, until it thickens to taste.

5. Remove the rind or leaves. Pour into the custard cups.

6. Dust with cinnamon and refrigerate covered.

NOTE: This pap may be made also with whole milk instead of coconut milk. Flavor instead with 1 1/2 teaspoons orange blossom water instead of the lime peel or sour orange leaves. Its Spanish name would then be *Manjar blanco*.

Serves: 6

CHAPTER XIII: COCONUT KISSES AND OTHER CONFECTIONARY

COCONUT KISSES

(Besitos de coco)

3 tightly packed cups grated coconut, p. 415
9 tablespoons all-purpose flour
3/4 cup sugar
1/2 teaspoon ground ginger
1/4 teaspoon salt
greased cookie sheet

1. Preheat oven to 325°F.

2. Combine all the ingredients well and form into little balls about 1 1/4" diameter.

3. Place in the cookie sheet and bake for 35 minutes.

4. Remove from the sheet while still hot and let cool on wire racks.

Yield: 30 kisses

COCONUT SQUARES

(Cocada)

4 cups coconut compote, p. 377
3 lightly beaten large egg yolks
2 tablespoons softened butter
2 ounces peeled and blanched almonds, chopped
buttered mold, 6" x 8" x 1 1/2"

1. Preheat the oven to 375°F.

2. Add the yolks and butter to the coconut compote and mix well.

3. Pour the mixture into the mold.

4. Sprinkle with the chopped almonds and press them lightly into the surface.

5. Bake for 50 minutes.

6. Let cool and cut into 2" squares.

Yield: 12 squares

COCONUT CANDY BARS

(Dulce de coco en barras)

3 cups grated coconut, p. 415
3 cups sugar
2 cups milk
1 teaspoon grated acid lime rind or 1/2 teaspoon grated fresh ginger root
1/8 teaspoon salt
1/4 teaspoon vinegar

1. In a heavy saucepan or *caldero* stir together all the ingredients and bring to a boil.

2. Reduce the heat to medium-low and cook for 50 minutes or until the candy separates from the bottom and sides of the pan. Stir three or four times, but do not scrape the bottom of the pan.

3. Pour on a greased surface or a double layer of waxed paper. Give it a rectangular shape about 3/4" thick, helping yourself with two moist spatulas.

4. Let cool for 25 minutes, then cut into 6" x 1 3/4" bars.

Yield: 6 bars

SWEET POTATO AND COCONUT CANDY BARS

(Dulce de batata y leche de coco)

1 pound white sweet potato
1/2 cup coconut milk, p. 416
1 1/4 cup sugar
1/4 teaspoon salt

1. Peel the sweet potatoes, quarter and boil until tender.

2. Puree the potatoes, add the coconut milk, sugar and salt. Blend well.

3. Cook, stirring constantly, over medium-low heat in a heavy

saucepan or *caldero* for 25-30 minutes, or until it separates from the sides and bottom of the pan.

4. Turn over on a marble slab, or any moistened hard smooth surface. Give it a rectangular shape about 1/2" thick helping yourself with two moistened spatulas.

5. Let cool for 40 minutes, then cut into 5 1/2" x 1 1/2" bars.

Yield: 6 bars

SWEET POTATO SAPODILLAS

(Nísperos de batata)

Follow the recipe for Sweet Potato and Coconut Candy Bars, p.368, but:

1. Add one egg yolk to the mixture before cooking.

2. Instead of cooling on a slab let cool on a platter for 30 minutes.

3. Form little balls by tablespoonfuls with your hands.

4. Roll lightly on ground cinnamon and top with a spice clove, and thus, they will resemble sapodilla fruits.

Yield: 24 sapodillas, 1 1/2" diameter

SUGAR FROSTED COCONUT FRUITS

(Frutitas de coco azucaradas)

3 cups grated coconut, p. 415
3 cups sugar for the candy
1 1/2 teaspoon grated acid lime rind
2 large beaten eggs
1/8 teaspoon salt
food colors
2 cups white granulated sugar for the frosting

1. Mix well the grated coconut, 3 cups sugar, beaten eggs and salt.

2. Bring to a boil over moderate heat in a heavy saucepan or *caldero*.

3. Reduce the heat to low, and cook stirring occasionally, without scraping the bottom of the pan, for 35 minutes or until the mixture is almost dry —240°F on a candy thermometer.

4. Divide the candy into 5 equal portions without scraping that stuck to the bottom of the pan.

5. Tint each portion with 3-4 dops of food color —red, orange, yellow, green, purple.

6. Sprinkle your hands with granulated sugar.

7. Make 10 small fruits with each portion shaping them up with your sugar-coated hands into an appropriately colored fruit, i.e., red apples, oranges, limes, peaches, plums, bananas, pears, cherries, etc.

8. Roll each fruit in the granulated white sugar and top with a stem made from a spice clove. If serving immediately, you may add natural small leaves, otherwise use artificial or candy leaves.

NOTE: You may tint the sugar for the frosting the same colors as the fruits. For each color, put 1/2 cup sugar and 2-4 drops food color in a jar. Shake well until the sugar is uniformly tinted.

Yield: 50 fruits

SOUR ORANGE PASTE

(Pasta de naranjas agrias)

8 or 9 sour oranges
sugar

1. Peel the colored rind of the oranges leaving the white pith intact.

2. Quarter and remove the flesh. Discard this, but save the white pith.

3. Soak the pith pieces in water to cover for 6 hours changing

the water every hour. If the pith is too thin, soak only for 5 hours.

4. Drain and cook in water to cover for 30 minutes over moderate heat —20 minutes if the pith is thin.

5. Drain well and chop finely —do not puree— in a food processor.

6. Measure the amount of chopped pith and mix with an equal amount of sugar.

7. Bring to a boil in a heavy saucepan or *caldero* over medium-high heat. Reduce the heat to moderate and cook for 30 minutes or until the candy separates from the sides and bottom of the pan. Stir occasionally for the first 15 minutes, continually for the rest of the time.

8. Spread the paste in 3 portions about 1/2" thick on a marble slab or any hard, smooth surface. Form into 3 rectangles about 3" x 8", helping yourself with two moist spatulas. Smooth the surface.

9. Let cool, wrap with plastic and refrigerate.

NOTE: The cooking of the paste must be closely watched after the first 15 minutes as it may be ready in less than the indicated time. This is determined by the moistness of the pith.

Yield: 3 paste bars

SHORTBREAD COOKIES

(Mantecaditos)

1/4 pound vegetable shortening
1/4 pound butter
1/4 teaspoon salt
2 large egg yolks
1 1/2 teaspoon almond extract
3 cups all-purpose flour
3/4 cup plus 2 tablespoons sugar
multi-colored décors (non-pareils)

1. Beat the shortening and butter together until soft and well blended.

2. Add the salt, yolks and almond extract. Blend well.

3. Sift together the sugar and flour and add to the rest by cupfuls. Blend well after each addition. You will get a grainy batter.

4. Preheat the oven to 325° F.

5. Make 1 1/8" diameter balls with the dough, rolling it in your hands. Compact the dough as you roll.

6. Place on a large ungreased cookie sheet lined with parchment paper leaving space between them to allow for expansion.

7. Make a light indentation on the top of each ball with your finger tip and sprinkle some décors over it.

8. Bake for 25-30 minutes until golden in color.

9. Remove from the cookie sheet carefully with a spatula and let cool on a wire rack. Store tightly sealed.

Yield: 75 cookies

PETIT MERINGUES

(Merenguitos)

1/2 cup egg whites (4 medium eggs)
1/16 teaspoon salt
1/4 teaspoon cream of tartar
1 1/3 cup sugar
1/2 teaspoon grated acid lime rind
food colors
cookie sheets, lined with waxed paper

1. Beat the egg whites with the salt and cream of tartar until they form soft peaks in a clean and dry bowl.

2. Add the sugar gradually, 1/3 cup at a time, and beat for 2 minutes after each addition.

3. Add the acid lime rind and beat for 2 minutes, or until you get stiff peaks.

4. Preheat the oven to 275°F.

5. Divide the meringue into as many portions as you want colors. Tint each portion with 2 to 4 drops food color depending on the deepness of color you want. Blend well.

6. Drop the meringues in the cookie sheets by level teaspoon measures, working with two teaspoons; or if using a pastry bag, into circular shapes about 1/2" diameter. Leave enough space between them to allow for expansion.

7. Bake for 30-35 minutes.

8. Remove from the paper and let cool on wire racks before storing tightly sealed.

Yield: 150 petit meringues

GLAZED CASHEWS

(Pajuiles abrillantados)

Follow the recipe for Cashew Compote, p. 377, but:

1. Cook the cashews in the syrup until you reach 248°F on a candy thermometer.

2. Remove from the pan and let drain on wire racks for several hours or until almost dry.

3. Roll in sugar and keep in a tightly closed container.

Yield: 16 glazed cashews.

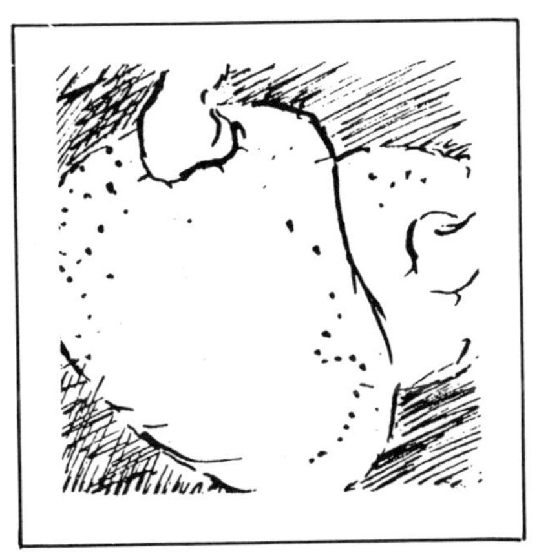

CHAPTER XIV: FRUIT AND VEGETABLE COMPOTES

CASHEW COMPOTE

(Compota de pajuiles)

16 ripe medium cashews —2 pounds
1 quart water salted with 2 teaspoons salt
3 cups sugar
1 1/2 cup water

1. Remove the nuts from the cashews. Remember the nuts are poisonous unless roasted.

2. Rinse the cashews and pierce all over with the tines of a fork.

3. Boil in the salted water for 15 minutes. Drain, squeeze gently, and dip in cold water for 5 minutes. Drain.

4. Bring to a boil the cashews, sugar, and 1 1/2 cup water. Stir to dissolve the sugar.

5. Reduce the heat to medium-low and cook for about one hour or until you reach the light syrup stage —222°F on a candy thermometer. Turn over occasionally.

6. Let cool and serve either at room temperature or refrigerated.

Serves: 6-8

COCONUT COMPOTE

(Compota de coco)

3 cups grated coconut, p. 415
3 cups water
4 cups sugar
1 teaspoon finely grated fresh ginger root
1/4 teaspoon salt

1. Bring all the ingredients to a boil in a heavy saucepan.

2. Reduce the heat to medium-low and cook for one hour without stirring until you get a light syrup —222°F on a candy thermometer.

3. Let cool to room temperature before serving or refrigerating.

Yield: 4 cups

Variation:

CHEWY COCONUT COMPOTE

(Dulce de coco amelcochado)

Follow the instructions for Coconut Compote, but use:

4 cups dark sugar instead of white sugar
1 teaspoon grated acid lime rind instead of ginger root

1. Cook for 65 minutes or until you reach 224°F on a candy thermometer.

Yield: 4 cups

GUAVA SHELLS

(Casquitos de guayaba)

4 pounds ripe, but firm, guavas
1 cup water
3 cups sugar

1. Peel the guavas with a vegetable peeler, halve, and scoop out the seedy core with a teaspoon.

2. Bring the guava shells, water and sugar to a boil in a heavy non-reactive saucepan.

3. Reduce the heat to medium-low and cook uncovered, stir-

ring occasionally, until you reach the light syrup stage —220°F in a candy thermometer— about one hour.

4. Let cool and refrigerate covered before serving with cheese or ice cream.

Yield: 12-16 servings

GUAVA, PLANTAIN AND SWEET POTATO COMPOTE

(Malarabia)

1 pound ripe medium guavas
1/2 pound white sweet potato
1 1/4 cup water
1/4 teaspoon salt
1 large ripe, but firm, plantain
1 1/2 cup sugar
1 large cinnamon stick

1. Peel the guavas with a vegetable peeler, halve, and scoop out the seedy core with a teaspoon.

2. Peel the sweet potatoes, dice 1/2" thick and put in the water and salt with the guavas.

3. Bring to a simmer in a heavy saucepan and cook covered for 10 minutes.

4. In the meantime peel the plantain by making three lengthwise incisions in the skin and pulling it off. Trim off the ends, halve lengthwise and remove the central fiber. Cut crosswise into 1/4" thick slices.

5. After the 10 minutes are over, add the plantain, the sugar

and cinnamon stick to the saucepan. Bring back to a boil by raising the heat, then reduce again to medium-low. Cook uncovered for 15-20 minutes, until the plantain slices are tender, and you get a light syrup —218°F on a candy thermometer.

6. Serve at room temperature or refrigerated.

NOTE: If the guavas are too sweet, add 1/2 teaspoon lemon juice 5 minutes after adding the plantain.

Serves: 6

MAMMEE COMPOTE

(Dulce de mamey)

1 four-to-five pound ripe, but firm, mammee
1 1/2 cup unsweetened pineapple juice
3 cups sugar

1. Peel the mammee and peel off the thin membrane covering the flesh.

2. Quarter the mammee and remove the seed. Peel off the tough part to which the seed adhered, and remove any small pieces of seed from the meat.

3. Cut the meat into 2" x 1" pieces. You should have about 2 pounds.

4. Mix the pineapple juice in a heavy saucepan with the sugar and stir until this is dissolved.

5. Add the mammee and bring to a boil.

6. Reduce the heat to medium-low, and boil uncovered until

you get a light syrup —220°F on a candy thermometer. A very ripe mammee will take 45-50 minutes; a harder one, as long as 65.

7. Stir occasionally and remove any scum that rises to the surface.

8. Let cool and refrigerate before serving with cheese.

Serves: 6-8

GREEN PAPAYA COMPOTE

(Dulce de papaya)

- 5-6 pounds green papaya
- 6 quarts water
- 2 tablespoons bicarbonate of soda
- 2 pounds white sugar
- 1 pound dark sugar
- 6 medium cinnamon sticks

1. Cut the papaya lengthwise into 1/4" thick strips. Peel them.

2. Dissolve the bicarbonate of soda in the water and soak the strips for 20 minutes. Do not go over this time to prevent toughening.

3. Rinse and drain the strips.

4. Place the papaya strips in layers sprinkled with the sugars in a large heavy-bottomed pan. Keep the pan over medium-low heat while doing this.

5. Cover and cook for 30 minutes.

6. Uncover and add the cinnamon sticks.

7. Cook uncovered for 1 1/2 hours or until the strips become

translucent and golden, and until you get a light syrup —222°F on a candy thermometer.

8. After the first hour turn over the strips so that those on the bottom are at the top.

9. Cool and refrigerate covered before serving with cheese.

Yield: 12-16 servings

RIPE PLANTAIN COMPOTE

(Plátanos maduros en almíbar)

3 large ripe, but firm, plantains
1/4 pound butter
1 1/2 cup water
1 1/2 cup sugar
2 cinnamon sticks
crumbly white cheese

1. Peel the plantains by making three lengthwise incisions in the skin and pulling it off.

2. Trim off the ends and divide in two crosswise.

3. Fry in the butter, turning often, over low heat for 25 minutes or until tender and golden.

4. Bring the water, sugar and cinnamon to a boil in a saucepan and add the plantains.

5. Reduce the heat to medium-low and cook for 25-30 minutes, turning once, or until you get a light syrup —218°F on a candy thermometer.

6. Let cool and top with the crumbled cheese before serving.

Serves: 6

DRIED PRUNES COMPOTE

(Compota de ciruelas secas)

1 pound dried pitted prunes
2 1/2 cups water
1 1/2 cup sugar
2 medium cinnamon sticks
2 teaspoons lemon juice

1. Soak the prunes in the water for 2-3 hours depending on their moistness.

2. Drain, but save 1 1/2 cups of the soaking water.

3. Bring to a boil this water, the sugar, prunes and cinnamon in a heavy saucepan.

4. Reduce the heat to medium-low and cook uncovered until you reach a light-syrup stage —220°F on a candy thermometer— about 25 minutes.

5. Remove from the heat and add the lemon juice.

6. Let cool and serve with cheese.

Serves: 6-8

SOUR ORANGE SHELLS

(Orejones de naranja agria)

6 large sour oranges
water
2 cups white sugar
1 cup dark sugar
1 1/2 cup water
2 large cinnamon sticks

1. Peel the sour oranges with a vegetable peeler without taking off too much of the white pith underneath.

2. Quarter the oranges and remove the flesh.

3. Put the white pith quarters in water to cover for 8 hours, changing it every hour.

4. Rinse and drain.

5. In a heavy saucepan bring to a boil the sugars, cinnamon and 1 1/2 cup of water.

6. Add the pith quarters, reduce the heat to medium-low, and cook for some 40 minutes or until you get a light syrup —222°F on a candy thermometer.

7. Serve at room temperature or refrigerate covered.

Serves: 6-8

STAR-GOOSEBERRY COMPOTE

(Dulce de grosellas)

6 cups ripe large star-gooseberries
3/4 cup water
3 cups sugar

1. Rinse the star-gooseberries and boil in water to cover for 5 minutes. Drain. Boil a second time in fresh water if they are too tart. Drain.

2. Mix the sugar and 3/4 cup water. Bring to a boil, stirring until the sugar is dissolved, in a heavy saucepan.

3. Add the star-gooseberries, reduce the heat to medium-low and cook for 45-50 minutes or until you get a light syrup —224°F on a candy thermometer. By this time, the star-gooseberries will have turned red. Stir occasionally.

NOTE: Since star-gooseberries cannot be pitted, you have to remove the pit from your mouth after eating the flesh of the fruit —very much like unpitted olives.

Serves: 6-8

TOMATO COMPOTE

(Compota de tomates)

2 pounds ripe, but firm, tomatoes
1 1/2 cup water
3 cups sugar
2 medium cinnamon sticks
julienned peel of 1/2 orange

1. Drop the tomatoes in boiling water for 1-2 minutes. Cut off the stem end and peel with a paring knife. If the tomatoes are firm enough, sometimes they can be peeled with a vegetable peeler.

2. Cut in half crosswise and squeeze with your hand to seed. Remove any remaining seeds with your finger.

3. In the meantime, bring the water, sugar and cinnamon to a boil in an uncovered heavy pan. Reduce the heat to medium-low and cook for 15 minutes.

4. Add the tomato halves and the julienned orange peel. Raise the heat to bring to a boil, then reduce to medium-low. Cook uncovered for 1 1/2 hours or until you get a light syrup —224°F on a candy thermometer. Remove any scum that rises to the surface.

5. Let cool, then refrigerate covered before serving.

Serves: 6-8

CHAPTER XV: ICE CREAMS, SHERBETS AND LINDBERGHS

VANILLA ICE CREAM

(Mantecado de vainilla)

3 cups whole milk
2 cups heavy cream or undiluted evaporated milk
1 cup sugar
1/4 teaspoon salt
4 teaspoons cornstarch dissolved in part of the milk
2-3 large egg yolks, lightly beaten with some of the milk
2 teaspoons vanilla

1. In a heavy saucepan mix all the ingredients well, making sure that you have dissolved the sugar.

2. Bring to a very slow simmer —do not let boil— and cook for 5 minutes or until it is thick enough to coat a spoon. Stir occasionally.

3. Let cool and refrigerate until cold after straining.

4. Pour into the chilled canister of a two-quart crank freezer, fit in the chilled dasher, and churn according to the machine's instructions —about 20-30 minutes.

5. Pack in a covered container and put in the freezer for 2 hours before serving.

Yield: 2 quarts

Variation:

VANILLA-LIME ICE CREAM

(Mantecado de vainilla y limón verde)

Follow the instructions for Vanilla Ice Cream, but add 2 teaspoons grated green acid lime rind.

Variation:

GREEN ACID LIME ICE CREAM

(Mantecado de limón verde)

Follow the instructions for Vanilla Ice Cream, but use 2 teaspoons grated green acid lime rind instead of the vanilla extract.

CHOCOLATE ICE CREAM

(Mantecado de chocolate)

2 1/2 cups whole milk
2 1/2 cups heavy cream or undiluted evaporated milk
2 1/2 ounces bitter chocolate melted in a double boiler
1 cup plus two tablespoons sugar
1/4 teaspoon salt
1 tablespoon cornstarch dissolved in some of the milk
1/4 teaspoon almond extract
1 1/2 teaspoon vanilla
2 large egg yolks, lightly beaten with some of the milk

1. In a heavy saucepan mix well all the ingredients, making sure you have dissolved the sugar.

2. Bring to a very slow simmer —do not let boil— and cook for 5 minutes or until it is thick enough to coat a spoon. Stir occasionally.

3. Let cool and refrigerate until cold after straining.

4. Pour into the chilled canister of a two-quart crank freezer, fit in the chilled dasher, and churn according to the machine's instructions —from 20-30 minutes.

5. Pack in a covered container and freeze for 2 hours before serving.

Yield: about 2 quarts

SOURSOP ICE CREAM

(Mantecado de guanábana)

2 to 2 1/2 pounds soursop
4 cups whole milk
1 1/4 cup heavy cream or undiluted evaporated milk
1 1/2 cup sugar
1/4 teaspoon salt
5 teaspoons cornstarch dissolved in part of the milk
2 large egg yolks lightly beaten with some of the milk
3/4 teaspoon almond extract

1. Cut the soursop crosswise into 3/4"-thick slices. Peel, remove the seeds and any hard core. Shred.

2. Measure 2 1/2 tightly packed cups and puree in a food processor or blender with 1/2 cup of the milk. Pass through a colander to remove any fibers.

3. Measure 1 1/2 cup of this puree and set apart.

4. Bring the rest of the milk, cream, sugar, salt, cornstarch, yolks and almond extract to a very slow simmer in a heavy saucepan. Do not allow to boil. Stir occasionally.

5. Simmer for 5 more minutes, stirring, until it is thick enough to coat a spoon.

6. Let cool and strain over the saved soursop puree. Blend well and refrigerate.

7. Pour into the chilled canister of a four-quart crank freezer. Fit in the chilled dasher and churn according to the machine's instructions —20-30 minutes.

8. Pack in a covered container and freeze for 2 hours before serving.

Yield: about 2 quarts

GUAVA ICE CREAM

(Mantecado de guayaba)

2 1/2 pounds guavas, preferably a mixture of sweet and sour ones
4 cups whole milk
1 1/2 cup heavy cream or undiluted evaporated milk
1 3/4 cup sugar
1/4 teaspoon salt
4 teaspoons cornstarch dissolved in part of the milk
4 egg yolks, beaten lightly with some of the milk
6-8 drops red vegetable color

1. Peel the guavas with a vegetable peeler. Halve and puree in a blender or food processor.

2. Pass through a sieve to remove the seeds. Measure 2 cups and keep aside.

3. In a heavy saucepan mix well the rest of the ingredients, making sure that the sugar is dissolved.

4. Bring to a very slow simmer stirring all the time. Do not let boil.

5. Cook for 5 minutes or until it is thick enough to coat a spoon.

6. Let cool, mix with the guava puree, add the food color and refrigerate until completely cold.

7. Pour into the chilled canister of a four-quart crank freezer, fit in the chilled dasher, and churn according to the machine's instructions —about 20-30 minutes.

8. Pack in a covered container and freeze for 2 hours before serving.

Yield: about 2 quarts

MANGO AND RUM ICE CREAM

(Mantecado de mangó y ron)

2 cups peeled ripe mango, cut into 3/4" pieces —3 half-pound mangoes
1 cup whole milk
1 1/2 cup heavy cream or undiluted evaporated milk
1/2 cup plus two tablespoons sugar
1/8 teaspoon salt
1 large egg yolk lightly beaten with some of the milk
2 teaspoons cornstarch dissolved in part of the milk
1/3 cup rum

1. Puree the mango pieces in a food precessor fitted with the steel blade and measure one cup.

2. In a heavy saucepan mix well the rest of the ingredients, making sure that the sugar is dissolved.

3. Bring to a very slow simmer, stirring all the time. Do not let boil.

4. Cook for 5 minutes or until it is thick enough to coat a spoon.

5. Let cool, mix with the mango puree, and refrigerate until completely cold.

6. Pour into the chilled canister of a 2-quart crank freezer, fit in the chilled dasher, and churn according to the machine's instructions —about 20-25 minutes.

7. Pack in a covered container and freeze for 2 hours before serving.

Yield: about 1 1/2 quart

COCONUT SHERBET

(Helado de coco)

6 cups coconut milk, p. 416
1 1/2 cup sugar
1/4 teaspoon salt

1. Mix well all the ingredients until the sugar and salt are dissolved.

2. Refrigerate, then pour into the chilled canister of a four-quart crank freezer. Fit in the chilled dasher and churn according to the machine's instructions —20-30 minutes.

3. Pack in a covered container and freeze for 2 hours before serving.

Yield: about 1/2 gallon

GREEN COCONUT SHERBET

(Helado de agua y pulpa de coco)

8 cups green coconut water
2 cups tender green coconut meat
2 1/4 - 2 1/2 cups sugar depending on the sweetness of the coconut water
1/4 cup water
1 tablespoon unflavored gelatin

1. Puree the coconut meat in a blender or food processor and mix with the coconut water and sugar until this is dissolved.

2. Warm the 1/4 cup water and dissolve the gelatin in it. Add to the coconut mixture and refrigerate until cold.

3. Pour into the chilled canister of a four-quart crank freezer. Fit in the chilled dasher and churn according to the machine's instructions —20-30 minutes.

4. Pack in a covered container and freeze for 2 hours before serving.

NOTES: This recipe uses the immature, green coconut, usually found unhusked, not the brown, ripe, husked coconut sold in markets. The water is the clear liquid inside, not the coconut milk extracted by squeezing the grated flesh of the ripe coconut. The flesh of the immature, green coconut is a translucent, gelatinous substance clinging to the inside of the shell. When ripe, this is the familiar white, solid flesh. Taste the coconut water of each coconut as you open it, as some turn out to be rancid.

Yield: about 2 quarts

ICE CREAM AND SHERBET CRANK FREEZING

(Método para congelar mantecados y helados en sorbetera)

1. Chill the canister and dasher.

2. Fill no more than 3/4 full with the chilled ice cream or sherbet mixture. This allows for expansion.

3. Put in the dasher and cover tightly with the lid. Set inside the crank freezer.

4. Alternate the ice and salt around the canister in the below stated proportions. Do not go beyond the draining spout or hole.

5. Crank until the dasher will not move any further. Some electric freezers will stop automatically.

6. To cure and further harden the ice cream or sherbet, either cover the crank freezer tightly with newspapers or burlap sacks, or pour the ice cream or sherbet into a covered container and freeze in your refrigerator for 2 hours before serving.

NOTE: Crank freezers vary, so it is a good idea to read their instructions before using. The above recipe is merely a guideline for the process of crank freezing.

ICE AND SALT PROPORTIONS TABLE FOR CRANK FREEZERS

(Tabla de proporciones de hielo y sal para sorbeteras)

Freezer Capacity	*Ice*	*Rock Salt*	*Table Salt*
2 quarts	8-10 pounds	1 pound (2 cups)	1 cup
4 quarts	12-14 pounds	1 1/2 pound (3 cups)	1 1/2 cup
6 quarts	16-18 pounds	2 1/2 pounds (5 cups)	2 1/2 cups

NOTE: Do not add more salt than that stated as the ice cream will become grainy and coarse in texture, and also because the freezing process will be hastened unfavorably.

REFRIGERATOR FREEZER ICE CREAM OR SHERBET

(Mantecado o helado en congelador de nevera)

1. Prepare any of the ice cream or sherbet mixtures in the previous recipes.

2. Pour into a shallow pan, or ice cube trays without their dividers. Cover and refrigerate in the freeer until almost hard —from 2-3 hours.

3. Cut up into chunks, put in a bowl and whip with an electric beater to aerate it, until it is smooth and has increased in volume.

4. Pack into a covered container and freeze until hard before serving.

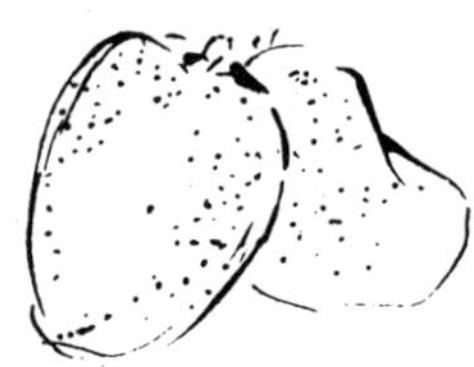

LINDBERGHS

(Límbers)

1 1/4 cup fruit puree
1 cup water
2/3 cup sugar

1. Mix well all the ingredients until the sugar is dissolved.
2. Pour into ice cube trays with dividers and freeze until solid.
3. Serve on pleated candy paper cups.

NOTE: Some of the traditional fruit flavors are guava, tamarind, soursop, mango and other tropical fruits. They can be made also by merely freezing in the ice cube trays any of the preeceding ice cream or sherbet mixtures. They are also made of syrups flavored with, i.e., anise, raspberry or the juices of tropical fruits.

Yield: about 18 lindberghs

CHAPTER XVI: BEVERAGES —COOL AND WARM

RIPE ACID LIME ADE

(Limonada)

1 quart water
3/4 cup strained ripe acid lime juice
3/4 cup sugar, or to taste

1. Stir all the ingredients together until the sugar is well dissolved.

2. Chill or serve over ice cubes.

Serves: 6

OATMEAL DRINK

(Refresco de avena)

6 cups water
3/4 cup rolled oats
3/4 teaspoon vanilla
sugar to taste

1. Soak the rolled oats in the water for at least 30 minutes.

2. Strain, add the vanilla, and chill.

3. Serve with sugar to taste.

Serves: 6

SOURSOP DRINK

(Champola de guanábana)

1 1/4 to 1 1/2 pound soursop
3 cups cold milk
1/2 cup sugar or to taste

1. Cut the soursop crosswise into 1" slices.

2. Peel, remove the pithy center and the seeds. Cut into chunks.

3. Puree in a blender or food processor with 1/3 cup of the milk.

4. Press through a potato ricer or through a colander with large holes to eliminate any stringy fibers.

5. Measure 1 1/3 cup of the puree and return to the blender along with the rest of the milk and sugar. Blend well. Add more milk if you prefer it thinner.

6. Serve over crushed ice or refrigerate.

Serves: 6

TAMARIND DRINK

(Refresco de tamarindo)

1 1/4 pounds shelled tamarinds
1 1/2 quart water
1 cup sugar, or to taste

1. Beat together the tamarinds and sugar in a bowl with a wooden spoon to separate the pulp from the seeds.

2. Add half of the water, stir well and strain.

3. Add the rest of the water, stir well and strain again.

4. Add more sugar if necessary and chill well before serving or pour over ice cubes.

Serves: 6

BANANA SHAKE

(Batido de guineo)

6 large ripe bananas, peeled and cut into chunks
1 1/2 quart cold milk
1 1/2 cup crushed ice
1/4 teaspoon vanilla (optional)

1. Puree the bananas over high speed in a blender.

2. Add the milk, crushed ice, optional vanilla and blend until well mixed and frothy.

Serves: 6

MABI DRINK

(Mabí)

1 ounce *mabí* bark (nakedwood, soldierwood) —about 45-50 3"-long strips
1 quart water
3 cups white sugar
1 cup brown sugar
2 quarts hot water
1 quart commercially-bought *mabí* drink for starter

1. Rinse the *mabí* bark strips and boil in a quart of water for 10 minutes over medium-high heat. Strain out the bark.

2. Dissolve the sugars in the hot water and add 3 cups of the water where you boiled the bark. Stir for 2 minutes.

3. Add the quart of starter *mabí* drink and beat for 5 minutes until frothy.

4. Pour into quart bottles leaving a 2 - 2 1/2" empty space at the top.

5. Cover the bottles with small paper cups or loose cheese-cloth.

6. Allow to ferment at room temperature for 24 hours.

7. Cover and chill well before serving.

NOTES: Taste the *mabí* starter before adding it at the third step. If it is too bitter, use only half. To make the *mabí* ferment faster, put in the sun for one hour. If the drink does not ferment enough in 24 hours, add 1 teaspoon of rinsed, uncooked rice to each *mabí* quart. Let stand for 24 hours more and strain before chilling.

Yield: 4 quarts

SANGRÍA

3 cups red wine
3 orange slices, cut crosswise 1/4" thick, and halved
6 lemon slices, 1/8" thick
2 cups seltzer or soda water
up to 1/2 cup sugar (optional)

1. Put the orange and lemon slices in a jug and press slightly with a wooden spoon.

2. Add the wine and seltzer, or soda water.

3. Add ice cubes, or pour into tall glasses filled with ice.

NOTE: If using the optional sugar add it with the wine. Stir well until it is dissolved before adding the seltzer or soda water.

Serves: 6

CUBA LIBRE

12 ounces dark Puerto Rican rum
1 acid lime, cut into 6 segments
18 ounces cola

1. Pour 2 ounces rum into each glass.

2. Squeeze some of the lime juice of each segment into each glass and drop in the lime segment.

3. Fill with ice cubes, pour 3 ounces of cola into each glass, and stir before serving.

Serves: 6

ACID LIME FROZEN DAIQUIRI

(Daiquirí helado)

3 tablespoons strained acid lime juice
3 tablespoons sugar
9 ounces white Puerto Rican rum
6 cups crushed ice
maraschino cherries

1. Put all the ingredients, except the ice, in a blender. Process at high speed until the sugar is dissolved.

2. Add the ice and blend at high speed until it is frothy.

3. Serve in chilled glasses topped by maraschino cherries.

Serves: 6

BANANA DAIQUIRI

(Daiquirí de guineo)

1 1/2 ripe banana, peeled and cut into chunks
9 ounces dark Puerto Rican rum
1 ounce strained acid lime juice
1 tablespoon sugar
6 cups crushed ice

1. Blend all the ingredients, but the ice, until smooth at high speed in a blender.

2. Add the ice and blend until frothy.

3. Serve in chilled glasses.

Serves: 6

PINEAPPLE DAIQUIRI

(Daiquirí de piña)

4 pineapple slices, peeled, cored and cut into chunks
2 tablespoons lemon juice
4 tablespoons grenadine
9 ounces dark Puerto Rican rum
6 cups chopped ice

1. Put all the ingredients, except the ice, in a blender and blend at high speed until smooth.

2. Add the ice and blend at high speed until frothy.

3. Serve in chilled glasses.

Serves: 6

PIÑA COLADA

1 cup thick coconut milk, p.416
2 cups pineapple juice
1 1/2 cup Puerto Rican Rum, preferably light
6 pineapple wedges
6 maraschino cherries

1. Blend all the liquid ingredients in a blender or by hand.

2. Serve on tall chilled glasses filled with ice and garnished with the pineapple wedges and cherries.

Serves: 6

DORA ROMANO'S PRUNE LIQUEUR

(Licor de ciruelas secas a la Dora Romano)

1/2 cup sugar
1 cup water
1 pound prunes
1 quart white Puerto Rican rum
8 juniper berries

1. Mix well the sugar and water and boil over medium-high heat for 20 minutes or until you reach 220°F on a candy thermometer, and you have about 1/2 cup syrup. Let cool completely.

2. Put the prunes and juniper berries in a clean, dry, 1 1/2 quart mason jar.

3. Mix the rum with the syrup and pour over the prunes.

4. Close the jar, shake gently, and keep in a dark place for no less than 6 months. Stir gently every month.

5. Decant the liqueur if you wish to stop the aging process. Use the prunes over ice cream, or chop for cakes or other desserts.

Yield: about 4 1/2 cups liqueur

RUM AND COCONUT PUNCH — *COQUITO*

(Ron con coco —coquito)

2 cups coconut milk, p. 416
3/4-1 cup sugar
1/8 teaspoon salt
1/4 teaspoon ground cinnamon
1 egg yolk
2 cups white Puerto Rican rum or 1 1/2 cup rum, 1/4 cup brandy

1. Put the sugar, salt, cinnamon, egg yolk and 1/2 cup of the coconut milk in a blender or food processor. Process until the sugar is dissolved.

2. Add the rest of the coconut milk and blend.

3. With the machine running —on high if it is a blender—, add the rum gradually and process for at least one more minute.

4. Bottle and chill before serving in liqueur glasses, dusted with cinnamon.

Yield: 4 - 4 1/2 cups

CHILDREN'S *BUL*

(Bul para niños)

1 quart orange juice
1 quart pineapple juice
1 quart white grape juice
5 cups ginger ale
2 cups sugar

1. Mix well all the ingredients, making sure that the sugar is totally dissolved.

2. Serve on a punch bowl over ice.

Yield: 25 six-ounce servings

RUM AND BEER *BUL*

(Bul de ron y cerveza)

2 cups orange juice
2 cups grapefruit juice
1 quart pear juice
2 cups pineapple juice
2 cups white grape juice
2 cups dark Puerto Rican rum
3 cups light beer
8 ounces maraschino cherries
2 cups sugar

1. Mix well all the ingredientsw, making sure that the sugar is well dissolved.

2. Serve in a punch bowl over ice.

Yield: 25 six-ounce servings

BUL WITH SHERRY

(Bul con jerez)

2 quarts orange juice
1 quart grapefruit juice
1 quart pineapple juice
1 quart amontillado sherry
1 cup sugar

1. Mix well all the ingredients, making sure the sugar is well dissolved.

2. Serve in a punchbowl over ice.

NOTE: If using cream or dry sherry adjust the sugar down or up, accordingly.

Yield: 25-30 six-ounce servings.

SOUR ORANGE LEAF MILK

(Té de hojas de naranja agria con leche)

3 to 4 sour orange new leaves per serving
1 cup milk per serving
1 teaspoon sugar per serving

1. Rinse the leaves and cut into 4 segments each.

2. Bring the milk and the leaves to a simmer and cook stirring for 2 minutes.

3. Strain and sweeten with the sugar.

Yield: 1 cup

GINGER MILK

(Té de jengibre con leche)

1 two-inch segment fresh ginger root, rinsed and crushed, per serving
1 cup milk per serving
1 teaspoon sugar per serving

1. Bring the ginger and milk to a simmer and cook stirring for two minutes.

2. Strain the ginger and serve the milk sweetened with the sugar.

Yield: 1 cup

HOT CHOCOLATE

(Chocolate caliente)

8 ounces sweet chocolate, finely grated
6 cups milk
sugar to taste
cinnamon (optional)

1. Mix well the chocolate and milk and bring to a simmer.

2. Simmer at low heat for 5 minutes, whipping it all the time with a wire whisk, until it is light and frothy.

3. Serve hot with sugar and dusted with cinnamon to taste.

Serves: 6

COFFEE EXTRACT

(Café tinto)

1 1/2 cups boiling water
1 cup dark-roast fine grind coffee

1. Put the coffee grounds in the filter and compact them.

2. Pour just enough water to moisten the grounds, about 1/2 cup.

3. Add the rest of the water very slowly, until it is all used up.

4. Add to warm milk, mixing in the proportions you prefer.

5. Season to taste with sugar.

NOTE: This extract may be made also in an expresso machine. Follow the machine's instructions.

Yield: 4 ounces

CHAPTER XVII: REMAINDERS—SOME SWEET, SOME SAVORY

GRATED COCONUT

(Coco rallado)

Ripe coconut.

1. Shake the coconut to make sure that it is full of water, and thus still fresh.

2. Pierce two of the eyelets of the coconut with a pointed tool or ice pick. Drain the liquid and save for other purposes. (It is a very refreshing drink chilled in the icebox).

3. Break the coconut open by hitting it with a hammer about its widest part. Break into smaller pieces.

4. Remove the meat from the shell by prying it out with a strong short knife, such as an oyster knife.

5. Pare the brown skin next to the meat with a paring knife, vegetable peeler, or scrape it off with a hand grater.

6. Cut the meat into 1" pieces.

7. On a food processor fitted with the steel blade, process in small batches until it is well grated, or grate with a hand grater.

NOTE: In recipes that ask for grated coconut as an ingredient, not as decoration, do not use commercially packed grated coconut.

Yield: One large coconut —5" diameter— yields about 4 1/4 cups of grated coconut.

COCONUT MILK

(Leche de coco)

Process I

1. Grate de coconut, p.415, and measure.

2. Put the grated coconut in batches in a food processor fitted with the steel blade.

3. With the motor running, add half the amount of tepid water as grated coconut. Process 1 minute.

4. Let the mixture cool and squeeze by portions through a clean cloth kitchen napkin.

5. Measure this amount of heavy milk.

6. Determine how much more milk your recipe asks for, if any.

7. Measure that amount in water and add to the already squeezed grated coconut. Squeeze again as in step 4.

8. Add this milk to the heavy milk already measured to reach the amount needed.

9. Proceed with your recipe.

Process II

1. Grate de coconut and measure, p.415.

2. Add half the amount of water as grated coconut.

3. Squeeze through a clean cloth kitchen napkin by small portions.

4. Measure this heavy milk.

5. Determine how much more milk your recipe asks for, if any.

6. Measure that amount in water and add to the already squeezed grated coconut. Squeeze again as in step 3.

7. Add this milk to the heavy milk already measured to reach the amount needed.

8. Proceed with your recipe.

NOTES: If you are not using immediately, the milk will keep in the refrigerator, covered, for as long as 2 weeks. It also freezes successfuly. Stir after removing from the refrigerator or defrosting.

If you are using commercial canned or frozen coconut milk instead of fresh one, make sure it is unsweetened and pure. Do not use cream of coconut, or commercially packed grated coconut as these contain sugar and other ingredients.

Yield: one large coconut —5" diameter— will yield about 4 1/4 cups grated coconut, out of which you will get 2 cups of the first-squeezed heavy milk, plus whatever amount you need from the second, diluted, squeezing.

CURDLED MILK SWEET

(Dulce de leche)

13-ounce can evaporated milk
1 1/4 cup water
1 1/2 cup sugar
8 acid lime peel strips about 1 1/2" long
2 teaspoons cider vinegar

1. Combine in a heavy saucepan the milk, water, sugar and lime peel. Stir to dissolve the sugar.

2. Bring to a boil, reduce the heat to medium-low and stir in the vinegar to curdle the milk.

3. Cook at a very slow boil for 15 minutes.

4. Break the curdled milk with a spoon into clumps about 1/2 to 1" thick.

5. Reduce the heat to low and cook for 45 minutes or until the syrup thickens —220°F on a candy thermometer. Stir occasionally.

6. Let cool and refrigerate covered before serving.

Serves: 6-8

PICKLED EGGS WITH ROAST PEPPERS

(Huevos en escabeche con pimientos asados)

12 hard-boiled eggs, halved lengthwise
2 large frying peppers, roasted, peeled, seeded and cut into 2" x 1/2" strips, p. 119
2 medium onions sliced 1/4" thick
20 - 24 pimiento-stuffed small green olives
2 cups olive oil
3/4 cup vinegar
3/4 teaspoon salt
8 peeled medium whole garlic cloves
1/2 teaspoon peppercorns

1. In a non-reactive saucepan, bring to a boil the olive oil, vinegar, salt and garlic cloves. Reduce the heat to low and simmer for 15 minutes.

2. Add the pepper and let cool.

3. In a wide-mouth non-reactive jar, place the eggs, onions, peppers and olives —in that order— in four layers. Add one fourth of the sauce on top of each layer.

4. Cover and chill well before serving.

Serves: 6

SWEET RICE FRITTERS

(Frituras dulces de arroz)

1 1/4 cup plain boiled white short-grain rice
1/4 cup sugar
1/4 teaspoon salt
1 teaspoon melted butter
2 lightly beaten medium eggs
1/2 cup milk
1/2 teaspoon vanilla extract
2 tablespoons seedless raisins
2/3 cup all-purpose flour
1/2 teaspoon double-acting baking powder
vegetable oil

1. Mix all the ingredients except the flour and baking powder. Blend well.

2. Mix the flour and baking powder and blend well with the other ingredients.

3. Deep fry by large spoonfuls in the vegetable oil over moderate heat until golden brown —about 1 1/2 minutes on each side.

4. Drain on paper towels and serve hot as a side dish.

Yield: 18 fritters

FLUFFY RICE FLOUR AND CHEESE CRULLERS

(Almojábanas esponjosas de harina de arroz y queso)

1 1/2 cup sifted rice flour
1 cup milk
2 tablespoons butter
3/4 teaspoon salt
4 large eggs
1/2 cup grated parmesan cheese
shortening

1. Bring the milk, butter and salt to a slow boil.

2. Off the heat, stir gradually into the flour, adding only as much as you need to moisten it all well. Cool completely.

3. Stir in the eggs one at a time, beating after each addition.

4. Add the cheese and blend well. If the mixture is too thick, add one or two more tablespoons of milk.

5. Fry by tablespoonfuls in hot shortening —350°F— in one-layer batches until golden brown.

6. Drain on paper towels and serve warm as a side dish.

NOTES: The crullers may be served with cinnamon syrup, p. 329, but then reduce their salt to 1/4 teaspoon. Serve as dessert. The mixture may be prepared in advance and re-stirred before frying.

Yield: 48 crullers

GARLIC BREAD

(Pan con ajo)

1 pound French bread
6 pressed medium garlic cloves
1/4 cup olive oil or 6 tablespoons softened butter

1. Blend well the garlic and oil or butter.

2. Slice the bread lenthwise and spread the mixture between the two halves. Put them together again. Or slice the bread crosswise, without going all the way to the bottom, at 1" intervals. Spread the garlic olive oil or butter between the slits.

3. Toast lightly in a 350°F oven for about 10 minutes and serve warm.

Serves: 6

GARLIC TOAST

(Tostadas de ajo)

1 pound French bread cut into 1/2" slices
3 or 4 medium garlic cloves, peeled but whole
olive oil or butter

1. Put the bread slices on a cookie sheet in a 350°F oven. Toast, turning once, until lightly golden.

2. Remove from the oven and rub with the garlic cloves on both sides.

3. Dribble one side of each toast with olive oil or spread with butter. Return to the oven for 5 more minutes and serve warm.

Serves: 6

RECIPE INDEX

CHAPTER I: THE CORNERSTONES

CHAPTER II: SAUCES, DRESSINGS AND DIPS

CHAPTER III: FIRST COURSE SOUPS, FULL MEAL SOUPS

CHAPTER IV: THE PLANTAIN, THE GREEN BANANA, THE BREADFRUIT AND OTHER VEGETABLES

CHAPTER V: *PASTELES* AND PASTA

CHAPTER VI: FISH, SHELLFISH AND THE GREAT LAND CRAB

CHAPTER VII: THE CHICKEN, THE TURKEY AND THE GUINEA HEN

CHAPTER VIII: BEEF, PORK, VEAL AND KID

CHAPTER IX: RICE AND BEANS... AND OTHER GRAINS

CHAPTER X: CAKES, PIES, BEIGNETS AND TURNOVERS

CHAPTER XI: FLANS AND CUSTARDS

CHAPTER XII: PUDDINGS, POLENTA AND PAP

CHAPTER XIII: COCONUT KISSES AND OTHER CONFECTIONARY

CHAPTER XIV: FRUIT AND VEGETABLE COMPOTES

CHAPTER XV: ICE CREAMS, SHERBETS AND LINDBERGHS

CHAPTER XVI: BEVERAGES--COOL AND WARM

CHAPTER XVII: REMAINDERS SOME SWEET, SOME SAVORY

GENERAL INDEX

Este libro se terminó de imprimir
en septiembre de 1993
en los talleres de Artes Gráficas de
RAMALLO BROS. PRINTING, INC.
Calle Duarte #227, Hato Rey, P.R. 00917